Ralph Barker served in the RAF during the Second World War, in the course of which his Beaufort was hit in combat and he survived a crash on take-off in which his pilot and navigator were killed. He was transferred to non-operational flying after his crash and hospitalisation. After the war, he worked in civil aviation for a short time before rejoining the RAF to work in the secretariat until 1961. *Down in the Drink* (1955) launched a successful career as a writer. He has written books on the RAF, on terrorism and war at sea, and hundreds of feature articles for the *Sunday Express*.

For this edition of *Down in the Drink*, Ralph Barker has written a new story, 'Whitleys and Hampdens on Hamm'.

To the many
thousands of airmen whose
grave is the sea

RALPH BARKER

DOWN IN THE DRINK

THEIR DEADLIEST ENEMY WAS THE SEA

headline
review

First published in 1955 by Chatto & Windus

This edition published in 2008
by HEADLINE REVIEW
An imprint of HEADLINE PUBLISHING GROUP

1

Maps on pages viii, 60, 90, 178, 198, 254 © Peter Barker

Cataloguing in Publication Data is available from the British Library

ISBN 978 07553 1752 3

Typeset in Perpetua by Palimpsest Book Production Ltd,
Grangemouth, Stirlingshire

Printed in the UK by CPI Mackays, Chatham ME5 8TD

Headline's policy is to use papers that are natural,
renewable and recyclable products and made from wood grown
in sustainable forests. The logging and manufacturing processes
are expected to conform to the environmental
regulations of the country of origin.

HEADLINE PUBLISHING GROUP
An Hachette Livre UK Company
338 Euston Road
London NW1 3BH

www.headline.co.uk

CONTENTS

MAPS

GLOSSARY

A.I., Aircraft Interception – radar equipment fitted in fighter aircraft for this purpose.

aileron, main aircraft lateral control.

A.O.C., air officer commanding.

the bag, P.O.W. camp.

brownjobs, the Army.

the chop, get the chop, killed in action or on active service.

clamp the key down, lock the transmitter morse key so that a continuous note is radiated.

dhobi ghat, water-filled bath or pit for washing clothing.

D/R, D/R position, navigation by dead reckoning, position computed by dead reckoning.

E.T.A., estimated time of arrival.

feather, feather an engine, stop the propeller windmilling and thus causing drag when an engine fails.

flaps, kind of air-brake, used for increased lift on take-off and for reducing speed before landing.

flotation gear, inflatable built-in air-bags designed to give buoyancy to aircraft.

fluorescine, fluorescine bag, a chemical which spread a vivid green stain over a large area of water.

Force 136, a ground force operating behind enemy lines in Burma.

George, automatic pilot.

goolie chit, blood chit, a certificate printed in the appropriate language carried by aircrew as a safeguard against mutilation by hostile tribesmen.

kukri, heavy-bladed short-handled Gurkha knife.

Mae West, inflatable life-jacket.

ops, operations, operational sorties.

pitot head, measuring instrument used in aircraft to measure airspeed.

Roger, 'message received and understood'.

R/T, radio telephony.

sprog, inexperienced, newly trained.

static, electrical interference with wireless reception.

Sutton harness, safety harness.

three-point attitude, attitude of the aircraft in which the two main wheels and the tail wheel touch the ground together.

tour, operational tour, fixed number of flying hours or sorties constituting tour of operational duty.

u/s, 'broken'.

Wimpey, a Wellington aircraft.

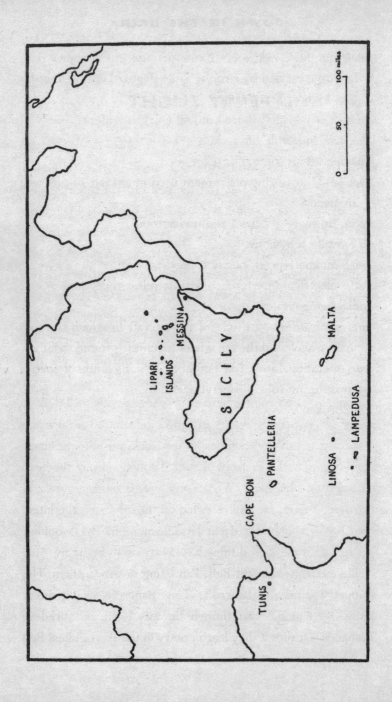

0   50   100 miles

MESSINA

LIPARI ISLANDS

S I C I L Y

MALTA

PANTELLERIA

CAPE BON

LINOSA

LAMPEDUSA

TUNIS

FERRY FLIGHT

SERGEANT Eric Bell swung the rear turret of the Wellington fully in all directions. This was the trip on which they would need to be on the top line. The leg from England to Gibraltar had been just another ferry flight. Now, as he looked back at the narrow runway sheltering against the great Rock, like a child in the lap of its mother, five miles behind them and a thousand feet below, he knew that the crucial test lay between here and Malta in the five or six hours immediately ahead. A mechanic by trade, Bell had taken quickly to air gunnery, and he fingered his guns lovingly, confident in the knowledge that he could dismantle and reassemble them more quickly even than the flight sergeant armourer at Gibraltar – he had done it under his nose. But the poet in him found time to admire and wonder at the majestic stillness of the Rock, misty in the after-noon sunlight. Lines from 'Home Thoughts from the Sea' crowded into his mind. What a mixture. Browning guns and Browning verses. He almost called up the others on the inter-com, but thought better of it in the same moment. They wouldn't get it. Or worse, they'd think he was trying to be funny.

But perhaps, thought Bell, I'm being unfair to them. The skipper, the massive Bancroft, 'Tiny' Bancroft, would surely know Browning, even though he was born and bred in Barbados. Or didn't they learn poetry in the West Indies? Bell

1

had a deep affection for his skipper. The rest of the crew he didn't know so well. Ferry crews were apt to be a scratch lot. He had flown with Robinson, the second pilot, Irving, the navigator, and Handley, the front-gunner and second wireless operator, several times before, but the first wireless operator, McNeil, was new to them all. At the last moment their original wireless operator had gone sick, and they had been given McNeil. Bell had been out drinking with him the night before they left England. McNeil was the only one of them who had done any operational flying. Bell felt that he was inclined to be just a little grand about it. That and the fact that he was a flight sergeant. McNeil wasn't much like the run of ferry crews. Perhaps it was because he was a regular. He didn't think McNeil would know much about Browning. And yet you never could tell with a regular. The most unlikely chaps lay in their bunks all day reading Freud.

Bell called his skipper on the inter-com. 'Hullo, Tiny,' he said. 'Rear-gunner testing.' One by one the crew made a test call to the pilot. Then Handley and Bell tested the guns. Already they had had to return to Gibraltar once because the guns had jammed. This time there was no trouble. Afterwards Bell heard Bancroft call Irving, the navigator.

'What sort of a wind have we got at fifteen hundred feet, Stan?'

'Not so good,' said Irving. 'What's the matter with eight thousand?'

'I don't think she'll make it,' said Bancroft. 'She started over-heating after we'd been climbing only a few minutes. They warned me that we might have overheating trouble while the sun was up.'

'Trouble is there's such a good wind at eight thou,' said Irving. 'It's a pity not to make use of it. Besides . . .'

'Besides what?'

'Well, you can't open her up a bit, I suppose? We're not making much of a groundspeed. I'm afraid we shan't get to Malta before dark.'

'Does that matter?'

'Only that we're supposed to get there at dusk.'

'Only that!' Bancroft's chuckle warmed the crew's heart. 'I'm not taking any chances with this overheating. We'll just plod steadily on. They'll be pleased enough to see us as long as we get there.'

'You don't think we ought to turn back?'

'We daren't go back again. Not unless an engine drops off or something.'

Bell settled down to a long trip. It was warm even in the draughty rear turret, and he took off his fur-lined jacket and sat in his khaki shirt and shorts, wearing nothing else but the revolver strapped round his middle. Arriving at Malta after dark might be a blessing in disguise. The business of approaching at dusk was only to make it harder for the Jerry fighters to pounce on them on the way in. This had surprised Bell a good deal at the briefing. Back in England he had learnt to believe that British fighters were more than a match for the Luftwaffe. It was hard to accustom oneself to the idea of Me 109s holding a kind of circus off Malta, with R.A.F. fighter pilots powerless to stop them. Bell didn't really quite believe it. He didn't seem to remember reading much about it in the papers at home. Yet the flutter he had felt in the pit of his stomach when he first heard the rumours at Gibraltar of ferry aircraft being shot down off Malta, and of being shot up after they landed, was still unpleasantly fresh in his memory. Instinctively his fingers felt for the triggers of his guns.

Occasionally Bell could see the white outline of the North African coast away to starboard, at the limit of visibility, perhaps thirty to forty miles away. He heard the navigator say they should be opposite Algiers, but although for a moment he fancied he could see the reflection of white buildings, he could discern nothing. Some time later he watched another Wellington overtaking them on a parallel course. They must be on the right track.

At length he saw the horizon tip and felt the bank of the aircraft as they turned south past Cape Bon to avoid flying over Pantelleria. Even so, they were near enough to see aircraft landing and taking off on the island. The Wimpey laboured on against headwinds and at an altitude far too low for economical cruising. Night was already coming upon them as they turned east on to their final leg into Malta.

'Hullo, Mac,' called Irving, the navigator. 'Can you tune in the Malta beacon now? We'll get the visual indicator working and home straight in.'

'I'll try,' said McNeil, 'but I'm having a spot of receiver trouble. Can't seem to pick up Malta. I'll see what I can do.'

McNeil tuned his receiver continually to try to pick up the beacon. According to his briefing notes it should be transmitting. What could be the matter? His radio equipment had been perfectly serviceable so far. Now, just because someone had asked him for something, he was having trouble. And on his first trip with a new crew. That made it even more infuriating.

'Any luck yet, Mac?' asked Irving.

'Not yet – give me a chance.'

Bancroft felt for the first time a vague disquiet. McNeil was a very experienced wireless operator – surely there must be something seriously wrong if he couldn't raise Malta. He felt that he still had to deal tactfully with McNeil. It had been pretty tough on him, being pitchforked into a strange crew and posted overseas at short notice. Bancroft had had no time to weld him into the crew. He realised that the atmosphere of this trip must be very different from the sort of trips with regular airmen that McNeil would be used to. Discipline was different in the regular Air Force. Rank meant much more when it was something you had sweated for years to attain. Bancroft felt that he and his crew, and the many other wartime men like them, had brought with them from civilian life some inner discipline of their own, which compensated to a large extent for their lack of experience of Service atmosphere and tradition. But it was hardly fair to expect McNeil to recognise this at once. It would take time.

McNeil, still unable to pick up Malta, was applying himself to the task of finding out what was wrong with the set. Here his training came to his aid.

'How far do you think we are from Malta, Stan?' asked Bancroft.

'About fifty miles, I should think,' said Irving. 'There's a black-out on the island at night and we shall have to keep our eyes peeled. Alter course five degrees to port, will you? I'd sooner we missed Malta to port than to starboard.'

Bancroft altered course and checked the new heading with Irving. Malta could be a hard place to find even in daylight. If they missed it in the darkness it would be better to carry on to Sicily and get a pinpoint there rather than waste petrol searching for Malta. Worst of all would be to miss Malta to starboard and plough on into the void of the central Mediterranean. The next land in that direction was Greece and Crete – nearly a thousand miles. Long before that they would run out of petrol.

'Have you got the Malta beacon yet, Mac?' called Bancroft.

'Just coming up now.'

Bancroft saw that the needles on the visual indicator had sprung to life and were hanging over to the left. He turned to port and the needles centralised. Everything was all right after all.

'Come on, Stan,' he said to Irving, 'we'll go aft and get some sandwiches and tea. Robbie, you take over for a bit. Just keep those needles centralised and we'll soon be there.'

Robinson took over the controls while Bancroft and Irving sat at the navigation table in the fuselage, munching sandwiches and drinking tea. The night air was cool and Bancroft slipped off his parachute harness and Mae West and put his battledress on. Irving shivered at the knees. They ate raisins and chocolate. There was no need to worry now that they were homing on the Malta beacon.

Suddenly they were conscious that the aircraft was no longer flying a straight and level course. Then Robinson's voice came up on the inter-com.

'There's something wrong with these needles. They won't centralise properly. I think we're flying round in a huge circle. Are you sure it's the Malta beacon, Mac?'

'It's Malta's call-sign all right,' said McNeil. 'Just a minute. I'll tune them in again.'

Bancroft heard the conversation on the inter-com and hurried forward with Irving. He took over from Robinson and saw for himself that the needles were behaving erratically. Handley called them from the nose.

'Land on the port side!'

Bancroft peered out of the cockpit to his left. He could see nothing. 'What is it – Malta?'

'It's a long, dark coastline,' said Handley. 'Looks like we're off Cape Bon again.'

'Forget those needles,' called Irving. 'Steer north-east and we'll try and hit Sicily. Give me a moment to work out a course.'

How suddenly the atmosphere of a flight could change. A moment ago they were relaxed and confident. Now they were very near panic.

'How about letting Mac call Malta for a bearing?' asked Irving.

'We're supposed to keep wireless silence, aren't we?'

'Yes – except in emergency.'

Bancroft considered for a moment. If they had to break

wireless silence it was better to do so early rather than late. He called McNeil.

'Go ahead, Mac.'

McNeil began transmitting on the Malta control frequency straight away. He could get no reply. He called them again and again without result.

'It's no good,' he said. 'They won't answer. There must be an air raid on.'

'That might explain the behaviour of the needles,' said Robinson.

'Did you make that a priority call?' asked Bancroft.

'Yes.'

'Why not make it an S O S?' suggested Irving.

'All right. Make it an S O S, Mac.'

'O.K.'

But even the S O S brought no answer. There seemed no doubt that there was something wrong with the set.

Bancroft hated doing it, but he felt that he must give his second wireless operator a chance to get a message through. He called Handley.

'Reg, you go back and have a go. Can't do any harm.'

Handley scrambled out of the front turret and back to the radio. Under McNeil's glowering eye, he re-tuned the transmitter and rebroadcast the S O S. Still there was no reply.

They kept on their north-easterly course, peering ahead for the coast of Sicily. The night was dark and the moon had not yet risen. In these conditions they might be near or even over land and yet not see it.

Handley, back again in the nose turret, suddenly shouted over the inter-com. 'Look, chaps! Away to starboard! Flak! That must be Malta!'

'Good show, Reg,' said Bancroft. 'That'll be Malta all right.' He watched the flak and flaming onions climbing lazily into the sky. 'How far away, Stan?'

'Ten to fifteen miles by the look of it.'

Bancroft checked over his petrol gauges. What did they do now? It would be suicide trying to get in to Malta during an air raid. Even if they managed to make a safe landing they would be a sitting target on the runway. They'd been told at briefing to hold off to the south of the island if they arrived during an air raid. Malta were supposed to broadcast a coded signal when there was an air raid in progress. Probably they had, and McNeil had been unable to pick it up. Bancroft reckoned that they could hold off safely for perhaps half an hour. Then shortage of petrol would force them to go in.

Bell rotated his turret so as to get a view of the flak over Malta. He had absolute confidence in Bancroft and was enjoying the grandstand view of the air raid. McNeil was still trying to get his radio to function. The rest of the crew watched the flak with a mixture of excitement and anxiety, looking for signs of an end to the raid but fascinated in spite of themselves when the flak intensified. Bancroft circled about five miles to the south of the island.

After about twenty minutes Bancroft decided that the flak had become more desultory. It was time to take their chance. The fuel would last them for perhaps another twenty minutes, and they might have trouble getting in. He set course for Malta.

There were one or two more isolated explosions and then the flak stopped altogether, leaving the night blacker than before. They kept going until they saw the white fringe of coastline, but once over land they saw nothing. Bancroft decided to fire off a couple of recognition signals. Robinson was disengaging the Very pistol from its stowage when Bell's voice, charged with urgency, came up over the inter-com.

'We've got company,' he said. 'I don't know how many there are. Two, I think. They look like Beaufighters. They're out of range at the moment. Perhaps they've come to lead us in.'

'That's decent of them,' said Bancroft. 'Give them the colours of the day, Robbie.'

Robinson locked the Very pistol and fumbled with the catch of the window. As he was doing so he heard the clatter of machine-gun fire. The Very pistol jammed against the window and fell beside him as Bancroft put the Wellington into a steep left-hand turn. When Bancroft pulled out he saw that the moon was coming up, low and clear and full. Whoever had fired at them would soon find them again. He called the crew.

'Everyone all right?' One by one they answered that they were. Bancroft was sure the aircraft had been hit. He checked his petrol gauges over and found them both showing empty. Surely they couldn't have used up all their petrol yet? They must have been hit somewhere in the fuel-tanks. He called the crew again.

'I'm going straight down,' he said. 'Look out for those

Beaufighters or whatever they are. I'm going to do a crash-landing.'

Bell winced. 'For God's sake don't try and land down there,' he said. 'Malta's as rocky as hell. Put her down in the sea.' The words were out of him before he realised it.

Bancroft could see the sense of what Bell said. North of Malta there was a long shining strip of water lit by the moon, as good a runway as they could hope for. He'd never done a ditching, but everyone said it was a piece of cake. He turned towards the moon, losing height rapidly. Handley and Bell watched anxiously for a return of the fighters. Everyone expected to hear the rattle of machine-gun fire at any moment. When Bancroft judged that he was about two miles out to sea north of Malta he turned until the moon was at his back. Then he sent Irving, Robinson and Handley back into the fuselage behind the main-spar, where they joined McNeil, who was sending out another S O S. Robinson made up for lost time by cramming sandwich after sandwich into his mouth and washing them down with great gulps of tea. You never knew how far away the next meal might be. Handley strapped the emergency water rations to his waist. Bell, still in the rear turret, turned the turret to the quick-release position and braced himself. He had one more word of advice for his skipper.

'Tiny.'

'What?'

'Don't put her down tail first, will you?'

Bancroft got as near as he could to a grin. 'Don't worry.' He throttled back his engines and began his final run. Thank God

11

the engines hadn't cut. The lighting was good – better perhaps than most of the runways at home. In the distance the shimmering water gave way to a dark fringe. That would be Malta. Thinking of Bell, he kept his speed at 110 knots and made a low skimming approach. The water was choppier than he'd thought. He eased the stick gently back and a moment later felt the sea hit them a terrific crack in the belly. Instantly the cockpit was full of water. McNeil, still tapping out his S O S, felt his hand forced off the key by the impact. Robinson and Handley were thrown violently forward. Just before they hit the water Irving was to pull the flotation-gear lever to inflate the belly of the aircraft so as to help keep it afloat. The tension of the moment, the jumble of bodies in the fuselage, and the need to brace himself for the impact of the ditching, all confused him, and he pulled the dinghy release by mistake. The Wellington was trailing the dinghy as it plunged into the sea.

Bell was delighted to find himself still connected to the aircraft. He had been terrified that the Wimpey would break its back. The impact had been no more violent than the sudden braking of a bus. In a moment he was up to the waist in water. He jettisoned his escape hatch and climbed out on to the tailplane, reaching up to the dinghy-release lever on the rudder. He groped, made contact, gripped, and pulled. He felt no response. Shouldn't he have felt or heard something if the dinghy had inflated? He peered forward along the fuselage but could see no sign of the dinghy, no sign of anyone. Was he going to be the only one to get out? He noticed that the port wing was twisted grotesquely up to the sky. The old crate was very nose-down. He must try to climb up and along the fuse-lage and see what he could do for the others. As he began to lift himself up, the Wellington rose on the swell and plunged down steeply on the far side, drenching him and forcing him to cling to the tail-plane. Convinced that the aircraft was about to sink, he inflated his Mae West and stepped off into the sea.

The buoyancy of the Mae West kept his head and shoulders well clear of the water. He struck out strongly to get away from the aircraft, and as he looked back over his shoulder he caught sight of the dinghy, floating calmly enough about twenty yards ahead of the Wellington, two silhouettes in it showing up clearly against the sky. He swam towards it, keeping clear of the sinking aircraft, and before he reached it he was hailed by three of the crew – Bancroft, Irving and McNeil. McNeil looked dazed and Irving had hurt his back, but all three were looking out for Handley and Robinson, the two missing members of the crew. Eventually they spotted one of them struggling with difficulty towards the dinghy. It was Robinson, and he seemed badly hurt. Bancroft jumped in after him and they dragged him aboard. There was still no sign of Handley.

Everyone began talking at once, telling of how they were affected by the impact and how they got out. All the men in the front of the aircraft remembered Handley going back from the front turret, but no one knew what happened to him after the ditching. McNeil thought he'd seen him disappear through the escape hatch in front of him. A wave of water had swept through the fuselage from nose to tail immediately on impact and they had each had the utmost difficulty in getting out.

Bancroft jumped back into the sea and made a complete circuit of the Wellington. The aircraft was waterlogged and sinking, and if Handley was still inside there was no chance for him. Shaking his head in dismay, he made his way slowly back to the dinghy, looking back at the Wellington after every few strokes, hoping against hope that Handley would appear.

Back in the dinghy, Bancroft ordered the water-chamber in the well of the dinghy to be filled so as to stabilise the dinghy in the choppy sea and help them keep as near the scene of the crash as possible, both for Handley's sake (in case he should be floating somewhere in the vicinity) and to improve their chances of rescue. He found the crew uncertain whether the dinghy was still attached by rope to the sinking aircraft. There was a moment of panic. Bancroft dived in again with Bell and they swam under the dinghy several times, but found no sign of a rope. As they hauled themselves back, the Wellington settled so deeply in the water that only the tail remained visible. Then even that disappeared. Whatever hopes they still entertained aloud for Handley, each man felt in his heart that the front-gunner had gone.

'Who pulled the dinghy release?' asked Bell. 'When I pulled it in the tail nothing happened.'

Bancroft looked at Irving. 'You'd better tell him,' he said.

Irving tried to turn round to speak to Bell, but groaned as his injured back prevented him. 'I pulled the dinghy release instead of the flotation-gear lever just before we ditched,' he said. 'When we hit the water we were trailing the dinghy.'

Bell had a vision of the dinghy being churned up by the propellers. He pressed his fingers into it gingerly to reassure himself that it was still stout and seaworthy. 'It's a wonder it wasn't cut to pieces,' he said.

'It must have been flung forward somehow,' said Bancroft. 'Anyway, we found it sitting right in front of our noses when we got out.'

They sat silent for a few moments, enjoying their luck. But the situation in the dinghy gave them very little cause for more than a fleeting satisfaction. Robinson was sprawled in the well of the dinghy with a badly lacerated leg; the cut was about five inches in length and went through to the bone. Irving's injured back meant that he needed a lot of room to keep at all comfortable, and McNeil was half dazed with concussion. Bancroft's left eyebrow was split open and the blood had caked all over his face, and Bell was bleeding from cuts in the hands and legs. As they twisted and turned to try and ease their discomfort they aggravated each other's injuries.

Their troubles were now increased by a severe storm. There was no rain, but the seas were so heavy that sometimes the dinghy was flung up by a wave at an angle of nearly ninety degrees. Yet somehow it shipped very little water. They emptied the water from the stabilising well and found that this made the dinghy even more seaworthy.

Bancroft pinned his hopes on the coming of daylight. Search aircraft and air/sea rescue launches would be sent out from Malta in the morning. One at least of the Beaufighter pilots must surely have recognised the aircraft as being a Wellington. Perhaps they'd both realised it, because there had been only the one burst. Anyway, some action would be taken as soon as they were reported overdue. McNeil's S O S should have been picked up by someone. There would be the radar plot at Malta, too – that should have told the ground plotters something. In any case they couldn't be more than a few miles off the shore. With daylight they would be able to see land and perhaps attract attention.

In the morning Bancroft examined the dinghy rations and equipment. He found at once that several items were missing, the most serious being a proper water ration. There was only one rubber water-bottle in the dinghy, and this proved on examination to be less than half full and to contain an opaque liquid revolting to the taste. Bancroft remembered for the first time that the emergency water ration from the aircraft had been strapped to Handley's waist.

How many of the discrepancies in the dinghy equipment were due to negligence, and how many to the manner in which the dinghy had been launched, Bancroft could only guess. There were three distress rockets, one canvas paddle and any amount of concentrated chocolate. The only other articles that seemed at all likely to be of value to them were their revolvers.

To dole out the water ration, Bancroft made use of the hollow wooden plugs designed for stopping up holes in the dinghy. They contained less than a small egg-cup. On the first day no one was given water except Robinson. McNeil, still suffering from concussion and a raging headache, complained bitterly at being left out.

The storm continued throughout the day and they all had to fight against seasickness, most of them succumbing at various times. Still it did not rain. But the most depressing feature of the storm was the poor visibility. They could see no further than a few hundred yards, and this gave them no chance of catching a glimpse of Malta and very little of being found by searching vessels or aircraft.

During the day they tended Robinson's injured leg as best they could. The first-aid bandages were intact, and they used these after bathing the wound in the sea. It was an extremely ugly gash and it completely incapacitated Robinson. Irving, too, felt very stiff and was at first unable to take his turn at paddling. Bancroft and Bell took it in turns to try to propel the dinghy in a southerly direction with the one canvas paddle. McNeil was still suffering from concussion and seemed unable to apply himself to anything. After the first few hours Bell paddled for most of the time. When Bancroft was using the canvas paddle Bell used a large silver cigarette-case, one of two he carried which had been given to him by the German Mercedes company when he completed his apprenticeship as a motor mechanic. He found that by closing his mind to his surroundings he could paddle without rest for hours on end. At these times he generally concentrated his thoughts on home.

They had a small pocket-compass in the dinghy equipment and this was sufficient for rough navigation. Telling the time was one of their chief difficulties as all their watches had stopped at ten past twelve, the time of the ditching. Towards late afternoon the sea was calmer, but visibility was very little better. Their most heartening moment came when Bell spotted a yellow object floating in the water some two hundred yards off. At first they thought it might be Handley, or his Mae West, but when they got to it they found it was a table from the aircraft. This encouraged in them the hope that they had not drifted far.

On the whole Bancroft still felt optimistic. They had proof that they were still in the vicinity of their place of ditching. Porpoises had been playing around them during the afternoon, and porpoises generally kept close to land. Besides, he had had such a clear view of Malta when he brought the aircraft in for the ditching that they could not be far away. The radio had given trouble and it might be unsafe to assume that the S O S had been picked up, but it seemed more than likely that Malta had refused to answer because of the air raid. McNeil had said that there was nothing wrong with his transmitter.

'What do you think about your S O S, Mac?' Bancroft asked him. 'Do you think it went out all right?'

McNeil returned Bancroft's gaze stupidly. Bancroft could see that he was making a great effort to remember. 'I . . . I think so.' His speech was slurred, but the sound of his own voice seemed to rouse him. 'I'm sure it must have done.' Bancroft waited as McNeil gathered his thoughts together and translated them into words. 'The receiver seemed to be duff, but the transmitter was showing aerial current. Someone should have picked it up.'

'Where were you when you sent it? Over Malta?'

The effort to remember seemed to have exhausted McNeil already.

'I don't know. I was still sending it when we ditched.'

'Long enough for them to get a bearing on us?'

There was a long pause. 'Yes. I think so.'

'Did you clamp the key down[1] when we ditched?' asked Bell.

McNeil turned slowly to face Bell.

'What?'

'The key,' said Bell. 'Did you clamp it down?'

'Yes. I must have done.'

Bancroft turned to Bell. 'Well, that's good enough. They'll have got a bearing on us all right. As soon as this weather clears up they'll be out searching for us.' He noticed that McNeil was still looking dazed and worried. 'Don't you worry, Mac,' he said. 'You did all right. Get some rest and forget about it.'

The night was calm, and Robinson, Irving and McNeil all slept a little. Bancroft and Bell sat on the edge of the dinghy, discussing their chances, keeping a look-out and waiting for dawn. When daylight came the visibility was good. There was still no sign of Malta.

Bancroft and Bell settled down to paddling again. There were no porpoises now. Both men were confident of rescue that day. They tried to steer a southerly course as before. 'If we miss Malta, there's always Africa,' said Bell.

---

[1] The instructions were that, immediately before ditching, the transmitter morse-key should be locked so that a continuous note was radiated, enabling ground stations who might have picked up the S O S to get a bearing.

During the morning they suddenly felt the dinghy brushing against something rough and rasping. The water swirled beside the dinghy and Bancroft pointed down in horrified excitement.

'Look there!' he shouted. 'It's a shark! It's a shark!'

They watched the water swirling and saw the ugly crescent of the mouth beneath the snout.

'They don't have sharks in the Mediterranean,' said Irving. His voice sounded strangely off-pitch.

'They do, you know,' said Bancroft. 'There's so much in the Med these days for them to feed on.'

They shuddered. For several minutes they watched the shark with a mixture of horror and fascination. Bancroft assured the rest of them that the shark was most unlikely to attack them. No one believed him. The shark was with them all day.

Keeping one eye on their new companion, they watched the sky and the horizon anxiously. There was no sound of searching aircraft, no sign of a rescue launch. Bancroft doled out a thimble of water to each man twice during the day, at ten in the morning and again at dusk. The sun was blistering. Everyone was wearing shorts except Bancroft, and their legs were raw. Robinson was still silent and looked ill. Irving was better, but McNeil's concussion had lessened his will to resist, and he persisted in giving way to the most pessimistic utterances on their prospects of rescue. Bancroft and Bell kept paddling in turns and snatched what sleep they could.

Next morning the shark was still with them, orbiting the

dinghy unceasingly. They tried hard to maintain their confidence that rescue was imminent, but as the lonely day wore on they found less and less reason for optimism. Surely, if someone had been searching for them, they would have seen or heard some sign by now? Perhaps they had drifted further than they thought during the storm. The table they saw might have drifted with them. And yet surely it couldn't have drifted away until the aircraft broke up. On the first day the weather would have prevented any attempt at rescue, but the last two days had been calm and clear. If they were so near Malta, surely they should have heard the noise of aircraft almost continually? There were aircraft coming and going all the time at Malta, German and Italian aircraft too. They had ditched north of Malta – surely German aircraft attacking Malta from Sicily must fly over them? There seemed no doubt that they were a long way from Malta, perhaps forty or fifty miles at least. Whether they were still north of the island, or whether they had drifted south or east or west, was anyone's guess. All they could do was try to make progress in a southerly direction and rely on the search that would surely be kept up for several days on the strength of McNeil's S O S.

Another thought occurred to Bancroft. They were a ferry crew, ferrying an aircraft to the Middle East. Bitter experience had taught him that transit aircrew were the lowest form of animal life in the Royal Air Force. To the operations-room boys at Malta they were nothing more than a liability. Aircrews were reckoned to be the least expendable of all currencies; but Malta might be forgiven for not risking a valuable searching aircraft in an area where the Luftwaffe had air superiority. Suppose they had done a quick search at the first opportunity and then given them up? Didn't that make sense?

Bancroft took a grip on himself. Whatever he did he must maintain an inward conviction that rescue would eventually come. He owed that to the rest of his crew, especially to the injured men. Any sign that his confidence was flagging might have a disastrous effect on morale. Already McNeil's depression was affecting the others.

He spoke to McNeil. 'How are you feeling today, Mac?'

Bancroft was completely unprepared for McNeil's response. He was unfamiliar with the effects of concussion and he didn't know what it could do to a man. McNeil burst into tears.

The tinge of kindness in Bancroft's tone had been the undoing of McNeil. The tears welled down his face as he tried to say that there was no sense in paddling because they weren't getting anywhere, that it was obvious that no one was looking for them, that nobody cared about them, that nobody had any idea where they were.

'But . . . what about your S O S?' asked Bancroft.

'They never got it,' said McNeil. 'Isn't it obvious? If anyone had picked it up they'd have found us by now. How do they know where to look for us, anyway? We're hopelessly lost and they haven't got a clue where we are. Can't you see?'

'But if you clamped the key down . . .' began Bancroft.

'Who said I did?' interrupted McNeil.

'Well, you did clamp it down, didn't you? Anyway, you said you did.'

'Did I?'

They watched anxiously as McNeil gazed at them helplessly, still trying to pierce the fog of his mind. At length Bancroft spoke, enunciating his words with great care.

'Look, Mac, it's important to us all. You must try and remember.'

McNeil seemed to get a grip on himself for a moment. 'I . . . I remember sending the S O S. I sent it three times . . . at least, I was sending it the third time . . . when we hit.'

'What happened then?'

'I hadn't had a chance even to brace myself. I was thrown forward . . . and then the next thing I knew I was up to my neck in water.'

'Then . . . then you didn't clamp the key down at all?'

'I don't see how I could have done. I didn't have a chance.'

'I see. Well, you did all you could, anyway.' Bancroft looked dully at Bell, and then looked quickly away, lest anyone should see the despair that he felt sure must be showing in his eyes. What McNeil had said meant the shattering of much that had given them reason for hope. Perhaps everything. It would be a moment or two before he could build their hopes anew.

'Look,' said Bell suddenly a few minutes later. 'The porpoises are back.'

'That means the shark's gone, anyway,' said Bancroft. He was beginning to build already.

For the rest of that day Bancroft and Bell paddled strongly towards the south. Wherever they might be in relation to Malta, their main hope of reaching friendly territory must surely lie to the south. Land might be nearer to the north, but there was no straight length of coastline that way and they might pass near islands, even near Sicily, without making contact. If he had been sure that enemy-held territory was close at hand, Bancroft might have aimed for it because of the injured men. But failing any clear idea of where they were, Malta or the coast of Africa seemed the best bet. He wondered how long they could last without water. Six or seven days, perhaps. He embarked on a little mental arithmetic, dividing the number of days into the possible distance between them and the North African coast, but he knew at once that the answer would be unpalatable and he shut it from his mind.

After the nagging uncertainty of the first two days, they derived profound comfort from a calm acceptance of their position. Now it was up to them. No waiting around for help from other quarters any more. They made up their minds about what lay ahead of them and steeled themselves for it.

After three days resting Irving found that his back allowed him more freedom of movement and he joined in the paddling. He was not able to put much weight into it at first, but he found the effort good for his soul. Irving's example encouraged McNeil to join in, and for a time he paddled strongly; but he was unable to sustain the mental effort, and within a few minutes he had let the paddle slip from his fingers. Even then he didn't grasp the significance of what he had done, and it wasn't until Bell saw the paddle floating some thirty yards away from the dinghy and shouted in alarm that McNeil came to life. They hardly had time to assess the risk of being attacked by a shark if they tried to recover it when the paddle filled with water and sank.

Bell produced his second large cigarette-case and took over the paddling from McNeil. But McNeil was penitent, and Bancroft allowed him to take another turn later in the day. Within a few minutes he had lost the cigarette-case.

The heat on this day was intense, and great rolls of skin like parchment began to peel off the legs of the men wearing shorts. Bancroft, Bell and Irving slipped their clothes off and immersed themselves in the water for a few minutes, but McNeil was a non-swimmer, and Robinson was in such a bad way that he was hardly able to talk. Worst of all, they were now unable to revive themselves with the priceless morning and evening tot of water. The last drop had been given to Robinson that morning.

All that night and throughout the next day Bell continued paddling with a steady rhythm that took no account of time or fatigue. He had passed his only remaining cigarette-case to Bancroft and was now paddling with one of the distress rockets. It was waterproofed and made a tolerably efficient paddle. When he finally rested towards late afternoon Bancroft told him that he had been paddling for sixteen hours at a stretch.

Robinson's lips and tongue were swollen and caked, and when he tried to speak they were unable to understand him. McNeil and Irving both had periods of delirium, and in one of these moments McNeil attacked Bancroft bitterly for allotting the major portion of the meagre water ration to Robinson. They were all demoralised by thirst, although Bell, with his ability to close his mind to his surroundings, seemed the least affected.

During the early afternoon Irving, crazed with thirst, urinated into an empty chocolate tin and kept it by him, sipping at it whenever he could bring himself to do so. Five days virtually without water, with concentrated chocolate as the only food, and without any bowel movement, had turned his urine into a thick yellow treacly liquid, extraordinarily repulsive to the sight and taste. Nevertheless he persisted in his attempts to drink it, finally mixing it with a piece of chocolate and trying desperately hard to swallow it. The others followed Irving's example, but Bancroft and Bell were so revolted that they were unable to swallow anything and afterwards felt sick and disgusted. Bell resolved not to try it again. When his mouth felt intolerably dry he rinsed it out with sea-water. Bancroft did the same.

McNeil kept insisting that they were making no progress with the paddling and that their situation was hopeless. But during the day they all felt a peculiar whirring sensation in their ears, and though it was some time before they realised it, the conviction grew on them that the sound they could hear was marine engines, perhaps the engines of craft searching for them. Visibility was restricted by heat haze, but they kept a ceaseless watch all round the dinghy, and towards dusk they all thought they saw land to the north – all except Robinson, who was in a more or less continual coma and took little part in the daily excitements and disappointments. But none of them was certain that the shadow he saw on the horizon was really

26

land, and as the sun went down they kept testing each other to see if they all saw land in the same place. It was not a strip of coastline they saw, but an isolated speck that might be no more than barren rock or a trick of the sun and the cloud. Their hopes were rekindled but they were all sceptical and there was no real elation amongst them.

On the morning of the sixth day Bancroft pointed excitedly to a school of turtles which splashed within a few yards of the dinghy. Each man drew his revolver, and they began taking pot shots at the turtles, but all the guns had rusted up except Bell's. Bancroft was acknowledged the best shot, and he borrowed Bell's gun, but although he fired round after round the turtles seemed impervious to gunfire.

'It's no good,' said Bancroft. He handed Bell the gun. 'Give me a knife, someone.' Bell found a curved knife in the dinghy equipment and handed it quickly to Bancroft.

'This is where we eat,' said Bancroft.

'What are you going to do?' asked Bell.

'There's only one way to catch a live turtle,' said Bancroft. 'Drop on its back and hack under the shell at the head. If you catch them in the right place they're yours.'

Bell was apprehensive. The turtles were each the size of the top of a coffee-table and they looked most dangerous mounts. Bancroft held the knife between clenched teeth and dived overboard, but he waited in vain for another school or a straggler to approach the dinghy, and the first school did not return. At length he climbed back into the dinghy and threw the knife down in disgust.

Bell still showed remarkable stamina in the way he kept paddling for many hours, and on this day he embarked on another marathon, closing his mind to his surroundings and concentrating his thoughts on his wife. Was it true that it was possible to reach someone spiritually close and mentally attuned by concentration of thought? With the speed and certainty of a cinematic cut, he projected his mind back across the many hundred miles he had covered, into his home. His concentration was so intense as to be almost hypnotic. If there was such a thing as telepathy he had surely found it. The well-remembered things of home were almost real enough to touch. He had been completely absorbed in this way for some time when a shout from Bancroft brought him back to his surroundings with a sickening shock, like hearing one's own voice in a dream.

'It's an aircraft!' Bancroft was yelling. 'I tell you it's an aircraft! Look!' Bell tried to follow the pointing finger, but both he and Bancroft were too excited for accuracy. McNeil and Irving, too, had come to life and were scanning the sky, and even Robinson showed animation and turned his head in the direction of the sound.

'Get a distress signal ready,' shouted Bancroft.

Bell had the signal in his hand. He had been paddling with it for two days. He began to tear off the waterproof case, wondering if there was the remotest chance that the signal would still be serviceable. There were two more in the dinghy pack, but they would take a moment to find. As he tore the last of the waterproofing away he could hear the unmistakable whine of aircraft engines. When he looked up he saw the silhouette of a three-engined aircraft not more than a mile or so away, flying at perhaps a thousand feet. There was no such thing as a British three-engined aircraft. He felt the thoughts of all the others heavy around him as the disappointment came and was digested and gave way to gratitude that anything bearing promise of rescue could come so near.

'It's a Junkers 52,' croaked McNeil.

'Have you got the rocket ready?' shouted Bancroft.

Bell was intent on timing the flight of the rocket to converge exactly with the course of the aircraft and burst where the crew could not help but see it. His fingers sought the friction-tape which would ignite the rocket. 'Wait till you see the whites of their eyes,' he said.

'For Christ's sake fire the thing,' shouted Bancroft. 'What the blazes are you doing with it?'

Bell sat coolly watching the approaching aircraft, enjoying every moment of it, determined to make this his finest shot. It seemed to the others that the aircraft had almost passed overhead when at last there was an explosion and a rush of air beside them and they saw Bell gasping in agony and holding his arm limply at his side. The aircraft was still at a thousand feet and almost directly over the dinghy. The rocket was at five hundred feet already and spiralling upwards, right into the path of the aircraft.

'My God,' said Irving, 'it's going to hit it.'

Bell's arm was completely numb. He watched as a man might watch who had fired his last round at some predatory creature of the air. His aim was true and he knew that the paths of the two objects would meet. The rocket burst with a shower of coruscation at exactly the height of the aircraft and directly in its path.

For several agonising moments there was no reaction from the aircraft. Then it banked to port and began a wide circuit of the dinghy, to the accompaniment of a cracked cheer and shouting from the dinghy. A moment later they saw the port window of the pilot's cockpit pushed back and a Very pistol pointed out. Three green stars exploded above their heads and fell slowly, leaving a trail of smoke. They were overwhelmed by a sense of joy and comradeship as it was borne upon them that rescue was at hand.

'It isn't a Jerry,' said Bell. 'Look at those markings. What is it? An Eyetie?'

'It's an Eyetie all right,' said Bancroft. 'Can't be a Junkers 52, then. Unless the Eyeties are flying them. What's the name of that Italian three-engined job?'

'Something like . . . Savoia 79?' suggested Bell.

'That's it,' said Bancroft. 'Savoia 79. They're Eyeties all right. I wonder what they'll do?'

As they watched, the Italian aircraft completed a second circuit of the dinghy and then made off in a northerly direction, at right angles to its original course.

'She wasn't heading that way before,' said Bancroft.

'I wonder if she's gone to get help,' said Irving.

The Savoia persisted on her new course for some minutes, watched anxiously by Bancroft and his crew. Then it turned deliberately west again, back on to its original course.

'Where are they off to now?' queried Irving.

'They're not coming back this way,' said McNeil.

'I've got it!' exclaimed Bancroft. 'Don't you see what they're trying to tell us? That's the direction of the nearest land – the heading they flew away from the dinghy on before they turned back on course! They can even probably *see* land up there. It's up to us to take the hint. Come on, Dinger, do your stuff.'

'You realise what it means?' asked Bell.

'What?'

'We'll be heading north – away from Malta.'

'How do we know that we haven't come south of Malta?'

'We don't,' said Bell. He handed Bancroft one of the two remaining rockets and the two of them set to work to try and make progress in the direction indicated by the Italian aircraft. In spite of the incentive they now had, neither Irving nor McNeil was physically able to take a turn at paddling, though Irving took charge of the navigation and did what he could to encourage them. McNeil was sceptical of Bancroft's interpretation of the aircraft's change of course and thought they would do better to stay where they were.

'They've found us,' said McNeil. 'After six days adrift we've been found. Now we're trying to disappear again.'

'God helps those who help themselves,' said Bancroft. 'They'll be out looking for us, we know, but there's no doubt about what they were trying to tell us.'

McNeil made no further comment, and Bancroft was relieved. There was no certainty that the Italian aircraft had pointed the way to the nearest land. What they had probably done was point to the nearest Axis-held territory. Malta might be much nearer in a different direction. But speculation of that kind would get them nowhere. Rescue must surely be on the way, and meanwhile they had something to aim at.

Whether they were making any impression on the distance that separated them from land was uncertain, but they kept doggedly on until the next day, when the heat of the sun eventually forced them to rest. There was no sign of any search party. Bancroft had the same thought now that he'd had when they were expecting rescue from Malta – would the Italians send anything so vulnerable as a rescue launch out into the Mediterranean to pick them up? And yet the solitude of the past week made him wonder whether they could be in the Mediterranean at all. Perhaps somehow they'd got into the wrong sea.

He tried to visualise a map of the Mediterranean. Suppose they had stooged on past Malta without seeing it, and suppose the land they thought was Malta had in fact been Sicily. Or even Italy. Could they possibly be north of Sicily? That hardly agreed with his interpretation of the behaviour of the Italian aircraft. Could they even be in the Adriatic? They had been airborne long enough. Nine hours from Gibraltar to the ditching, when they should have made Malta in six. And yet there were the headwinds and the slow groundspeed. And the air raid at Malta, and the Beaufighters. No, they couldn't have been that much out. He turned to discuss the possibilities with Irving, but checked himself just in time. No sense at this stage in sowing further speculation and doubt.

One thing was certain — if rescue didn't come soon it would come too late to save Robbie. He hadn't spoken for two days and his tongue and mouth were swollen to twice their normal size. He looked desperately ill. He was probably dying. Irving and McNeil both had their moments of lucidity, but for much of the time they were in a sort of delirium, muttering unintelligible or inconsequential things. He wondered if their minds would ever recover.

Towards midday Bancroft and Bell, scanning the horizon in search of some rescue craft, both spotted what looked like a seaplane in the same moment. Now came their worst mental torture so far. They recognised the plane as an Italian Cant seaplane, and by the height at which it was flying and its regular changes of course it was obviously carrying out some kind of search. It was flying low over the water three to four miles off, turning ninety degrees on to a new course every few minutes, and undoubtedly searching the whole area. And yet Bancroft could see that unless they changed their present area of search they would be most unlikely to discover the dinghy.

'How about sending off a rocket?' asked Bell.

'They might see it,' agreed Bancroft. 'We'll try it next time they head this way.'

Bell stripped one of the rockets of its casing and made ready for the firing. It was a tense moment. Their only means of propulsion were the two rockets, and yet their value as signals was infinitely greater than their value as paddles. If they could attract the attention of the Italian crew, the Cant would almost certainly be able to alight by the dinghy and at least embark some of the injured men. They might all be safe by dark. The prospect was so infinitely desirable that they could not prevent their thoughts from dwelling on it. But would the Cant crew see a signal at this distance? Surely there was at least a chance.

The seaplane was now nothing more than a speck on the horizon. It carried on its course away from the dinghy until they were gripped by the fear that the search had been abandoned. They sat immobilised, silent, statuesque. Then at last the seaplane turned on to a course parallel to them, and at length turned again so that the dinghy lay right in its path. The power of movement returned to them. This was their chance.

'How long will they stay on this heading?' asked Bell.

'I've been trying to do a rough time-check for each leg,' said Bancroft. 'I think they're changing course about every three minutes. We'd better wait about two minutes.'

Bell tried to count the seconds as he kept his eye on the approaching seaplane. How did one time two minutes? It wasn't long enough to boil an egg. He thought suddenly of the years of his boyhood, when they had stood in the playground at school on a cold November morning each year, waiting in heavy silence between the gun that fired at eleven o'clock and the maroon that shrilled at two minutes past. Remembrance Day. He tried to recall how long two minutes had seemed then.

Bancroft roused him to action. 'Right, Dinger, let it go.' Bell tore the friction-tape, holding the rocket at arm's length, dreading the shock of the explosion. A moment later his arm was limp at his side again and the rocket was racing skywards with a whoosh that filled his ears. The seaplane came steadily on.

'They haven't seen it,' said McNeil.

'Too early to say,' said Bancroft.

Bell narrowed his eyes and watched for a long moment. 'At least they'd have dipped their wings if they'd seen it,' he said. 'This time I think Mac's right.'

'For Christ's sake fire the other rocket,' yelled McNeil.

'Hold it!' shouted Bancroft. They wouldn't fire their last rocket yet. Not yet. Besides, the three minutes were up.

A second later the seaplane turned on to a new heading away from the dinghy. It did not turn again. Bell picked up the last rocket from the well of the dinghy and began paddling impassively. He did not turn to watch the seaplane merge into the horizon.

The morale of the men in the dinghy, stimulated by the excitement of the day before and sustained by the sight of the searching seaplane, now fell to its lowest ebb. Heat and thirst distracted them, and Irving and McNeil fell into almost continual delirium. Even Bancroft and Bell began to lose their grip. They lapsed spasmodically into a torpor in which they dreamed of cascading water and lemons and luscious fruit. Still Bell paddled when he could.

During the afternoon Bell noticed that the inflated rim of the dinghy was worn right down to the canvas where his arm had brushed against it countless times. At first he thought that this was another hallucination. He could not believe that he could have done so much damage without noticing it earlier. The discovery brought a new fear, fear that the air in the pneumatic rim might begin to escape from this weakened area. They plied it gently with their fingers and it seemed still firm and durable. Bell did no more paddling that day.

'Why didn't you let me stay on that island?' Irving suddenly demanded of Bell. 'There was water there, and yet you paddled past it.'

'What are you talking about?' asked Bell in astonishment.

'That island,' said Irving. 'That island where there was water. We could have stopped there, but you would keep on paddling.'

Bell, roused in that moment from hallucinations of his own, wondered if what Irving said might be true. He turned a distracted look at Bancroft. Bancroft shook his head. Reassured, Bell told Irving he'd been dreaming, and soon Irving had retreated again within himself, muttering now and again but aggressive no longer.

This is how it's going to be, thought Bell. One by one we shall go off our rockers. We shall lie here for perhaps three or four more days, dying slowly one by one, unbeknown to the next man until we start to smell, and then unburied because no one will have the strength to tip us over the side.

I shan't let this happen to me, thought Bell. He remembered the two morphia tablets he had in his pocket. He'd picked them up in an old first-aid pack months ago, and had carried them ever since. One would bring oblivion and two would be lethal. When the time came he would take them both. Better not tell the others. He still had his revolver, but somehow he didn't fancy that way. It would be the morphia tablets for him.

Similar thoughts were running through Bancroft's mind. He tried to assess their remaining expectation of life. Robbie would surely die within twenty-four hours. Irving and McNeil might linger on for three or four days. He and Bell might outlast them, but they would be the unlucky ones, having the longer time to contemplate certain and lingering and frightful death. He turned to Bell.

'I shan't wait for it, Dinger,' he said. 'I'll fight as long as I can, but before I lose my reason I shall go over the side.'

'Just like that?' Bell had a horror of drowning, a horror that had been with him all his life. Death he could contemplate, but not death by drowning.

'Just like that. It's the best way. Everyone says it's the best way. They even say it's pleasant. Quite pleasant. That'll be the way for me.'

'I shall end it too,' said Bell. 'But not that way.'

'Why not? It's so easy. And so fitting. And it's not messy. Besides, it disposes of the body. That gun of yours will make an awful mess. Who's going to clear it up? Look, I'll show you.'

While Bell watched uncertainly, Bancroft peeled off his clothes and stepped over the side of the dinghy. He plunged under the water and began to sink. Bell watched him go, down into the pellucid water, deeper and deeper until he seemed to be near the bottom. Bell could see the stones lying on the sea-bed. The water rippled around Bancroft as he sank, and suddenly Bell could see him no more.

He tried desperately to pierce the depths again, but all he could see now was the reflection of his own burnt face staring down. He waited. Bancroft was a long time down there. What was he doing? Trying to frighten me, thought Bell. He realised now just what the survival of his skipper meant to him. Without Bancroft he was alone with a dying man and two others who were delirious.

He called out 'Bancroft! Bancroft!' and realised in the same moment that he had never addressed his skipper by his surname before. Somehow there seemed nothing strange about it now. He had read somewhere that sound carried under water and he shouted again. 'Bancroft!' There was no need to give up just yet. There was still a chance – plenty of chance. Anyway, Bancroft had no right to leave him alone.

Suddenly the water opened in front of him and Bancroft shot clear, breathing fiercely and bloodshot round the eyes. He climbed unsteadily back into the dinghy.

'That's how I shall do it,' he said.

McNeil, whom Bancroft had thought was too far gone to take any notice of what he and Bell were doing, began to babble and weep at the return of his skipper. Bancroft spoke to him and was gratified to see him make a real effort to regain control. At length McNeil turned to Bell.

'Pray for us, Dinger,' he said.

'Why ask *me*?' demanded Bell. He looked away from McNeil and out towards the horizon. 'I've got no right to pray. No right to pray for myself, even, let alone for others. I never prayed when things were going right. I can't expect to be answered now.'

Bell kept his gaze averted. He knew in his heart that he had given McNeil the wrong answer, but it was too late to change it now.

Late on this seventh day, as the sun began to go down, Bell suddenly pointed wildly to the north. 'Look!' he shouted. 'Look! Can't you see it? It's Land! Land!'

They followed his trembling finger, and one by one they identified a sugar-loaf shape on the horizon which some trick of the light had exposed for the first time.

'It *might* be an island,' said Bancroft cautiously. 'My God, I believe it *is* an island.'

'Or it might be a rock,' said McNeil.

'Yes,' said Bell, deflated, 'it might be a rock.'

For twenty minutes, until the light began to fail, they strained their vision for further glimpses of land in the same direction in vain.

That evening, while the rest of the crew were asleep or in a coma, Bancroft and Bell discussed their chances of reaching the dark hump of land they had seen. They sat together on the edge of the dinghy and conversed in low tones, knowing that any plan they might form must be carried out by them alone. The rest of the men in the dinghy could be nothing more than a hindrance to them. Perhaps even a fatal hindrance.

'I wonder if we're getting anywhere with the paddling,' ruminated Bancroft.

Bell hesitated. 'I don't know,' he said. 'Most of the time we've been trying to make way to the south. Then when the aircraft pointed north we faced the other way. I don't think we've got far in either direction.' It was a bitter admission to have to make. Bell had borne the brunt of the paddling throughout.

'I've been thinking the same way,' said Bancroft. 'All I can suggest is that we must try and get a bit closer to land, and then swim for it.'

'And leave the others?'

'Yes. Their only chance will rest on whether we can make it or not. In fact, their chance would be better than ours.'

'How do you get that?'

'We might fail. If we made it we could certainly send someone back to pick them up, but if we didn't, well, they'd still have the same chance as they've got now.'

Bell considered this for some time. At length he said, 'Well, I'm game. Whatever you say goes.' Keeping well clear of the worn patch, he began paddling again towards the spot where they had seen the sugar-loaf hump.

'There's another thing that's worrying me,' said Bancroft a little later. 'What do we do if Stan or Mac go completely crazy? It could happen, you know. Could we leave them alone like that?'

'Why not?'

'They might be dangerous to each other. Or to Robbie.'

'If one of them gets that dangerous . . .' Bell shrank from the implications of what he had wanted to say.

'What?'

40

'Well, you know what they do in submarines.' He fingered his revolver.

Bancroft was silent for a while, alone with uneasy thoughts. Then he said, 'I can't think that they're strong enough to be dangerous to us. Not now, anyway. We'll have to chance what they may do to each other. Or to themselves.'

'I hope you're right,' said Bell.

'Keep going, Dinger. Try and get some sleep tonight and we'll see where our friend the sugar-loaf is tomorrow. We'll make it somehow.'

Bancroft lay awake for a long time, worrying about Bell's gun. He knew that one by one they were losing their sense of judgement and proportion. McNeil, because of his concussion – with the manner of his being shanghaied into a strange crew as a possible contributory reason – had been the first. Robinson was unconscious most of the time anyway. Now Irving had begun to imagine things. Could any one of them be trusted to behave rationally and objectively in any given set of circumstances? Could any one of them be trusted with a gun?

Arguments in the past few days had been frequent; almost every little incident had been made the excuse for acrimony. It wasn't just McNeil, either. He and Bell and Irving had been just as bad. They were all getting on each other's nerves. Was it right to allow so one-sided an argument as a gun to be in anyone's possession?

Bancroft decided that it very probably wasn't. Bell was asleep. It would be a simple matter to relieve him of the gun and throw it overboard.

Taking care not to rock the dinghy, he reached across Bell's waist, undid the holster, and pulled lightly at the revolver. In a moment he felt the weight of it in his hand. Better not to let Bell know of his decision, or why he had made it. Better not to discuss it with anyone. In the morning the gun would be gone and there would be nothing Bell could do about it. He fingered the gun regretfully for a full minute, still uncertain whether he was doing right, and then, making up his mind, he allowed the gun to slip quietly through his fingers into the sea.

Next morning Bancroft and Bell were awake at dawn, looking confidently for a sight of land. There was an early-morning mist, and when the sun came up a heat haze obscured the horizon. Sickened with disappointment, they fell silent, waiting listlessly for the weather to change. Bell noticed in an abstract kind of way that his gun was gone. It didn't seem to matter any more. He made a cursory search of the dinghy and then gave it up. Someone must have heard them talking. Perhaps Bancroft had decided that the responsibility of having the gun was too much for them in their present state and heaved it overboard. He didn't care so long as one of the others hadn't got it. Instinctively he felt for his morphia capsules. They were still there.

All day they were tormented by raging thirst, which they tried to relieve from time to time by gargling and dowsing their heads in sea-water. They did not try too hard not to swallow just a little water. They found it freshening. Irving had at last given up trying to swallow his own urine, and he followed their example, but Robinson resolutely refused to take sea-water and persisted in drinking his urine. During the day they discovered small jelly sea-horses about the size of a florin resting on the sea-foam, and they put them on their tongues until they melted. They were fishy and salt to the taste, but seemed less salt than sea-water, and the cool moisture brought fleeting relief.

Bancroft put some of these pieces of jelly in Robinson's mouth. Robinson seemed to be unconscious most of the time, but occasionally his lips moved as though he wanted to say something. No sound ever came. Bancroft was astonished to find him still alive. He had been convinced that he was dying two days ago. Robinson's mouth and tongue were a ghastly sight, swollen unrecognisably and caked with white. Yet he seemed able to swallow the moisture from the jelly. Bancroft gave all he found for the next hour or so to Robinson. Bell and Irving did the same.

'I can't think how he's lasting out,' Bancroft said quietly to Bell. 'I can't think that there's any chance of his ever recovering.'

'What do we do if he dies?'

Bancroft's voice fell to a whisper. 'Pitch him over the side, I suppose.'

'That's what'll happen to us all, one by one,' said Bell.

'Do you think his blood would be any use to us?'

Bell did not flinch at this question. It seemed a natural one. He had thought of it himself already.

'We could try it.'

'If he dies,' said Bancroft, 'we'll cut a vein in his leg at once.'

Bell nodded. 'All right.'

That afternoon a tiger shark, nearly twice the size of their previous visitor, swam round the dinghy, twisting and turning on its back and showing a hideous necklace of teeth as it did so. They shuddered at the sight of it, but their emotions had been drained from them and they hardly felt fear.

'He looks big enough to tip us over,' said Bell.

'He is. Seven feet long, I should say. Don't move. If he does look like attacking us, splash the water as much as you can with both hands. Do what I do.'

They watched apprehensively. An hour later they lost sight of it. Had it made off or was it about to attack them unseen? They waited in taut trepidation. At length they saw the wake of the shark some distance away. When the shark finally left them they forgot about it instantly.

Late in the day the haze cleared and they were overjoyed to find that they had drifted a little nearer land. The sugar-loaf hump had changed into a rocky lump sticking straight out of the sea, with a thin faint line of coastline beyond it. But land still looked remote and unattainable, and although Bancroft and Bell both paddled for a while, the effort needed to make any real progress exhausted them quickly and they were forced to stop.

Bell was overwhelmed by a sense of frustration at the ease with which their plight could be changed into rescue and rehabilitation. For the want of a passing ship, a searching aircraft, some means of propulsion, five men who were now alive would be dead in . . . forty-eight hours, three days perhaps for some of them. It seemed so absurd, so wasteful, so unnecessary, so unreal. There were times when he didn't believe it could really be happening to him.

He tried to imagine his wife as a widow. How she would receive the news. He saw the telegraph boy rest his bicycle outside the house, felt the surge of fear his wife would feel as she saw the boy at the gate, the awful shock as she opened the door and saw the telegram. If they could reach the piece of land ahead of them he might perhaps be back with her in a week. Even less. But how were they to reach it? It was beyond them, utterly beyond them. It might as well be a thousand miles away for all the chance they had of gaining it.

The heat was intolerable and thirst gripped them all. Speech became impossible. It was not until nightfall that Bancroft spoke again.

'Tomorrow's our last chance,' he said. 'Tomorrow will be the ninth day. If rescue doesn't come tomorrow, we shall be done.'

They all slept a little that night. Bancroft and Bell found that they were no longer continually conscious of thirst, although they still dreamed of waterfalls and swiftly running streams and exotic fruits. They felt an immense burden of lassitude upon them, enervating but strangely pleasant and soothing after the long hours of mental and physical strain. Bell wondered if this was how Irving and McNeil and Robbie had felt in the last few days. Relaxed, and resigned. Probably it was the beginning of the end for them. But if this was dying of thirst it was better than the agonies of living.

When the sun came up next morning it no longer tormented them. For the first few hours it threw a shimmering haze which blanketed the land and reduced visibility to no more than a mile or so, but towards noon the haze lifted suddenly and they saw land again, perceptibly nearer but not quite in the same direction. Bancroft decided that they were drifting past an island. He and Bell tried paddling again for brief periods, but they made no impression and merely exhausted themselves.

'There's only one thing a man can do when he feels like we do,' said Bancroft.

'What's that?'

'Swim.'

Bell was startled from his lethargy. 'We couldn't swim that distance?'

'We might.'

'How far is it? Twenty miles?' Bell laughed. The skipper was slipping, too.

'I shouldn't think it's more than ten miles,' Bancroft said. 'How far can you see across water? About three miles? At eye-level I mean. At that rate I don't think that piece of low-lying land behind the rock can be more than ten miles.'

'We still couldn't swim it.'

'We could try.'

Bell shook his head dubiously, his eye focused a long way off.

'Suppose we try and tow the dinghy for a bit,' said Bancroft. 'We might close the distance a little that way.'

'There's a painter about somewhere,' said Bell. He groped about in the well of the dinghy. 'Is this it?'

'It'll do, anyway.' Bancroft had begun to take off his battle-dress, and Bell took off his drill. They slipped over the side and harnessed themselves to the painter like a team of horses. McNeil and Irving watched dumbly. Robinson was still unconscious.

They swam for nearly twenty minutes, but by that time they were tiring rapidly and seemed to have made no headway. Bancroft reluctantly decided to abandon the attempt, and the two men crawled back into the dinghy, weak and despondent.

When they had recovered their breath and dried out in the sun, they dressed again and began to discuss the attempt. They were certainly no nearer land. The effort of towing had exhausted them quickly, and paddling was almost as tiring and equally futile. They no longer hoped for rescue. At this distance from land the dinghy would never be seen by the naked eye. There was only one chance.

'It's no good trying to bite bits out of it any longer,' said Bancroft. 'We shall have to swim for it all right.'

'I told you before,' said Bell. 'I'm game to try.'

'It's not so stupid as it sounds,' said Bancroft. 'We've got our Mae Wests. We ought not to drown. We'll have to chance the sharks, of course. But sharks don't usually come far inshore. All we've got to do is take it steadily and we'll get there.'

Their strength was flowing back after the effort of the towing, and with it came a freshness and vigour which they attributed to immersion in the sea. The sun was descending and Bancroft decided they should make the attempt straight away.

'There's no sense in waiting. Every hour that passes leaves us weaker. By this time tomorrow it may be beyond us. We'll go tonight.'

Stripped of their clothes and wearing nothing but their Mae Wests, they prepared for the last throw. McNeil and Irving watched them silently, unable to comprehend what the preparations meant, yet vaguely aware that they were about to be abandoned. Bancroft leaned over Robinson to make sure he was still breathing. He seemed much the same as he had been for several days, palsied and insensible, his face red and raw and angry, his mouth swollen and his tongue distended. It would be too late to save Robinson.

'What do we do if we see a shark?' asked Bell.

'Kick your legs out. Make a splash. They don't like disturbed water. Anyway, if we stick together they may not attack us.'

Bell put the thought of sharks from his mind. That was the only answer. But that bit about sticking together. He wasn't quite clear on that.

'Suppose . . . suppose one of us gets tired,' he said. 'Suppose one of us feels like giving up. What do we do?'

Bancroft could read what was in Bell's mind. There was little doubt who was the stronger swimmer. When they had been towing the dinghy, Bancroft's stroke had been so strong that sometimes he had found himself pulling Bell as well. And yet he knew that Bell was a fair swimmer. He wouldn't have let him make the attempt otherwise. Besides, Bell had tenacity.

It was a quality that might prove even more valuable than prowess as a swimmer. He'd keep going till the end.

But he hadn't answered Bell's question. It might well be that they had an equal chance of making it. There was the danger of sharks. It was quite true that sharks were less likely to attack two men than one. Again, if a shark attacked one of them, the other might escape. And if one of them got into difficulties, it would be madness for the other to waste his energy in trying to support him or help him back to the dinghy. That would be the last chance gone for everybody. Still, as the stronger and more efficient swimmer, Bancroft was reluctant to accept responsibility for the decision.

'What do you think about it?' he said. 'It's up to you.'

Bell had been thinking about it already. His standpoint was essentially different from Bancroft's, but he had arrived at the same conclusion.

'If one falls down,' he said, 'the other presses on.' He knew that what he really meant was, if I can't make it, leave me.

Bancroft turned to Irving and McNeil. 'Chaps,' he said, 'we're going to try and get help. If we sit here for another day or so we shall all be as bad as poor old Robbie. If we reach land we shall send a boat out for you. If we don't, well, you won't be any worse off than you are now.' Bancroft waited for their reaction. Irving said, 'Good show, good show,' and McNeil nodded. Bancroft was satisfied.

'Suppose someone finds them and not us?' said Bell. He turned to Irving. 'Stan, old boy, if you get picked up tonight or tomorrow, make sure they look for us, won't you?'

Irving seemed to understand. 'Yes,' he said, 'of course I will.'

They started out about an hour before dark. Bancroft was confident that he could strike the right course even at night. They were almost clear of the dinghy when McNeil's voice carried to them across the water.

'I'll bet they don't come back for us,' they heard him say.

This was too much for Bell. He was already finding it just about all he could manage to keep up with Bancroft. He had begun to think of the sharks. If he got behind, they would pick him off easily. A straggler. It would soon be dark. Bancroft might be able to find his way, but Bell knew with hollow certainty that he would get lost without Bancroft.

'That's done me,' he said. 'That's knocked all the stuffing out of me. I'm going back.'

Bancroft could see it was no good arguing. When Bell made up his mind, nothing would change it. In any case, Bancroft was already beginning to wonder whether they had been wise in starting out so late in the day. It might be better to try again first thing in the morning. He swung round in the water and followed Bell back to the dinghy.

'Look, Dinger,' said Bancroft, 'for God's sake don't take any notice of what they say. None of them know what they're talking about. They haven't been responsible for their actions for days. We'll have another go in the morning whatever happens.'

'I'm sorry,' said Bell.

They put their clothes on again, but the air was chill, and

they shivered throughout the night, unable to rest or sleep. The knowledge of the task that lay ahead of them contributed to their restlessness, and the hours seemed interminable. The sky was obscured by cloud and there was no way of reckoning time. They awaited the coming of dawn with impatience.

They set off again at first light. Robinson and McNeil were asleep or unconscious, but Irving managed a cheerful farewell. It was a dull morning, but visibility was good and they could see the rocky coastline lying like a thin strip of cloud on the horizon to the north. Bancroft thought it looked nearer than the night before. He wondered if they might have drifted a little towards land in the night. Perhaps it was just a trick of the light.

Both men used the breast stroke, and Bancroft swam well within himself so as not to exhaust Bell. Occasionally they used the crawl for a few minutes for variety, and several times they turned over on to their backs to rest. Even so, after about an hour Bell found himself getting steadily behind. It was like the Boat Race. Once you got behind you were lost. Bell felt more and more like the losing crew. They always looked all-in at the finish. It was the moral effect of being behind. He decided to give up the chase. If he was to get there he must do it in his own time.

Bancroft was now forty or fifty yards ahead and well away to the right. Bell did not realise the significance of this. The currents were strong and Bancroft was being less affected by them.

Bell settled down to a steady tempo and tried to forget about Bancroft. There was only one thing for it. He must close his mind and keep on going till he hit something. Keep on going. Close his mind. Keep on going.

There was no feeling left in Bell's limbs, but they still answered the call of his resolution. He did not stop to rest now. If the ponderous rhythm of his stroke were broken he might never be able to set it in motion again. His numbed mind was a fit companion for his numbed body. A mind aware of the weakness of the body would have surrendered.

Bell kept going like this for many, many hours. At length, in the early afternoon, he found himself swimming against some dark precipitous static monster which all but engulfed him. His mind swam slowly back to consciousness. He saw that he was dominated by a huge crescent-shaped rock. There was no way of outflanking it. He tried to clutch at it but the lichenous deposit left by the sea robbed him of a hold. His mind ached intolerably with the flow of thought after hours of mental anaesthetic. His limbs were no weaker than before except that now he was aware of their weakness. He knew he had reached the end.

With unfeeling fingers he undid the straps of his Mae West and slipped it from his shoulders. Now he would drink. Buckets and buckets and buckets of sea. He relaxed his grip on the Mae West and closed his mind for the last time.

Meanwhile Bancroft, never losing sight for more than a few moments of the main features of the coastline, kept steadily on. After about an hour in the water he found that he was drawing away from Bell, and he steadied so as not to lose him. But he found that swimming just below his natural speed hampered him and destroyed his rhythm. He decided to settle down to his own speed again and keep Bell in sight if he could. For a long time he could see the bobbing head behind him by looking over his shoulder to the left. Dinger was going well enough. A bit off track, perhaps, but he would make out all right.

Bancroft's movements became instinctive and mechanical. He forgot about Bell. When he thought of him again he looked round but couldn't see him.

Bancroft reckoned from the sun that he had been swimming for about four hours. He turned over on his back and rested for two or three minutes, and then trod water while he tried to gauge how far he was from the shore. At first he thought he had made very little impression on the distance, but then he recognised the outline of houses and knew that he must have covered a fair distance – perhaps as much as halfway.

It never occurred to Bancroft now to wonder what land it was that he was approaching. Sufficient that it was land at all. He tried to regain his old rhythm, but after the rest he found it hard to recapture. Within a few minutes he had to rest again. The Mae West was still buoyant, but he determined not to relax too completely. The long immersion had chilled him and he was frightened of cramp.

With a conscious effort of will he set his limbs in motion again. Half-way, he thought. Only half-way. If only he'd never stopped for that first rest.

He knew that he'd reached the critical phase of his journey. The point of no return. That was it. The point of no return.

He had thought of his wife many, many times during the

past ten days. Now he forced himself to think of her continuously. He tried to think of things that had happened to them together, but the effort of remembering incidents was beyond him and he concentrated all his thoughts on remembering her face. Soon the old rhythm returned.

He did not rest again. He could see the cottages quite clearly now. Two white ones together and a darker one away to the right and further inshore. He had a warm feeling of triumph inside. He was going to make it.

He could see something nearer to him than the cottages that he could not properly recognise. Then he saw what it was. A boat of some kind, only a small boat, perhaps a fishing-boat, crossing his track. If he could attract their attention it would save him the long last mile to the shore. He remembered Robbie and Stan and Mac in the dinghy. He wondered if Robbie was still alive. If he could stop this boat and direct it to the dinghy there might be a chance for Robbie yet.

Somewhere tied to his Mae West he should have a whistle. His fingers groped round his left shoulder until they grasped it. He drew in all the breath he could find and blew a blast that faded almost before it began. He paused, and blew again, a long shrill blast that emptied his lungs. It was no good. He was too far away.

The fishing-boat passed quickly in front of him and hurried on, brisk and business-like. The shore looked much more distant now. With a supreme effort he gathered the last of his strength for the final assault. Channel swimmers sometimes gave up when in sight of the shore.

The cottages were very clear now. He swam like an automaton, with his head down, refusing to measure the distance to the shore lest he should underestimate it. His limbs were leaden and the weight of his head was almost insupportable.

When the rocky sea-bed scraped his knees he was too shocked to understand what it meant for a moment. He touched bottom, but his knees collapsed, and although well within his depth for the last hundred yards he still swam until he reached the shallows, floundering and splashing the last few yards until at last he lay prostrate on the beach.

The cottages looked more unattainable now than ever. If he had been in their back yard he could not have struggled to them.

He could feel his heart pounding into the sand. He had to find the others. He had to find Bell. He had to find someone who would help him look for them. He crawled a few inches and then collapsed again. He tried to shout, and was appalled and silenced by the feeble sound.

He saw movement of some kind further along the shore. He could make out the figure of a man staring down the beach. Whatever must he look like, lying there naked except for his Mae West. He tried to raise his arm, but the muscles would not obey his impulse. He remembered his whistle, but he could not find it.

He watched the man approaching cautiously. A fisherman by the look of him, rugged, unshaven, unkempt, weatherbeaten.

'Aircraft,' said Bancroft, his lips barely moving. 'Wellington.

Dinghy. More chaps out there.' He managed to raise himself on to one elbow, and point out to sea.

The fisherman seemed to understand. He left Bancroft and set off down the shore with purposeful, rolling gait. Soon he disappeared round a rocky point. Bancroft relaxed for the first time, satisfied now that he had made contact with a human being.

The fisherman reappeared a few minutes later in a small boat with several other men. They beached the boat alongside Bancroft and lifted him into it.

'Where am I?' asked Bancroft, trying to place the men from their appearance and tongue. 'Is this Malta?'

'Malta!' This seemed to amuse the fishermen greatly. 'Malta!' They laughed hugely among themselves. Then the first fisherman spoke.

'Filicudi.' He pointed inland. 'Filicudi.' Bancroft could make no sense of this. The fisherman tried again. He pointed eastwards. 'Lipari. Ye-es? Lipari.'

Bancroft struggled to remember where he had heard the word before. Lipari. Lipari! The Lipari Islands! North of Sicily! They must be mistaken. He could not remember why, but he knew that he ought to be somewhere near Malta. But north of Sicily! They must be pulling his leg. He shook his head.

'Italiano?' he said.

They nodded vigorously. 'Italiano.'

Bancroft wondered how loyal they might be to the Italian cause. Some of these islands were notoriously independent. Then he remembered his crew.

'Aviateurs,' he said, pointing seawards. 'Aviateurs.'

The islanders nodded their understanding. They took him round the rocky point to a little village, where he was carried gently from the boat to a bedroom in one of the houses. It was a plain, austere room, but scrupulously clean. They brought a doctor to him almost at once.

The doctor spoke a little English. He told Bancroft that the fishermen had already gone to look for his friends. Bancroft explained that there were three men still in the dinghy and a fourth in the water somewhere, trying to swim to the island. He told the doctor how Bell had drifted westwards during the early stages of the swim.

One of the women of the house came in with a small goblet of water, not much bigger than the thimbleful they'd had in the dinghy. 'One every hour,' said the doctor, and repeated it several times. 'One every hour.' Bancroft thought of the prescriptions on medicine bottles at home. Medicine was the same everywhere.

Bancroft was left alone. He tried hard to keep awake, thinking of the men still in the dinghy, and of Bell, some-where out there, still struggling on. Or, perhaps, exhausted and beaten. He wondered if the goblet of water had been drugged, he felt so sleepy. He closed his eyes and fell at once into a deep sleep. When he awoke three hours later it was to find Robinson, Irving and McNeil being put to bed by the good villagers. The doctor was tending them. Bancroft noted that it was pretty rough surgery. There was no sign of Bell.

'Are they looking for Bell?' he asked the doctor.

'They can't find him,' said the doctor.

Bancroft digested this slowly.

'Are they still looking for him?'

'It is no good,' said the doctor. 'He is not to be found.'

Bancroft's reactions were sluggish and his mind moved in slow-motion. At length he said, 'He must be found.'

The doctor shrugged. 'They did well to find the others. The other one has drowned.'

'He can't have drowned,' said Bancroft. 'He's a good swimmer. Besides, he had a Mae West.'

The doctor looked blank. 'Mae West?'

Bancroft felt that he was losing. 'Mae West,' he repeated. 'Rubber. Inflated rubber. Lifejacket.'

The doctor raised his eyebrows. 'Ah! Lifejacket.' He nodded in agreement. 'Then he may be . . .' he searched for the word . . . 'floating.'

'Of course he's floating,' said Bancroft. 'Now will they go?'

The doctor spoke in Italian to the women of the house. They disappeared. A few minutes later they returned and spoke to the doctor. The doctor returned to Bancroft and shook his head.

'They have searched already. They cannot find him.'

Weakened to the point of complete physical collapse, Bancroft yet found the strength to struggle from the bed to his feet. Dazed and unsteady, he was pounced on by the women and easily overpowered. He sank back on to the bed.

'What are you trying to do?' asked the doctor.

'Give me a minute to get my strength,' said Bancroft. 'I'll find him myself.'

'You will do no such thing,' ordered the doctor. He looked hard at Bancroft, and for a moment their eyes met. Whatever determination or despair the doctor read there, he turned on his heel and left the room. When he came back he spoke to Bancroft without looking at him.

'They have gone to find your friend,' he said.

Bancroft lay back on the pillows. A wave of nausea swept over him, and he closed his eyes tightly to shut out the seasick world.

The Italian fishermen had been most reluctant to spend any more time searching. Nowadays, with mines and aircraft and submarines, one didn't go to sea if one could help it. Even a little fishing-smack had been known to be fired on. But, like all good workmen, once they knew the job had to be done they did it thoroughly.

An hour later, bouncing among the rocks to the west of Filicudi, they found their missing airman, naked, half full of sea-water, but still clutching his Mae West, still very much alive.

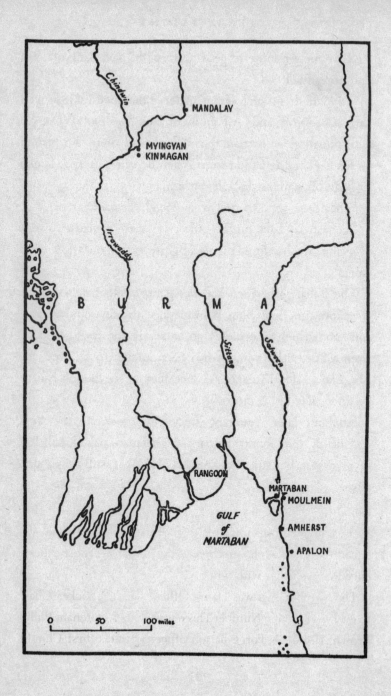

'CHAS'

IN the West, the summer of 1945 was an uneasy, restless hiatus between V.E. Day and V.J. Day. Election fever raged in Britain while the dust of defeat settled in Germany. But in the Far East there was war.

A fortnight before Hiroshima, the Allied armies were advancing on all fronts, poised in the Pacific for the final knock-out, yet not knowing that the last round had begun. A victorious advance was driving the Japanese from Burma, and the Americans were closing in on Japan. But men were still dying in flat-bottomed assault craft, risking their lives to drop a handful of pellets from the sky on a jungle railway-siding. The atom cloud was not even forming on the horizon. A fortnight before Hiroshima.

On the morning of 17th July, four Mosquito fighter-bombers took off from an airfield in central Burma, a short distance south of Mandalay, near the junction of the Irrawaddy and Chindwin rivers. They were led by Squadron Leader 'Solly' Joel, acting commanding officer of No. 110 (Hyderabad) Squadron. Joel had chosen three of the squadron's most experienced crews to go with him.

His Number Two was Flying Officer Charles Locke, 'Chas' to everyone. Flying Number Three was Flight Lieutenant Philip Brown, Royal Air Force liaison officer with the first Chindit column, the jungle sores still unhealed under his flying-suit. Number Four was Pilot Officer Jimmy Laver. When the day was over, it would be his task to record its fruits in the squadron history. Nothing emotional. Just the facts.

They took off from Kinmagan airstrip a few minutes before eight o'clock that morning. Their target was the railway station and sidings at Apalon, five hundred miles to the south, two hours' flying in a Mosquito. Apalon was on the Moulmein–Bangkok railway near Amherst, fifty miles south of Moulmein, in the narrow coastal strip of lower Burma that borders on Siam. The Japs were bringing supplies and ammunition by rail through to Apalon at night, and then waiting for darkness again before rushing them through to Moulmein. This was the infamous railway of death, in the building of which it was said a prisoner died for every sleeper laid. The railway was no stranger to the crews of 110 Squadron. They had flown through the narrow valley between the hills below Moulmein many times, low cloud and the threat of cumulo-nimbus forcing them to surrender the mobility of air routes and follow the natural course of river, road and railway.

The squadron had lost a number of good crews on raids in this area. The tactical limitations imposed by ubiquitous low cloud and the range of hills south of Moulmein robbed attacks on the railway of surprise. The Jap spotters saw aircraft flying down the valley and alerted all points south.

'We shall have the usual weather,' said Joel at briefing, 'ten-tenths strato-cu with large masses of cu-nim above it reaching

62

to forty thousand feet plus. Cloud base eight hundred feet. That means that the tops of the hills on either side of the valley will be obscured by cloud. We shall have to come right down low through the valley as usual, but I've worked out a little trick on the approach to the target to try and throw the Japs off the scent.

'What I propose we do is to fly down the mouth of the Sittang river and out into the Gulf of Martaban, and keep on in a southerly direction until we're almost abreast of Moulmein. Then we'll do a ninety-degree turn to port, leaving Moulmein away to starboard, and steer a course inland. The Japs at Moulmein are sure to spot us and this will give them the idea that we're on the way to an inland target. At the last moment we double back to the railway and come down between the hills towards Apalon. We may get some element of surprise that way. There's nothing very ingenious about it, but at least it's different.

'We shall bomb in pairs as usual, Locke as my Number Two and Brown and Laver Numbers Three and Four. We shall have four five-hundred pounders each, eleven-second delay jobs, so we can safely come in low and aim them into the railway station in a shallow dive.

'R/T silence on the way down, chaps, but as soon as the attack begins try and keep in touch while you're doing your bombing and strafing runs – we don't want any collisions over the target. Remember, this valley is damnably narrow – there simply isn't room to turn round. After you've finished your bombing run, get the hell out of the southern end of the valley. We'll rendezvous there and form up again for the trip back.'

Then the Army Liaison Officer had a piece to say.

'We've discovered recently that there's a P.O.W. camp very near Apalon. I don't expect you'd see it from the air, but you'll understand that its existence does make careful identifying of your target and accurate bombing even more important than usual.

'Force 136 have been in contact with this camp, and the prisoners have been warned that air attacks on Apalon are impending. What happened was that the Force 136 boys, operating a very long way behind the Jap lines, made contact with a party of P.O.Ws. at work in the jungle, and offered to kill their Jap guards and get the chaps back to our lines by submarine. The P.O.Ws. refused because they said the Japs would take it out of the sick men back at the camp. So do please be very careful about attacking the right target.'

Tucked well in to starboard of Joel, Chas Locke, flying Number Two, watched the Sittang river spread and open out into the Gulf of Martaban. It might have been an idea to bring Mae Wests on this trip. They would be flying over water for a time. But in the restricted space of a Mosquito cockpit, sitting side by side with Nicky, his navigator, he knew only too well the additional discomfort that resulted for both of them if they wore anything more than their already bulky equipment of jungle-green battledress-style khaki drill, with its plethora of pockets containing everything from mosquito-veiled hat to bog-paper, their jungle boots, helmets and goggles, parachutes and Sutton harness, kukri knife, .38 revolver and the canvas belt stuffed with the solid silver rupees which they knew as escape money. Escape money! Fat chance anyone had of escape in the Burmese jungle. No, they didn't want to be hampered by any more clobber. They wouldn't be more than a few minutes over the sea, and they wouldn't need to try and fox the Japs going home. They could head straight back to base, over land the whole way.

They turned east as planned before they reached Moulmein and flew inland at five hundred feet. When they were out of sight of Moulmein, they dropped down to tree-top height, turned south and swept round in a wide arc to strike the Moulmein–Bangkok railway. The cloud base lowered as they made for the gap in the hills.

It was bumpy at deck-level and the relative positions of the four Mosquitos changed like celluloid balls in a shooting gallery. On either side of them the 1,000-foot hills rose like the gates of a dry dock, shutting them in. Below lay the single-track line, strangely unsubstantial and insecure, like a toy railway. And on either side of the railway, the jungle.

'Switch over to fuselage tanks,' said Locke. He'd meant to tell Nicky to do this before. Nicolson leant back and turned over the petrol cocks. Locke noticed that the outer wing-tank gauges were reading practically empty. He usually liked to keep a few gallons in them for emergency. He couldn't remember when he'd last done a trip without keeping half an hour's petrol supply in his outer wing-tanks, just so as not to have all his eggs in one basket.

He'd distrusted the Mosquito fuel system ever since he'd had that pep talk from the technical expert on his conversion course in southern India. The fellow had been just a little too smooth. He could see him now, standing on the tarmac at Yelahanka in a smartly tailored bush-jacket with 'Technical Representative' on the epaulettes, white on a black background, long legs tapering into the inevitable pair of dung-coloured desert-boots. He and the other pilots on the course had stood under a Mosquito fuselage, staring up into the open bomb-doors. 'Here,' the expert had said, pointing at a connecting bracket that looked like some kind of distribution point, 'is the fuel collector box. The petrol feeds from the fuselage and inner wing-tanks through the fuel collector box to both engines. So, if one of your inner wing-tanks gets holed or runs dry, it doesn't mean that you're going to get an engine cut.' Locke was still gazing up into the fuselage, appalled at the nakedness of the belly of the aircraft when the bomb-doors were open. 'The outer wing-tanks, of course, only feed the individual engine on each side. So the answer is to work on those first, and if you're on a long trip, stay on them as long as you can before you switch over to the main distribution. That way you'll get the best endurance and be sure that if an engine does cut out on you at a crucial moment, at least you'll have exhausted the only supply of fuel on that side which you can't utilise for the other engine.'

'This fuel collector box affair looks a bit vulnerable,' Locke had said.

'We've got the bomb-doors open at the moment, so that

you can get a look at it. In flight you'd have the protection of the bomb-doors.'

'Not over the target,' persisted Locke. 'If you got hit in the fuel collector box over the target, that would puncture your whole fuel system, wouldn't it, apart from the outer wing-tanks?'

'Chance in a million,' said the expert.

Nevertheless, Locke had always kept half an hour's reserve in the outer wing-tanks, just in case. Until today.

He saw Number One waggle his wings and, looking ahead, he could make out the cluster of buildings which must be Apalon station, with several trucks standing in the sidings, powerless and still. He followed the leader into a shallow dive aimed at the station buildings. His altimeter began to unwind rapidly. He kept his eyes on the target.

'Bomb-doors open.'

Nicolson selected bomb-doors open. The airspeed shot above three hundred as they screamed down. Two hundred feet, a hundred and fifty feet, a hundred feet . . . For a split second he could make out every detail of the station – the camouflage paint on the sides of the trucks, a Jap soldier diving for cover. A high-speed photograph taken by the eye. Then he saw the leader's bombs go and he pressed the bomb-release button on the control column. In the same instant there was a terrific crack and a roar as the whole aircraft kicked like a viciously spurred horse. The cockpit was full of smoke and dust, and below the rudder pedals appeared a gaping hole in the floor. His feet were almost scraping the tree-tops. Both engines were going broom-bang, broom-bang, broom-bang, rhythmically, like a mad orchestra. He pulled back the stick and held his breath until the aircraft answered, staggering up over the trees like a pheasant into wind.

A babble of voices seemed to burst like shrapnel in his ears. 'Chas, you've been hit! Chas, you've been hit!' There were a dozen things to do, but first he reached down to his left and switched on his R/T, just to show them that he was still the same old Chas. 'You're bloody telling me,' he said.

The fuel-pressure warning lights were glowing red. He shouted at Nicolson. 'Change to outer wing-tanks!' He hadn't run them dry, there must be something left there. He watched Nicolson manipulating the fuel cocks. The engines picked up quickly and seemed to run sweetly. At least they had a few minutes.

They must have been hit in the fuel collector box. That would explain why the engines had kept cutting and picking up, cutting and picking up. So it had happened at last. Today of all days, when he'd run the outer tanks nearly dry. He knew how a man felt when his house burned down the day after his insurance policy lapsed. He knew how a lot of men had felt, screaming over the jungle in their last moments, looking desperately and hopelessly for somewhere to put down. As much chance as of landing in the middle of a Cup Final crowd without killing anybody.

'There's white smoke streaming out behind you.'

'What are you gonna do, Chas?'

'It's not smoke, it's petrol.'

68

'Chas, close your bomb-doors.'

'Can you make base, Chas?'

'Get a bit of height and bale out, Chas.'

'Shut up! I can't even talk to Nicky!' Locke waited while Nicolson selected bomb-doors closed again and again, vigorously pumping the emergency lever each time. Nothing happened. They were jammed. Jammed bomb-doors for a crash-landing. That was just lovely. It meant the whole hydraulic system – undercarriage, flaps, everything. Fortunately, although the controls were sluggish and sloppy, the aircraft was still climbing all right. The height comforted him and helped him to think.

'I'll tell you what we'll do.' It was Philip Brown on the R/T. 'I know the jungle, I know how to live in it, I know how to get around in it. You two bale out and we'll bale out over the top of you. You stay put and I'll find you. Then we'll make for the coast and try to work back to the British lines.'

It was a mad scheme and Locke dismissed it instantly, wondering with a kind of awed gratitude at the man who had proposed it. Fancy anyone even thinking of such a thing, let alone putting it forward as a suggestion, with all its implications. What about Brown's navigator, dragged to the brink of a precipice, surely against his will? No, there was only one chance. Strike across the Gulf of Martaban for the coast off Rangoon. It couldn't be more than fifteen or twenty minutes' flying. They might just make it.

One thing he knew for certain – he wasn't coming down behind the Jap lines while the aircraft still flew. No bastard

Jap was going to get *him*. He thought of the P.O.Ws. contacted by Force 136 refusing an offer of freedom, freedom from the most frightful toll of cholera and dysentery and beri-beri and inhuman treatment, to spare their sick comrades further hardships. Somehow he felt he just didn't have that kind of courage.

But there was Nicky to think of. He must give Nicky the chance to bale out. There wasn't much hope for them if they failed to reach the Rangoon coast. Even the pilot's notes didn't recommend ditching a Mosquito at the best of times, and they generally told you that you could do anything with an aircraft except marry it. The words came back to him. 'Whenever possible, bale out rather than ditch.' And with the bomb-doors open, and no Mae Wests . . .

'We've got about a thousand feet, Nicky,' he said. 'That'll be enough height. You'd better bale out, old son.'

'What are you going to do?'

'I shall stick. Have a shot at crossing the gulf. At least there are more of our chaps and fewer Japs on that side. No bastard Jap's going to get me.'

'That goes for me too,' said Nicolson. 'What makes you think you can get across the gulf without a navigator, anyway? Let's go.'

Locke felt a great warmth towards Nicky.

'O.K., old son, but if we ditch we've probably had it.'

'We'll chance it.'

Locke called the others on the R/T. 'I'm going to have a shot at crossing the gulf with what I've got left in my outer wing-tanks. There's not much there, but it's a chance. If I can put her down on the beach on the Rangoon side we may manage to keep out of the Japs' way until the Army gets through. Nicky's coming with me.'

'We'll stick with you.'

Nicolson gave Locke a course to steer to cross the gulf. They had about a thousand feet and Locke decided this would have to be enough. No sense in wasting petrol in trying to climb. It was almost exactly a hundred miles across the gulf at this point. He reckoned they had petrol for perhaps sixty or seventy miles. Perhaps eighty. Perhaps ninety. Perhaps even a hundred. There would have to be enough for a hundred. But if they could only get in sight of land that might be enough. The air/sea rescue boys could probably find them and pick them up. There was a dinghy stowed in the fuselage directly behind them. It was supposed to release and inflate automatically on impact. If it did they would be all right.

He watched the others formating on him. It was good to have company at a time like this. Joel called him on the R/T.

'Hullo Chas. I'm going to gain height so that I can get in radio touch with base. I'll give them your course and position and so on. I'll climb to about six thousand and keep a watch on you from there.'

'Good show, sir.'

Two aircraft formating on him and one above him sending position messages and transmitting for a radio fix! Even if they came down in the sea there would still be a chance.

'Half-way across,' said Nicolson.

If only the old tub would keep going for ten more minutes.

He looked again at the needles on the petrol gauges. They still showed empty. They must be running on air. He peered ahead, his eyes waiting for the first glimpse of land to swell into focus, his ears still attuned to every beat of the engines.

'If these outers dry up,' he said to Nicolson, 'we'll at least try the others. There might be enough in them to keep us going for a minute or two.'

They must be nearing the coast now. They had certainly come more than seventy miles. Any second now they might see land. Any second now the engines might cut. Any moment now.

'Look!' shouted Nicolson. 'Land dead ahead!'

'Land ahoy, Chas!'

'Can you see it, Chas?'

Locke could already make out the details of the coastline some ten miles distant.

'I shall put her straight down on the beach,' he said. He turned off his R/T and spoke to Nicolson on the intercom. 'Looks like we're going to make it.'

In the same moment the engines coughed and spluttered their derision. Locke put the nose down desperately. 'They might pick up again,' he shouted. The screech of the slip-stream took the place of the roar of the engines. They coughed and spluttered again and finally cut.

'Turn on to main tanks, Nicky! Jettison escape hatch!'

Nicolson already had his hand on the petrol cocks, and he turned them over instantly. The engines cut dead. The main tanks were bone-dry. He jettisoned the hatch.

Locke pushed the nose down again and kept his speed above two hundred. The stalling speed of a Mosquito in this condition would be about a hundred and eighty. He called the formation.

'That's the lot,' he said. 'The tanks are bone-dry. I'm ditching.'

'Good luck, Chas.'

'Good luck, you two.'

'Good luck.'

How nice it must be, sitting up there with two good engines and plenty of gas, wishing somebody else good luck.

They had so nearly made it. Land was so close that they could see the palm trees fringing the shore. Perhaps seven or eight miles short, that was all. But the air/sea rescue boys ought to be able to reach them here. At least they would know where to look.

The sea was calm and they rushed down towards it at a hundred and eighty miles an hour. Locke levelled out gently. 'Keep the tail well down, Chas,' said Nicolson. His tone was full of confidence and encouragement. Locke could have hugged him.

The tail streaked prettily along the surface of the sea, braking the aircraft gently. It was the perfect tail-down ditching. The men in the three aircraft circling overhead saw the water pluming out behind the ditching aircraft like the wake of a yacht. But when the nose dipped to make impact with the water, the open bomb-doors churned into the sea and a wall of water struck the rear bulkhead and snapped and splintered the wooden fuselage like a rotten tea-chest. The nose of the aircraft was guillotined, its tail severed, its back broken. Volumes of water cascaded skywards like waves beating on a mole. Then the surface slowly smoothed out, leaving two jagged pieces of wreckage on the still sea. Dismay and the certainty of tragedy filled the minds of the men who watched.

As the aircraft broke up Locke was conscious of the scream of rending metal and wood, and of a huge mass of water smashing over the front of the cockpit. He was vaguely conscious, too, of Nicky being thrown forward beside him, and simultaneously he was flung out into a strange darkness. Here, at last, was death. It had had to come eventually.

Locke felt himself going down, down to unknown depths, his consciousness dwindling and evaporating until his whole being was concentrated in a pinpoint of light between his eyes. As he went he felt his body being struck all over by bits of wreckage. There was no answering pain. He waited for the final chunk of wreckage to strike his head and extinguish the pinpoint of light. He knew that if that tiny light disappeared it would mean oblivion.

He struggled to follow the light that he recognised as himself. Hope and fear were gone, thought and reason too, shocked out of him when he was flung into the sea. Everything was eerie and silent, like a dream. It was not until he began to feel the need for air that he realised he was still alive.

He felt his movements strangely constricted, and then he realised that his parachute and harness were hampering him.

He snapped the quick-release box and struggled free. He had no idea what depth he had reached, but it seemed to him that he was at the bottom of the sea. He knew that if he could not breathe freely soon the light in him would be extinguished.

The pinpoint of light seemed to be receding into the distance, and yet he had a sensation that he was becoming a whole person again. He saw that the water around him was changing to a paler green. The pressure on his lungs seemed lighter, and yet he could hold his breath no longer. Almost at the same moment as he began to gasp and so let water into his lungs he broke the surface.

Somehow he was alive. Dazed with concussion and shock, he felt no elation, only surprise.

He looked quickly round and saw in the same moment the wreck of the Mosquito, the fuselage and the tail unit some distance apart, and, drifting speedily away to the south, the dinghy. It must have floated clear when the aircraft broke up. He was suddenly aware that every bone in his body ached as though it had been twisted and tortured and hammered. His head was numb and he put his hand up to his forehead. His helmet was gone, torn off, he supposed, when he was flung through the nose. When he withdrew his hand it was covered in blood.

He looked up and saw the three Mosquitos wheeling round overhead, like angry birds. He saw land in the distance, unattainable yet unbearably near. When he looked back at the wreckage he saw the tail unit founder and sink.

He had no hope of reaching the dinghy. Already as he measured the distance he saw that it was increasing. If he reached it he would be safe. If he failed there would be nothing. But he thought he could reach the remains of the wreck. Shattered and broken as it was, bits of it might float for an hour or two. An hour was a lifetime. He did not look beyond it.

The fuselage of the aircraft was pointing towards him, torn and jagged like a pulled Christmas cracker. He tried to strike out towards it but found that both his legs were useless. Every movement he made applied instruments of torture to his aching limbs. Jesus. It wasn't possible to feel such pain without fainting.

The wreckage looked tantalisingly close. He felt like a well-beaten horse called upon for an effort in the last furlong. The whip of death lashed him and he set his teeth and put his head down, shutting his eyes tightly to exclude everything but the thought of his goal. Presently he opened his eyes and looked straight up into the jaws of the smashed fuselage.

The front part of the fuselage was under water and he floundered and flopped his way to the rear of the broken centre strip, his clothes like lead weights and his head nearly awash. Then he grabbed hold of the wreckage and supported himself thankfully, all but exhausted. For the moment he was safe. Now for the first time he thought of Nicky, and was ashamed.

He had seen nothing of Nicky. Not from the moment of ditching. He looked desperately around, but knew as he did so that it was hopeless. Again and again he shouted Nicky's name. The only sound which came was the slapping and gurgling and sucking of the sea around the wreck and the drone of the aircraft circling overhead.

He knew dimly that he had no right to be alive. Nicky must have bought it when they ditched.

He could not bear to think about it. He could not bear to think that Nicky had gone. He had to shut it from his mind. He would think about it later.

The aft end of the broken piece of fuselage sprouted the torn and twisted wires of the electrical system, tangled like the roots of chickweed. He plunged his hand in amongst the wires to gain a leverage, and a violent shock passed into and through his body, holding him erect for several seconds. He did not relax his grip, hanging on fascinated, and the shock subsided. Then he began to pull himself up into the shelter of the broken fuselage.

At once the pain was so excruciating that he felt himself about to pass out. He bit his lip fiercely but sickness and nausea still overwhelmed him. Then the horizon blurred over and he knew he was going to faint. If he fell back into the sea unconscious he would drown. He remembered the whisky flask in his flying-suit. He had saved some of his spirit ration month by month to fill that flask. Many a night in the Mess tent when the party spirit was at its height and the whisky was running low he had been tempted to have a swig or two from his flask. But he had never done so. You never knew when you might be forced down in the jungle, when a flask of whisky might keep you alive. Well, he wouldn't want it for the jungle now. He fumbled for the flask, unscrewed the metal cap, put the neck of the flask to his lips and drank. Warmth and strength coursed through him and he felt ridiculously elated.

He tried again to pull himself up and this time he succeeded. He sat in the end of the wreckage, like a chicken hatching from its shell. Water flopped and eddied around the jagged fuselage and effervesced like an alkaline at his waist.

He looked up and saw a solitary Mosquito about two thousand feet above him, still circling. He waved without hope of being seen. The other chaps must have pushed off. Short of petrol. He wondered if he had been seen at all. They wouldn't see him from up there at two thousand feet, anyway. That was certain. Soon the last Mosquito turned and flew off to the north. Back to base. Base. A clammy, humid airstrip cut from the hostile Burmese jungle that suddenly seemed the most desirable place on earth.

He took another swig from the flask to boost his morale. They would be sure to send someone out to look for survivors. Provided they looked closely enough they would find him. Provided they came soon enough. Already he fancied that the wreckage was settling deeper in the water. The sea was swirling round his knees. The buoyancy of the empty petrol-tanks would keep him afloat for a time. He didn't care to think for how long.

He was still suffering agonies from his injuries, and he thought of his first-aid kit. He would see what he could find there. But although he ached in every limb, his most pressing need was water. Somewhere in the fuselage there was a water-tank. He looked round and saw it immediately to his right.

He reached up and tried to disconnect it from its housing, but twisted his back as he did so and nearly fainted with the pain. He grabbed hold of the water-tank, but it clung tenaciously to the fuselage and would not loosen. It was all too bloody funny. Here he was dying for a drink, someone had thought to put a water-tank just where he could reach it, and he couldn't get at the water inside it.

He took another swig from his flask. It slaked his thirst momentarily and lightened his burden. He surveyed himself and decided that he must have broken both his legs. His right leg was broken somewhere near the ankle and his left knee was swollen to the size of a small football. All the time the pain in his back was agonising. He pulled out the first-aid kit and noticed that it was stamped 'Air Ministry'. The package was sheathed in a rubberised fabric and his numbed fingers felt for the joint. Somewhere you were supposed to tear across the dotted line. He couldn't find it. Waterproof, he thought. Everything's bloody-well waterproof so that I can't get at it. He tried to read the instructions on the package but he could not concentrate. He remembered that he had a little air-tight tin of tablets that Doc Harbinson had given him back at Kinmagan. He tugged again impatiently at the cover of the first-aid pack. Air Ministry. That was funny. Nothing from Air Ministry was ever any good, anyway. He flung the package into the sea.

He found the tin Doc Harbinson had given him and poured the tablets he wanted into the palm of his hand. Sulphonamide. That was the stuff. Six tablets. He had no idea what to do

79

with them. There was a hole in his right leg about the size of a florin. He rammed tablets in the hole until he had filled it and levelled it off. That looked tidier. Then blood began to trickle down into his eyes again from his head and he broke the last tablets up and rubbed the powder into his forehead. The bleeding seemed to stop.

His first-aid operations had seemed strangely protracted and he realised that he was losing his sense of time. He couldn't remember how long he'd been there. He thought it might have been half an hour since the ditching. Might have been longer, though. Might have been any time.

He was suddenly aware of a noise in his ears, and looking up he saw two Spitfires overhead at about a thousand feet. They'd come for him! They were here! He scanned the horizon for the rescue launch in vain. But nothing mattered now that they'd found him. He watched the Spitfires eagerly, waiting for them to come down and take a look at him. They stayed at a thousand feet. They weren't even waggling their wings at him. He wondered uneasily whether they had seen him, whether anyone had seen him up to now. Why didn't they come down to the deck? Silly bloody clots.

Oh, it stood out a mile. No one had seen him. They were just carrying out a routine check for floating survivors. He waved frantically and shouted impotently. Where were they heading now? South? They must be looking for the bloody dinghy. There's no one in that, you clots! I'm here! In the bloody aircraft! Oh, Christ.

The Spitfires flew off and his eyes followed them helplessly. He felt intensely lonely. He'd had it. They'd looked for him, and now they'd gone off to report a few bits of wreckage and an empty dinghy. The chaps on the squadron would say the aircraft broke up when it hit the water. Not a chance for anyone. He'd had it.

He lifted the flask to his lips and tilted it despairingly until it was upside down. It was empty. He had no recollection of finishing it. He was losing his sense of proportion and the empty flask was the worst tragedy of all.

The water was above his waist now. It must be seeping into the petrol-tanks. He wouldn't have much longer. Perhaps half an hour. Perhaps an hour. Then the wreckage would submerge and take him with it. He broke off a small piece of jagged wood from the splintered fuselage with the vague idea of having something to help him float when the kite eventually sank.

He looked back towards the coastline, but the land was gone. He must have drifted a long way south, far out to sea. Even if anyone was looking for him they would never find him now.

He began to think about death. It stared him in the face, inevitable, inexorable. It was like the sword of Damocles. Drip, drip, drip in the petrol-tanks every moment, and the wreckage sank deeper and deeper. There was absolutely no escape and he resigned himself to it.

He had been resigned to death for many months. That was how you became on a squadron. At first you worried your-self stiff at the thought of getting the chop, a thought so much more insistent and probable on operations than the prospect of danger which you looked forward to in your training days and dismissed because it couldn't happen to you. Then one by one you saw your friends and contemporaries killed, people you'd thought of as immortal like yourself. You realised that death was something personal. It could happen to you. From then on you lived with the certainty of it day and night. It became a part of you, waking and sleeping. You became accustomed to the idea of sudden and violent and personal death. You were resigned to it and merely hoped it would be over quickly and painlessly when it came.

Sudden death. People prayed to be preserved from sudden death. But it was the kind of death he was conditioned to. Not this lingering kind.

So this was how it was all going to end. He was struck by the pity of it. He thought of his family. They would take it pretty hard, especially at this stage in the war. He felt more pity for them than for himself. He'd played his life the way he wanted it and he hadn't expected to survive the war anyway.

He supposed he ought to be feeling fear and awe and humility. It wasn't respectable to be smug in the face of death. He ought to be concentrating on spiritual things. He ought to be making his peace with God.

He'd never gone much on God and religion and all that stuff. He'd managed all right without it. He had believed in the essential goodness of man, and in the example of Christ, but he had rejected the doctrines and the dogmas and he had rejected God. Now that all hope was gone, now that death was sure, how did he feel?

He was pleased to find that he felt the same. People were fond of saying that even atheists turned to God at the end. Well, here was an agnostic who did not, *could not*. He could not make himself believe now in things his whole way of life had rejected.

How could he pray for forgiveness to a God he didn't believe in for living the lusty and boisterous life he would go back to at once if rescue came?

He thought of Richard Hillary. Hillary had been right. His agnosticism had remained steadfast in the face of his Last Enemy. With the true agnostic it must be so. Ernest Pyle had been utterly wrong when he wrote that there were no atheists in fox-holes.

He turned his thoughts away from God. He had always been sufficient unto himself, and he would stay that way. He would play it the way he'd always played it. If there was anything to come afterwards he would soon know.

The water was up to his armpits now. There would only be a few more minutes. The sea was rougher and sometimes water splashed into his face. He had nothing left but the determination not to give in.

He had a queer vibratory sensation in his ears, and for a moment he allowed himself the luxury of thinking that it might be a motor-launch. Then he saw two aircraft fly directly overhead. The Spitfires were back. He watched them with a vague interest, emotionless, dispassionate. It was nice to have company again, but it was all so futile. They were up there and he was down here. What was the good of that?

This time the Spitfires came right down low and dived straight at him, waggling their wings. He did not even have the strength to wave back. Still, they must have seen him this time. He watched them break off and circle at two or three hundred feet, and then turn and dive towards him again, beating up the wreck. It was comforting to watch but pretty useless. Why hadn't they sent a launch out?

His ears detected a different engine noise and looking up he saw a Lysander struggling across the sky, hardly seeming to move in comparison with the fleet Spitfires. He saw the rear-gunner fling something over the side of his cockpit and seconds later there was a great splashing cascade of water thirty to forty yards away. When the water subsided he saw a large yellow dinghy floating away downwind on the troubled sea. Very nice of everybody, but still bloody useless. Didn't they know he was injured? Didn't they know that he suffered the most appalling pain even when he tried to lift himself higher in the wreck?

He began to wish that the Spitfires and the Lysander would go away and leave him to his fate. Parting from life would be easier without their poignant reminder of the clamour and thrill of living.

The water was nearly up to his neck now. Sometimes, as the wreckage rode the swell, he had to hold his breath when the crest of a wave broke in his face. The sea was getting heavier all the time and he struggled hard to keep his head and shoulders clear. Shots of intolerable pain paralysed his every movement, but somehow he raised himself a few inches.

He had to think about the moment when the wreckage would sink. It might founder at any time. He would cling to it as long as it floated, but when it went under he would somehow struggle clear and float for as long as he could. They shouldn't say that Chas Locke gave in easily.

The chug-chug note of an unfamiliar engine suddenly reverberated in his ears, and he tried to crane his neck to see where it was coming from. The noise came closer, and his heart gave a wild leap as he recognised an air/sea rescue aircraft almost hovering beside him, all biplane and stay-wires and wing-tip floats and amphibianism. A Sea Otter! A plane that could land on the sea!

He believed instantly in the certainty of rescue, and a smile transformed his face and stretched his cheeks until they ached. He felt like a schoolboy given an unexpected half-holiday. Excitement flowed through him like electricity. He was saved! He suddenly noticed that the sun was shining and that the world around him was beautiful and sparkling and new.

The Sea Otter began circling the wreck and Locke wondered at first why they did not land beside him at once. Then he remembered the swell and wondered if they intended to risk a landing at all.

The pilot seemed to make up his mind, and Locke watched the amphibian fly off purposefully downwind and then turn up into wind for an approach. He lost sight of it for some time as it flew behind him, but was too exhausted to turn his head. The plane touched down about a hundred yards away and the landing was a good one. Then it began to taxi towards the wreckage. The sea was still rough and the Sea Otter stopped some thirty yards distant, evidently afraid of ramming the wreck. A figure appeared in the nose of the plane, standing up in the open-air front turret in a Mae West, holding a rope.

The amphibian began to describe a circle of a radius of about twenty yards around the wreckage. The figure in the front cockpit made ready to fling the rope. Christ, thought Locke. They're trying to lasso me.

The fellow in the Mae West flung the rope and it fell yards short. Even the splash of water as the rope lashed the sea hardly reached him. Silly bloody idiot. He had a Mae West on – why didn't he jump in and pull him out? Perhaps they were frightened of sharks. That was funny! He'd been here for God knows how long and that was the first time he'd thought of sharks.

Round came the Sea Otter again, taxying downwind, and a second time the rope fell short, disturbing the water like a hooked fish. The third time the rope struck the wooden fuselage somewhere behind him and he clawed at it ineffectually. Then it was thrown too late, and then too soon. Each attempt was punctuated by a full minute as the Sea Otter completed another circuit of the wreck before the rope could be thrown again.

The sea was rougher than ever now, churned up by the taxying amphibian. The water broke over his head continually and he was almost completely submerged. He had to snatch a breath in between the moments when he was dragged under water. Oh, it was pricelessly funny, pricelessly funny, drowning while a rescue aircraft taxied round and round and a man in a Mae West played cowboys with a rope because he wouldn't get his feet wet. It was just too pricelessly bloody, bloody funny.

The Sea Otter went on circling, five times, six times, seven times, the plunging rope lashing the sea just a little nearer the wreckage each time. Gasping and gurgling, buffeted and sinking, Locke nevertheless managed to grab the rope the eighth time. He eased the loop over his shoulders and under his armpits, and a moment later felt himself yanked from the wreckage and dragged across the surface of the swell to the wing-tip of the plane.

Two more members of the crew appeared on the wing and lifted him up. The pain was excruciating and he begged them to leave him alone. They tried to help him along the wing, but were deterred by his curses and yells. They left him to drag himself painfully towards the open cupola in the back of the fuselage. Then they lifted him and laid him in the bottom of the aircraft directly under the cupola. He could not stand being carried further.

He lay in the fuselage, utterly exhausted, half-drowned, marvelling at the pain that one man could endure. He lay quite still, his mind and body unable yet to enjoy the triumph of rescue. He saw the canvas first-aid bag, buckled and sealed with sealing-wax, lashed above him, and he thought, now it will come, sweet relief, oblivion.

He watched the orderly moving about with blankets, nervous but important.

'Got a cigarette, old son?'

The orderly pursed his lips and looked uncertainly for'ard. He shook his head. 'Sorry, sir, no smoking in the aircraft.' The clot. 'Don't be bloody tiresome,' said Locke. 'Give me a cigarette.' It was an order from an officer and the orderly fumbled for cigarettes and matches.

Locke's eye kept roving to the first-aid bag. When was the clot going to open up and give him the treatment? The Sea Otter was bouncing giddily over the swell, trying to take off. Every bump was sheer purgatory. Why on earth didn't he pass out? Surely it wasn't possible to feel such pain and still remain conscious.

The seaplane made six runs before it eventually climbed away, shattering the last of Locke's resistance and reducing him to the brink of unconsciousness.

The orderly, too, had his eye on the first-aid box. It was his first rescue. He knew if he opened up the box it meant breaking the seal, accounting afterwards for anything he used, putting in demand notes for replacements. Perhaps even a court of enquiry. Drugs were short in Burma. They would soon be back at base and the doctors could take over. Orderlies were trained to keep the patient comfortable and warm and quiet. They weren't supposed to give more than superficial first aid. Yet he felt that he must offer to do something.

He bent over Locke, tucked the blankets round him, and took a deep breath.

'Would you like a couple of aspirins?' he said.

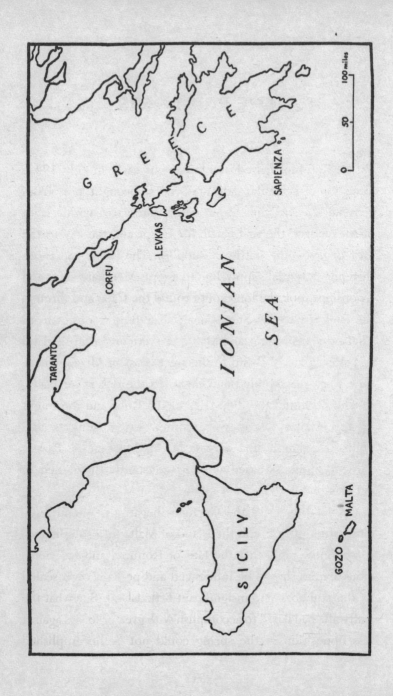

THE PRISONERS

WHEN Rommel halted at El Alamein early in July 1942, after the spectacular advance which brought him from Cyrenaica across the Libyan desert almost to within sight of Alexandria, the real battle for Egypt and the key to the East began – the battle of supplies. The Allies had more than one potential supply-line to Egypt. Merchant ships and troopships took the long route round the Cape and through the Red Sea to the Suez Canal; aircraft flew direct from England via Gibraltar and Malta, or were crated in England and transported by ship to the west coast of Africa, where they were reassembled and flown to the desert air-bases. But for Rommel the industries of the Ruhr and the might of the Afrika Korps were joined by a tenuous and vulnerable supply-line across the Mediterranean. R.A.F. torpedo-bombers based at Malta constantly threatened to cut this line.

On 1st July 1942 the Germans began a new and ferocious attempt to bomb the island of Malta into submission. It was intolerable that the fate of Rommel and his victorious armies should be influenced and perhaps even sealed by this stubborn and insignificant little island. But what the Luftwaffe had failed to accomplish with greater forces against less opposition in the spring could not be accomplished now. In the first ten days of July over a hundred enemy aircraft were shot down for the loss of less than a quarter that number. By the middle of July the enemy's losses were so heavy that dive-bombing was stopped. Malta was free to continue its vital offensive role in the battle of Egypt.

On 28th July 1942 a Malta-based Spitfire on dawn reconnaissance over the enemy coastline and coastal waters in the eastern Mediterranean spotted an enemy oil-tanker escorted by five Italian destroyers, with air cover, hugging the coastline off the island of Sapienza in southern Greece, intent on getting out of range of Malta's strike aircraft before cutting across the Mediterranean into Tobruk harbour. The Spitfire turned quickly for home. As soon as the pilot was within R/T range of Malta he called the controller and transmitted a sighting report. Nine Beaufort crews on stand-by were called out for immediate take-off.

Beaufort crews in the Middle East, on the rare occasions when they changed from khaki drill shorts and shirts into their walking-out uniforms, were apt to look like a bag of coloured sweets, a kind of Empire assortment. Australians and Canadians were almost as numerous as men from the Old Country; South Africans and New Zealanders were in it too. The blood spilled in the Mediterranean by the men of the torpedo-bombers was the rich red blood of a civilisation.

To Lieutenant Ted Strever of the South African Air Force, newly arrived in Malta, this was torpedo strike number three. He had for his navigator a Lancastrian, Pilot Officer W. M. Dunsmore, of Liverpool. His wireless operator/air gunners (the Beaufort carried two Wop/A.Gs.) were both New Zealanders, Sergeant J. A. Wilkinson of Auckland and Sergeant A. R. Brown of Timaru. Wilkinson and Brown had been shot down with another crew ten days previously. Their pilot and navigator had been wounded, and they had been re-crewed with Strever and Dunsmore.

Shortly before nine o'clock on that July morning, Strever and his crew took off in the formation of nine Beauforts detailed to attack the oil-tanker. It was a hot sunny day and the Mediterranean reflected the sky's pale blue. As they taxied out the aircraft was stiflingly hot, and they were glad when they were clear of the runway and the slipstream rushed in through the free gun hatches on the port and starboard sides. The Beaufort carried twin Brownings in the wings and in the turret, which was half-way along the fuselage, and a single free gun on either side just forward of the turret. Going into action the wireless operator manned these two side guns.

When the nine Beauforts were airborne they formed up into pairs and set course east-north-east for Sapienza. Soon they were skimming along at 160 knots, low over the sea, glad to be clear of the danger of being jumped on by fighters in the Malta area. Dunsmore, Strever's navigator, released his straps and clambered from his seat alongside Strever down into the perspex nose. Brown, on the look-out for fighters immediately after take-off, tested the two free guns and then began a listening watch on the strike frequency. Wilkinson tested his guns and then rotated the turret gently from side to side, scanning the sky. They settled down to a period of nearly two and a half hours' flying before they would reach the position radioed by the Spitfire pilot. The rippling Mediterranean rushed by fifty feet beneath them. In the turret, Wilkinson watched Malta until it became a white cloud on the sea.

At a quarter-past eleven Brown began to pick up a cluster of blips on his search radar. He called the crew, and soon Strever and Dunsmore saw the strike leader waggle his wings and begin a gentle turn to starboard. Strever tucked in behind him. In the distance, perhaps eight miles away, they could see the Axis convoy, made up of a heavily laden merchantman and five destroyers with fighter cover, sneaking along in the shadow of Sapienza, peaceful and almost still. They turned into the attack, Strever still holding the Beaufort down fifty feet above the sea. He wondered if they had been seen. He looked quickly left and right and saw eight other Beauforts converging on the hub of the convoy like the spokes of a bicycle. They were all here so far.

This moment, as the sea raced by underneath and the ships grew bigger second by second, was fantastically exhilarating, perhaps the most exhilarating experience of modern war. A sense of speed, a breathless, glorious feeling of intense danger, a feeling of personal combat, a grandstand view of the target as it steamed ponderously and unconcernedly to spectacular destruction — all these things made up the unique excitement of torpedo-dropping. Last came the agony of suspense as the tin-fish ran towards its intended victim, the inevitable exposure of the belly of the aircraft as you broke away past the waiting destroyers, and then − if you were still in one piece − then you saw the instantaneous ball of fire as the torpedo struck and the whole ship exploded into a sheet of flame brighter than the sun.

The convoy was steaming away from them, and in order to get a beam shot the Beauforts swung away to port towards Sapienza and then turned back to make their run from the coast. There were two Beauforts going in ahead of Strever. The tanker was judged to be making about twelve knots and Strever laid off deflection on the torpedo-sight attached to his windscreen and called to Dunsmore to come out of the nose and sit beside him to drop the torpedo. The destroyers looked incredibly close and he wondered why they hadn't opened up yet.

Then he saw a fierce rain beating on the water a few yards ahead and realised that they were flying through machine-gun fire. Tracer rushed at his eyes and then at the last moment swerved away over his shoulder and was gone. Puffs of smoke hung around them, so still that they must be some distance away. He jinked as much as he dared at this height, then steadied the aircraft as the range closed to a thousand yards. He was used to the deceptiveness of distance over water but he could hardly believe that they were still more than half a mile away. Out of the corner of his eye he saw the Beaufort on his left pull up suddenly like a marionette on a string and then hang helplessly in mid-air before it turned on its back and crashed down into the sea. No chance for the boys in there. The merchantman looked incredibly close, eight hundred yards away. Strever called Dunsmore.

'Now!'

Dunsmore pressed the release button. 'Torp gone.'

Strever opened the throttles and they careered on until they passed directly under the bows of the tanker. Brown, at the side guns, saw the buttons of the tanker's gun-crew glinting in the sun. As they swept past the tanker's bows they ran into a curtain of fire from the escorting destroyers. Wilkinson called to say that the torpedo was running hard and true a few feet below the surface, but his message was drowned as the port engine cracked like a broken leg and Strever wound on right rudder trim as he swung the aircraft out of range.

Instinctively he turned the Beaufort back towards Sapienza. The port engine was a smoking wreck and the starboard engine was running roughly under the strain. Smoke began to filter through the fuselage, and with it came a clammy, cloying smell of oil. The oil-pressure reading on the port engine had fallen to zero and the starboard-engine pressure was falling rapidly. With no height it was hopeless to try to reach the coast. Better to ditch her now than risk a sudden engine failure and an uncontrolled dive into the sea.

He throttled back the good engine and called the crew. Brown sent out an S O S, but at this height there was scant hope of its being picked up. He clamped his key down and left the wireless seat to brace himself. Wilkinson came out of the turret. The sea had roughened and as Strever eased back the stick he felt the aircraft being buffeted in gusting winds. The ditching was heavy and up in the nose Strever and Dunsmore at once went under.

As soon as the aircraft came to a standstill Wilkinson, sitting by the free gun hatch on the port side, jumped out on to the wing and tugged at the dinghy release. Brown made his way back to the same hatch, and as he left the aircraft he saw Wilkinson about to step into the dinghy. The whole tail unit had snapped off just aft of the turret and was floating on its own a hundred yards away. Brown stepped quickly into the dinghy beside Wilkinson.

They watched the half-submerged Beaufort anxiously for some sign of Strever and Dunsmore. It looked impossible to make any rescue attempt with the front cockpit below the surface. Then quite suddenly Dunsmore appeared clutching the navigation bag, followed by Strever, and the two men clambered into the dinghy beside Wilkinson and Brown. Half a minute later the Beaufort ducked like a whale beneath the waves, less than twenty yards away.

Safely in the dinghy, they took stock of their position. They had the navigation bag, containing maps and codes and Very pistol and emergency rations, the dinghy rations, and the dinghy equipment. Dunsmore had a deep gash in his arm, and Wilkinson produced the medical kit from the dinghy equipment and administered first-aid. They were about five miles off Sapienza — enemy territory that now took on a cloak of friendliness and held the hope of succour.

To the east they could see the oil-tanker, very low in the water but apparently not on fire. In the other direction they saw the last of the Beauforts disappearing towards Malta. Overhead, a Baltimore reconnaissance plane circled at 20,000 feet, perhaps fixing their position. Malta must be three hundred miles away. Suddenly they realised how near the Mediterranean was to being 'Mare Nostrum', Mussolini's sea.

To attempt any other course than to reach Sapienza hardly occurred to them. Even that might prove beyond their powers. The decision to begin paddling towards the island was taken silently, unspoken. They stared sullenly towards Sapienza and captivity.

They paddled in the broiling heat of midday for three-quarters of an hour without making much headway. Already they were hot and thirsty and dispirited. They felt sure that the Italians had seen them go down and had left them to their fate. When they saw a Macchi 202 in the distance they watched it apprehensively, ready to dive overboard should they be attacked. The Macchi circled at five hundred feet and then made off.

The fact that the Macchi had not opened fire encouraged them to hope that rescue might be on the way. A few minutes later Wilkinson pointed excitedly towards the north.

'Look!' he shouted. 'A seaplane! Could it possibly be one of ours?'

They watched the seaplane approaching steadily. Soon they could make out three radial engines and the clear outline of the floatplanes. No British aircraft were got up to look like that. It was an Italian Cant Z 506B.

The floatplane flew directly overhead and they watched awkwardly, sure that they had been seen and yet reluctant to signal for assistance. Soon the Cant returned and began to circle the dinghy, and presently it landed about fifty yards away. Rescue – and captivity – was at hand.

The Cant came to a stop and Strever and his crew began paddling towards it. They made little progress and the two groups of men eyed each other speculatively. Then Strever, bowing to the inevitable, stripped and dived over the side, covering the distance to the Cant in swift, strong strokes. When he reached it he was courteously received by the Italian crew, who hauled him aboard and showed a charming anxiety to be friendly. He wondered if they knew about the tanker.

Drawing on an unsuspected histrionic ability, Strever explained in pantomime what had happened and the Italians nodded delightedly, offering him a large tot of brandy and a cigarette. Strever, trying hard to remember what he knew of the Geneva Convention, refused neither. The Italians then handed him a length of rope, one end of which was fastened to the Cant fuselage. Strever swam with it back to the dinghy. When he reached it he gave the thumbs-up sign.

'We're in,' he said.

In Strever's absence they had put all the guns and maps and codes in the navigation bag, fastened it securely and dumped it over the side. Strever climbed back into the dinghy and the Italians hauled on the rope. Soon they were all aboard the floatplane.

The captain of the Cant said his name was Alessandro Chifari. His crew consisted of a navigator, flight engineer and wireless operator. When the rest of Strever's crew had been given a tot of brandy, Chifari told them in pidgin English to sit aft and not to move about. The flight engineer jeered at them genially. 'For you the war is over — yes?' No one felt inclined to argue.

The engines were restarted and Strever and his crew could feel the motion of taxying. The sea was rough and there was no attempt to take off. From their position in the aft of the fuselage they could see nothing. Strever gathered from the pilot's dumb-show that there were bombs or depth charges on board and that they were taxying towards the channel behind Sapienza into smoother water for the take-off. After an uncomfortable half-hour the water seemed calmer, and the engines roared as the pilot opened the throttles. The take-off run seemed interminable and they thought uneasily of the depth charges. The noise inside the fuselage was deafening, and after the take-off speech became impossible. They had little idea of their direction, but they kept careful note of their airborne time in case some clue should offer itself when they landed.

The flight lasted exactly two hours. Strever felt fairly sure that they had travelled in a northerly direction. When the Cant finally came to rest they were disembarked on to a jetty and an escort party took charge of them. They wondered whether they might be already in Italy. They were taken by car to what Strever thought must be the local headquarters. Here they were interrogated. Question after question about their last operation, about their base, about aircraft strengths at Malta, about their squadron, was fired at them, but they resolutely refused to give any information other than name, rank and number. No real pressure was brought to bear and eventually they were taken to the Officers' Mess. There was a carefree atmosphere amongst the Italians, as though the war were a long way away, and Strever felt more sure than ever that they had flown nor-nor-west that afternoon and were still on one of the many islands off south-western Greece.

At the Officers' Mess they were given civilian clothes to change into, which were welcome as their khaki drill was soaked in sea-water. Four huge plates of macaroni were then placed in front of them, and as they had not eaten for over twelve hours they tucked in with a will. When they thought the meal was over, four steaks were brought in. After the ubiquitous tinned stew of the previous weeks, their appetites were voracious and they ate the steaks with gusto. The meal ended with more brandy and cigarettes, and they were given the run of the Mess for the rest of the day. Later in the evening they were given writing materials and told that they could write to their next of kin.

'Where are we?' asked Strever.

The Italians would not answer this question, so Strever tried another tack.

'Where are we going?'

'Taranto,' said one of the Italian officers. That meant that they were definitely not yet in Italy. Later the only Italian officer who spoke any English told them that they were to be flown to Taranto next morning for internment in a prison camp. 'That is bad,' said the Italian ominously. They'd got more out of the Italians than the Italians had got from them.

'Tomorrow bad, tonight good,' said the Italians. They realised even more fully what was meant when they were taken to bed. Four of the Italians had given up their two double rooms so that their prisoners should pass a comfortable night.

Strever paired off with Dunsmore, and the two New Zealanders shared the second room. Guards were posted in the passage and outside the windows. They began to feel at last that they were prisoners, and found the realisation disturbingly and surprisingly unpleasant. Their captors' words echoed in their minds. *Tomorrow bad.*

On the wall of the New Zealanders' room was a map of the Adriatic Sea and the Grecian coast. Brown and Wilkinson turned towards it eagerly. Somewhere on that map was the spot in which they were spending the night. They plotted the approximate position of the Axis convoy, and then looked for land some two hours flying in a northerly direction.

'We're somewhere here,' said Wilkinson, tapping the map. 'Levkas – or perhaps as far south as Corfu. It's a hundred to one we're somewhere in that area.'

'There's Taranto!' said Brown. 'Should be about an hour and a half's flying.'

Wilkinson did not speak again for some time. When he

did eventually break the silence, Brown was nearly asleep.

'I'm going to get out of this mess if I can,' he said.

They were awakened at seven o'clock next morning, and breakfasted well on eggs (the first they'd seen for many weeks), bacon, tomatoes, toast and coffee. While they were at breakfast they were left alone for a few moments. Instantly they began to discuss the possibility of escape.

'I've worked out where we are,' said Wilkinson. 'Either Levkas or Corfu. Taranto can't be more than about two hundred miles. If we don't do something quickly we'll be in a P.O.W. camp by lunch-time.'

'Not a hope here,' said Dunsmore. 'We've as much chance of eluding them here as a bunch of film-stars at a world première. Better wait till we get to Taranto.'

'You know what they say,' said Strever. 'The best chances come immediately after capture. Once they get us to Taranto there'll be no more of this being fêted like transatlantic flyers. Life'll start to get tough then.'

'Has anyone thought of trying to capture the aircraft and fly it to Malta? Malta's about three hundred and fifty miles, I reckon.'

'I've thought of it, Wilkie,' said Strever. 'I thought of it yesterday. We probably had a better chance then than we'll get today. They're bound to mount a guard on us now. Still, we'll keep our eyes open.'

'Look out,' said Brown. The guards had arrived to escort them to the jetty. They had no further chance to discuss escape.

The whole Italian headquarters staff seemed to have preceded them to the jetty to see them off. Everyone wanted to shake hands with them and take pictures, and as they boarded another Cant floatplane – not the same one as the previous day, and a different crew – a battery of cameras clicked into action. Strever could not help contrasting the carefree atmosphere here with the grim bitterness of life at Malta. Life here was leisurely and luxurious and food and drink plentiful. Life at Malta was hectic and austere. It was hard to believe that their two countries were locked in a desperate battle for survival. Strever tried hard to recapture the bitter enmity of the fighting, but the gaiety of his captors disarmed him. Resenting the feeling of goodwill that abounded, he stepped quickly into the plane.

The Cant crew consisted of pilot, second pilot, engineer, wireless operator/observer, and a corporal acting as escort, armed with a .45 revolver that looked as though it had been rescued from a museum. Strever and his crew entered the plane first, followed by the guard. Then came the Italian crew, in high spirits, each carrying two or more large cases, which they dumped in the fuselage. They were going home on leave. The flight was part and parcel of the party, and the holiday spirit was already abroad.

The Italian pilot introduced himself. 'Captain Gatetama Mastrodrasa, at your service.' He grinned, showing a set of incredibly white, even teeth. 'We go to Italy on leave. I see my bambino' – he rocked an imaginary baby in his arms – 'for the first time. For you, it is bad.' He shrugged his shoulders and opened the palms of his hands, then turned on his heel and went forward to the pilot's seat.

Space was restricted in the crew compartment of the Cant and the nine men were in close proximity to each other. Pilot and second pilot sat in the front of the perspex cockpit, with the corporal escort standing behind and between them, facing backwards. Next came the wireless operator and flight engineer. In the back of the elongated crew compartment Strever and his crew squatted on the floor.

They were airborne at 0940. That meant that they ought to reach Taranto about 1110, barring accidents. They sat quietly and tried to look relaxed and resigned. Nevertheless the corporal's belt and holster fascinated them. How quick would he be on the draw? What firearms might the other members of the crew have ready to hand? And if they could turn the tables on the Italians, what then? Could they effectively subdue the whole crew and at the same time fly an unfamiliar aircraft and navigate it from an unknown point to a tiny island notoriously hard to find, without radio and perhaps without maps?

Well, it might be worth a try.

Staggering along under an overload of men and luggage, unable to climb above a thousand feet, where the air was sickeningly bumpy and unbearably hot, the Cant made slow and unsteady progress towards the heel of Italy. Four men faced the prospect of years of imprisonment. Four men were going on leave. Poised between the two parties, a kind of neutral umpire, stood the corporal guard.

The corporal sat down behind the pilot. It was a bad day for a non-flyer; a wretched day for a ground type with a queasy stomach. The corporal felt the sweat pouring from his forehead. Yet he felt cold. He longed to set foot on the sure earth again. How long had they said? Ninety minutes? They could hardly be half-way yet. He found himself swallowing incessantly. His head ached intolerably and he longed to lie down. Up-currents and down-draughts played battledore and shuttlecock with his stomach. He gritted his teeth fiercely, determined not to be sick. His eyeballs felt like roundshot. His jowls drooped. His energy was spent and he felt an overwhelming apathy. If only the plane would crash or something. Anything to get down on the deck.

Wilkinson sat facing the wireless operator/observer, whose log sheets were strewn on the navigation table between them. Behind the observer sat the corporal, his face a ghastly parchment. Wilkinson looked at his watch. 1025. They must be about half-way. They daren't leave it much longer. Perhaps a fighter escort might be sent to meet them. Soon they would be picked up by the Italian coastal radar. It was now or never.

Somehow he had to distract the observer's attention and get his hands firmly planted on the airsick corporal's gun.

The only trick he knew was a schoolboy affair. You pointed suddenly out of the window and while your victim turned his head away you had him momentarily at your mercy. Schoolboys were used to the trick and didn't always buy it. He would have to take a chance with this fellow.

'Look!'

The observer turned his head, and instantly the window clouded into an opaque blackness and then splintered into stars as Wilkinson's fist sank into his jaw. There was no recoil. Wilkinson allowed the impetus of the punch to carry him past the table; then he jumped over the observer's slouched body and snatched at the corporal's revolver. His hands closed over it greedily and he tore at it with all his strength. Next moment the pistol was in his hands, and as the corporal fell back into the pilot's lap he handed the pistol to Strever, who had quickly backed him up, leaving Dunsmore and Brown to attend to the observer and flight engineer. The corporal fell between the pilot and the control column, and as he struggled to free himself he fouled the controls and sent the floatplane into a steep dive. Wilkinson, flung forward like a piece of loose cargo, caught the corporal by the scruff of the neck and with a Herculean effort lifted him clear.

By this time Strever was pointing the gun coolly in the pilot's ribs, believing the day had been won, unaware that the second pilot was in the act of turning a Luger on him.

Brown, holding down the stunned observer, saw the Italian second pilot swing triumphantly round with the Luger. Another second and their dreams of capturing the aircraft would be over. The nearest missile to hand was a seat-cover. He gathered it and hurled it with one movement, like the throw of a classic cover-point. The seat-cover flew through the air unerringly, striking the Luger and knocking it from the second pilot's grasp. Instantly there was a free-for-all as the two crews struggled for possession of the Luger. Strever kept the pilot covered while Dunsmore hooked the Luger out of the scrum back to Wilkinson. The morale of the Italian crewmen was broken.

But Captain Mastrodrasa was not done with yet. He kept the Cant in a steep dive, determined to foil the Beaufort crew's escape by landing the Cant on the sea.

Strever brandished the revolver before his eyes, and then raised it as though he would smash in the Italian's skull. The horizon came down from above them like a blind as the Cant floatplane slowly levelled out.

Meanwhile Dunsmore and Brown were busy tying up the rest of the crew with a length of mooring hawser. Dunsmore tied them up while Brown seized a monkey-wrench from the tool-kit and stood poised above them.

'One move out of you lot and I'll dong you,' he shouted, swinging the wrench. The Italians understood the gesture — and the onomatopoeia. The Italian captain, too, was hustled back to be tied up, but every time Dunsmore thought he had them firmly secured, the Italians shook their heads and wriggled their wrists to show that they could still free themselves. Eventually Dunsmore tied them up with their trouser-belts.

Strever took over the controls and turned the floatplane ninety degrees to port of their previous track in the rough direction of Malta. For one glorious moment they relaxed, breathless and dishevelled, flushed and exultant, revelling in a sense of freedom and power, undisputed masters of the plane in which they had been travelling to Italy two minutes earlier as prisoners of war.

But their jubilant mood passed swiftly as the hazards of the flight ahead of them crystallised in their minds. Dunsmore sat at the navigation table and worked out a course, but they were still uncertain of their take-off point and previous track and had only a hazy notion of their present position. Dunsmore turned the navigation compartment upside down but could find no maps. Evidently the Italians were confirmed coast-crawlers.

Strever, steering the approximate course given him by Dunsmore, was acutely conscious of the dangers facing them. Malta was nearly twice as far as Taranto. They did not know the speed or the endurance of the Cant. Navigation without maps and with an airspeed indicator registering in kilometres was the purest guesswork. If they ran out of petrol and failed to get within sight of Malta, no one would know where to look for them, neither the Italians nor the British. It was essential that he discuss their situation with Dunsmore. Two heads were better than one. He called Dunsmore.

'Get that second pilot untied, will you? I'm going to put him in the seat and come back for a conference.'

The Italian second pilot was duly released and pushed into the pilot's seat.

'Keep on that heading,' shouted Strever, gesticulating and pointing to the compass. And so that the Italian should be in no doubt as to their destination he added 'Malta, Malta.'

The Italian turned to him in anguish.

'Malta?' The word meant only one thing to the second pilot. His eyes bulged. 'Spitfires!' He made a motion describing machine-gun fire and the demise of the Cant. Strever grinned and went back to talk to Dunsmore. They would cross that bridge when they came to it.

Strever and Dunsmore together ransacked the aircraft for maps in vain. Then between them they began to reconstruct on a blank sheet of paper the approximate slant of the Greek coast up towards the Adriatic, the thin heel and toe of Italy, the appendage of Sicily, and somewhere south of Sicily two arbitrary blobs that represented Malta and Gozo. It was like sticking a pin in a list of runners. They showed their cartography to the Italian navigator, who shook his head violently. They freed his wrists and he snatched Dunsmore's pencil and made swift corrections, like a lightning artist. Strever and Dunsmore replotted their position.

'What do you think?' asked Strever.

'I don't think we can be far out,' said Dunsmore. 'I've been squinting at the compass all the time and plotting a mental course. Keep on this track for another half-hour. If we see nothing by then, we'd better turn due west and make a landfall on the toe of Italy or on Sicily. Then we can set course again for Malta.'

'If we've still got any petrol,' said Strever. They would look funny running out of petrol off Italy or Sicily with five Italian prisoners. That would put them right back where they started. The whole thing was beginning to look like a game of touch, in which for the moment the Italians were 'he'.

Strever went forward to keep an eye on the Italian second pilot. Brown got into the gun turret and kept watch for other aircraft, while Wilkinson tried to pick up the Malta beacon on the radio. The radio controls were extremely complicated, and he could find no trace of any homing device on the receiver. He thought he might be able to make the transmitter work, but in doing so they would probably give themselves away to the Italians. Better to leave well alone.

As the floatplane plodded on in a south-westerly direction, Strever took over the controls from time to time to familiarise himself with them and to guard against any attempt at re-turning the tables by the Italians. After they had been on the Malta heading for an hour without any sight of land, Dunsmore went forward and spoke to Strever.

'Time's up,' he said. 'We'd better try and make a landfall.'

Strever turned the Cant to starboard towards the Italian coastline, and they watched anxiously for a sight of land. They must now be overdue at Taranto, and aircraft might be searching for them. It would be too soon yet for an air/sea rescue search, but aircraft already airborne might be alerted. Apart from the Cant and its crew, the capture of an entire Beaufort crew must be something of a prize.

It was not long before they sighted land, almost certainly the heel of Italy, but they were too far distant yet for an accurate fix. Strever brought the Cant down low over the sea to avoid the Italian coastal radar. As they neared the coast they saw a ship steaming across their path. Strever held on grimly, waiting for the flak to rise, but none came.

'Get a load of that,' he said. 'Packed with Jerry soldiers.'

'I'll make a note of its position and course, anyway,' said Dunsmore. 'They'll be pretty interested back at base.' He laughed nervously, aware that he had said something that sounded strangely anachronistic.

'Junkers 52 formating on us,' shouted Brown from the turret. Strever held his course, hardly daring to look round, feeling like a thief. Brown waited until the German aircraft was some three hundred yards distant and then dipped his guns in salute, ready to fire at them instantly if the Junkers 52 looked at all belligerent. After two or three tense minutes, in which even the German aircraft itself seemed to be eyeing them suspiciously, it pulled away to the north. Strever and Dunsmore then bent to the task of making a landfall and setting course for Malta.

As they neared the toe of Italy Strever glanced once again at his watch. 1130. They had been airborne for an hour and fifty minutes, and it might be another hour or more before they reached Malta. They must get their fix and turn south as soon as possible.

Brown noticed that the Italian flight engineer was struggling with his bonds and that his face was strangely contorted. He kept pointing forward until Brown realised what he was trying to say. The petrol-tanks needed changing over.

Brown untied the engineer's hands and went forward with

him. The Italian switched the cocks over and then pointed dramatically to his watch. They understood his meaning clearly enough. The petrol-tanks would run dry by 1230.

Strever eyed the Italian critically. It might be a trick to persuade them to abandon the idea of attempting to reach Malta. Somehow he didn't think so. He swung the aircraft round on a southerly heading and waited for Dunsmore to give him a course for Malta. Working from an improvised map was hazardous, but visibility was good. They would see Malta all right.

For the next hour they lumbered steadily on, scarcely a word being spoken, each man thinking his own thoughts. If they missed Malta they would stooge on into nothingness. A moment would come when they must stop heading south and begin a square search for Malta. Choosing that moment was the problem. If they stopped too soon they would find nothing. If they kept on too long they would have no endurance left for any kind of search.

Suddenly the Italians became voluble. 'No benzine,' they shouted. 'Benzine kaput.' The gauges were reading zero. Strever himself could see that. He called Wilkinson and Brown.

'We must be pretty close to Malta,' he said. 'For God's sake keep a sharp look-out. And we'd better release the Eyeties. You know what sort of reception we'll get from Malta. We can't leave these devils tied up if we're going to get shot down.'

'Do you think they'll try anything?'

'I'm certain they won't,' said Strever. 'They know even better than we do that we're nearly out of gas. See that they put life-jackets on. And keep them as quiet as you can.'

Wilkinson and Brown released the rest of the Italian crew and then continued scanning the horizon. The two gunners had never really considered the possibility that Strever and Dunsmore might fail to find Malta. Now they could see the exploit that had begun so triumphantly tapering away into disaster, a disaster they were as helpless to prevent as their prisoners.

Five minutes later Brown shouted at the top of his voice, wildly and ecstatically, 'Malta!'

Strever corrected him. 'Gozo,' he said, 'but I think I can see Malta too.' The time was 1240. The last and perhaps most dangerous lap lay ahead.

The tension increased as the outline of Malta began to sharpen. They wanted to be seen, in case the petrol-tanks ran dry in the next few minutes: but on the other hand they knew well enough the kind of reception a single Italian aircraft would get from Malta's Spitfires. Strever handed the controls over to the Italian again and made him fly the aircraft almost at sea-level. If things went badly for them they could always make a quick landing on the sea.

What a surprise the chaps would get at Malta! Creeping in under the island's radar screen, they were now only three miles off-shore. Malta looked pale and beautiful, serene and indomitable. Another few moments and they would be there. The whole aircraft seemed to hold its breath.

It was as they sighted the wireless masts above Valetta that the ten Spitfires came rushing at them out of the sun.

Dunsmore instantly took off his white singlet and trailed it out of the cockpit in token of surrender. In the turret Brown spun the guns about as the recognised signal to show the fighters he was not going to fire. But the ten Spitfires, strung out in follow-the-leader fashion, came relentlessly on.

The first Spitfire opened up at point-blank range with cannon and machine-gun fire and the smooth surface of the Cant's starboard wing splintered and twisted into an ugly pock-marked sheet of scrap metal. Strever shouted to the Italian pilot to come down on the water. As the floatplane slewed round drunkenly on the sea the three engines coughed and spluttered and then cut dead. They had run out of petrol.

Immediately the aircraft was still, Strever and his crew rushed out on to the wings and waved frantically to the Spitfire pilots. The whole formation was circling overhead. Mercifully, the fighter boys flipped their firing buttons to safe and, after a long look at the Cant to satisfy themselves that it was properly winged, they returned in formation to Malta. Strever and his crew watched them disappear. Already the air/sea rescue boys would have been alerted, and they waited impatiently to be picked up, longing to set foot again on Malta, produce their prisoners and tell their story.

Now that the incident was so nearly ended, Strever and his crew felt a sharp twinge of conscience at the way they had treated the Italians. What a way to repay the kindness of their captors from the moment of rescue right up to the start of this trip! But the Italians were cheerful and seemed to bear no illwill. They opened their voluminous bags and brought out the brandy and wine and cigarettes they had been taking on leave. When the air/sea rescue launch arrived one and a half hours later, its crew were greeted by nine mellow men.

On reaching Malta they were taken to the nearest Officers' Mess, where as a special change from tinned stew they were given the besieged island's rarest delicacy – bully-beef. They had eaten infinitely better as prisoners. Afterwards they escorted the Italian crew to the island prison-camp, pleaded for the best accommodation, and with some misgivings bade them farewell.

THE BALANCE SHEET

THE last hour of the long night anti-submarine patrol in the Bay of Biscay was always the longest, like the last mile home. The clock on the dashboard of the Wellington, lit by the faint glow of the fluorescent lighting, pointed to ten minutes to four, the kind of hour when peaceful men slept soundly in their beds. Triggs, sitting at the controls, wondered at the inconsistencies which had brought him, a peaceful man, all the way from Australia to fly night patrols in a Wellington twelve hundred feet above the Bay.

Yet it was a peaceful enough night. Even a pacifist might carry out these night patrols without much offending his conscience. With a heavy layer of 10/10ths cloud at three thousand feet, the night was so dark that visibility was almost nil. But back in the fuselage McLean was operating the anti-submarine radar. If he got a U-boat contact, they would home on to it until the range was too close for radar, and then they would switch on the powerful Leigh Light which illumined the sea dead ahead for over a mile. Not so long ago, U-boats had been able to cavort below them unmolested on dark nights such as this. Now, radar and the Leigh Light could turn the darkest night into day.

Somehow, in spite of the conditions, tonight's trip had been plagued by uneasiness and uncertainty. Everyone had been on edge, everyone had had in the back of his mind the feeling that something was wrong. And indeed there had been much in the behaviour of both engines to undermine confidence. But they were the kind of niggles for which a man hesitated to turn back. Triggs had decided to press on and carry out the patrol.

Now it was the last hour before dawn. Back in south-west England, other crews of other squadrons would be taking off to continue the endless patrol. With the first light of dawn they could set course for base, leaving the cares of the night behind them. Nothing to report.

Devonshire's voice broke into Triggs' thoughts from the rear turret. 'There's an awful lot of sparks from that starboard engine, Skipper. Do you think it's O.K.?'

'Sparks? What are they like?'

'Like . . . like a cluster of stars.'

'You can cut out the poetry, anyway. Have another look.'

'There's more than ever now. I can still see them trailing behind us when they're a hundred yards back.'

Triggs eyed the oil-pressure gauge. It was steady for a moment, and then he watched with alarm as the pressure dropped quickly to zero. He began to close the throttle slowly, correcting with starboard rudder. The engine sounded rough and laboured, and then it seized suddenly and completely, the propeller hanging limp and still like a useless limb. He quickly cut the fuel supply to the dud motor to lessen the risk of fire, and increased the revs on the good engine.

'Send an S O S, Arthur. Tell them we're on one engine.'

'Right.'

He called Badham, his Australian navigator. 'Give Arthur our D/R position, Col.'

'O.K.'

Cartwright transmitted the S O S on the control frequency and then wound out his trailing aerial so as to repeat it on the long-wave distress frequency. He felt the aircraft losing height rapidly and wondered whether his messages would be received. It had been a poor night for wireless and there was usually static interference back in England during August. They ought to have more height to have a fair chance of getting a message through. He repeated his S O S on the control frequency and then changed to the distress frequency without waiting for a reply.

Triggs opened up the port engine to 3½ lbs boost and 2450 revs per minute, keeping the airspeed at 120 miles an hour. He watched the engine temperature rising, complaining under the strain. In spite of the increase in power on the port side they were still losing height.

'Jettison everything you can,' he called, 'parachutes, flame floats, all loose equipment.' As he spoke he pressed the depth charge jettison button, wondering for a brief instant whether some unwary U-boat might get the surprise of its life. The altitude needle still moved slowly anticlockwise. The port engine temperature went on rising.

'Prepare for ditching, chaps. We'd better ditch into wind, Col. What's the direction?'

'Two hundred and eighty degrees true,' said Badham.

'Strength about thirty miles an hour. I reckon the waves are breaking about two to three feet high running downwind with the swell. There's quite a bit of a swell on, too. Depth about sixteen to twenty feet and tops about two hundred yards apart.'

'Good show, Col.'

Walker, the second pilot, helped Triggs into his safety harness and then jettisoned the pilot's escape hatch before lying down feet forward in the fuselage next to the wireless operator and bracing himself against the ledge on the floor. Badham jettisoned the astro-dome, operated the flotation gear and then braced himself below the open astro-dome against the main spar of the aircraft. Devonshire rotated the rear turret to port and jettisoned the turret door. Cartwright went on transmitting his S O S, determined not to take up his ditching position until the last possible moment.

Triggs kept the aircraft heading for base and tried to work out his ditching problems. He knew that this mark of Wellington, shorn of a nose turret and carrying a load of special anti-sub radar equipment aft, was very liable to become tail-heavy. He had two hundred and eighty gallons of petrol on board and wanted to get rid of it, partly as a precaution against fire and partly for the buoyancy effect of the empty tanks after the ditching; but he was concerned lest the loss of weight of the petrol forward should unbalance the aircraft still further. He decided that with a choppy sea and appreciable swell the biggest danger lay in the actual ditching. They would be out of the aircraft in quick time in any case.

Then there was the question whether to ditch into wind or parallel with the swell. They rarely amounted to the same thing. There were two schools of thought. You could land into wind but against the wave crests, in which case you could reduce speed more easily, but had to take the chance of the aircraft tripping on one wave crest and then diving straight into the next. On the other hand, if you landed parallel with the swell but across wind, your speed was higher and you hit the water crabbing to one side. With the tops of the swell two hundred yards apart he ought to be able to land into wind without tripping on a wave crest. Crabbing to one side on one engine sounded pretty desperate.

Triggs flipped on his inter-com and began a running commentary on the ditching. 'I'm going to ditch now just as soon as I can. No point in trying to stay airborne. The port engine's getting too hot. I can't judge our height too well, so I'll rely on the radio altimeter. I reckon we're down to about a hundred feet. Fifty feet.' He switched on the landing light, illuminating the white wave crests. There seemed to be an awful lot of sea. 'The radio altimeter's reading zero. Reckon we must be submerged by now. Funny if we ran into a sub.' He saw the swell rush past underneath and judged his height as thirty feet. The heavy equipment amidships was making the Wimpey extremely tail-heavy and very difficult to handle. He daren't use any flap in case it pulled the nose up still further. 'Height about thirty feet. Speed seventy-eight knots. Turning into wind. We'll be about thirty degrees across the swell. Closing the throttle and holding off.' He closed the port throttle, put the propeller into coarse pitch and turned off the petrol. 'Holding off a few feet over the water. Hold tight.' He held the Wimpey in a three-point attitude, watching the speed fall away. 'Seventy knots. Sixty-five knots. She must hit.'

He felt the tail strike the water and the sea towered above him. Then they seemed to hit the top of the swell and the aircraft stopped instantly. The bump was lighter than a belly-landing on a runway. No one was thrown out of position except Cartwright, who was flung forward and cut his eye.

The cockpit filled with water up to the instrument panel immediately and Triggs thought they were going to sink nose first. Then he saw water pouring up through the front para-chute hatch in the floor of the aircraft and cascading down through the astro-hatch above him. The influx of water seemed to right the aircraft.

He released his harness and stepped out of his seat, his eyes on the escape hatch above his head. Knee-deep in water, he stumbled as he made for the hatch and realised he was stepping on a body. Walker, the second pilot, was lying on his face unconscious. He lifted him up out of the water and jammed him half-way through the escape hatch, then climbed out himself and pulled Walker through the hatch after him. Walker was still unconscious and he dragged him out on to the wing.

In the fuselage, Cartwright helped McLean up through the astro-hatch and then followed him, leaving Badham to operate the dinghy release. Badham jerked the lever firmly and then prepared to climb out through the hatch.

'The emergency rations!' shouted Cartwright into the aircraft. 'They've come adrift and got washed away.' Badham remembered something floating past him immediately after the ditching. He saw an emergency pack lying on top of his navigation table and went back to retrieve it. Then he passed the pack up to Cartwright and climbed out.

'Where's the dinghy?' shouted Badham as he thrust his head and shoulders clear.

'Did you pull the release?'

'Of course I did.' Badham went back into the sinking aircraft and pulled the release again and again but still the dinghy refused to blow out. By this time the water had risen up to his armpits and he struggled to raise himself up again through the hatch. His mind grappled with the awful truth that the dinghy had failed to release and that as the aircraft went down they would be flung into the sea. He was appalled by the sheer contrast between the warmth and security of the aircraft and the cold, unfriendly sea.

Cartwright saw that Badham was coping and he turned to find the outside manual dinghy release. His fingers closed over it and he pulled, again and again, like a man playing on a pin-table when the last ball has gone. 'It's stuck,' he said. 'It's stuck.' He could think of nothing else to say.

Triggs shook Walker out of his concussion and held him upright. Standing up on the wing, they were up to their knees in water as the aircraft plunged in the heavy seas. Cartwright and McLean were still struggling with the dinghy release. Walker had recovered and Triggs left him, making for the dinghy stowage. He ignored the manual release and wrestled with the stowage with his bare hands. Soon he had prised off the lid and pulled out the dinghy.

Devonshire, dazed when the turret began to rotate as the tail struck the sea, recovered quickly as the water rose to waist level. He freed himself and climbed out of the turret along the top of the fuselage to the wing. As he arrived on the wing the dinghy began to inflate and the crew climbed aboard, keeping the dinghy anchored to the wing by their weight.

'Where's the emergency pack?' shouted Triggs, still standing on the wing.

'I gave it to you, Arthur,' said Badham.

'I put it on the wing while I was trying to release the dinghy.' Cartwright stared round helplessly, realising that anything lying on the wing must have been washed off as the sea rose.

'It can't have gone far,' said Triggs. The landing light was still burning, throwing an eerie phosphorescence around them. 'There it is!' shouted Triggs, pointing to a dark shape bobbing about on the surface near the propeller. He plunged into the sea, swam out beyond the port engine and secured the emergency pack. He made his way through heavy seas back to the wing, handed the pack into the dinghy and dragged himself on to the wing. The wing was several feet under water and only six inches of the fuselage was still clear of the sea.

The dinghy was floating to leeward of the Wellington and Triggs stayed on the wing, pushing the dinghy gently towards the wing-tip so as to avoid fouling the aerials. When he felt the wing-tip sinking beneath his feet he grabbed hold of Badham, who helped him aboard. As he turned to take a last look at the sinking Wellington the only part still visible was the uppermost extremity of the tail fin.

Triggs judged that they had been about a minute getting the dinghy out and perhaps another half a minute retrieving the emergency pack and getting clear. Perhaps two minutes since the ditching. Not a second more. He looked up and saw that the tail fin had disappeared.

The dinghy had already shipped three or four inches of water and the six men sat three on either side, baling out continually, at first using their cupped hands, and then as more and more water slopped in over the side they each removed a shoe and kept baling with a steady rhythm. Badham had underestimated the height of the waves and swell from the air, and the dinghy was buffeted and tossed without respite. They were already soaked at least to the waist and the spray breaking over the side completed their discomfiture. Seasickness overtook them, but with the high seas persisting there was no chance for anyone to give in and hang his head over the side. They were sick continually until they had nothing left to bring up but their stomach-juices, and still they retched and choked. The water in the dinghy yellowed and muddied sickeningly, and still they bent to bale it out.

After nearly an hour and a half of continuous baling they began to make some impression on the level of the water. Soon they were able to use their handkerchiefs to mop up the floor of the dinghy. But when dawn came it brought an even fuller realisation of their plight. The seas were mountainous and visibility was down to half a mile. Triggs examined the dinghy equipment and emergency pack. There were rations and water in sufficient quantities to last them for several days, and all the dinghy equipment seemed to be intact. He noticed with surprise that there were only two distress rockets.

An hour and a half since the ditching, thought Triggs. Time enough to have got back to Chivenor. Five-thirty. That would just about have been their E.T.A. He wondered if anyone had picked up their S O S. Another half-hour or so and they would be posted overdue.

An hour after dawn they were still afflicted by intense depression following the early violent seasickness. But in spite of their miserable condition, Triggs and Badham were slowly regaining their normal outlook of cheery optimism. They were alive and the dinghy had proved itself in heavy seas, and they had no doubt they would be rescued soon. This part of the Bay was always a scene of activity, day and night. They were only about eighty miles off the Brest penin-sula, right in the path of the anti-U-boat patrols. They were certain to see aircraft, and sooner or later an aircraft would see them. They would probably see German aircraft as well. Luftwaffe fighter patrols were always about, ready to pounce on the unwary. Then there was the French tunny-fishing fleet. In the eight sorties they'd done since the squadron became operational three weeks ago they'd seen several tunnymen.

The chances were that they would be spotted from the air by the Germans and picked up eventually by a tunnyman. Even if the Coastal boys saw them first they would only attract the attention of the Jerries. And they were much too far away, and much too near the French coast, for any real hope of an air/sea rescue operation from the U.K. The thought of ending up as prisoners of war damped their spirits momentarily.

'How far are we off Brest, Col?'

'I'll work it out for you.' Just like Col, thought Triggs. Still a Coastal navigator to his fingertips. He half expected him to produce a sextant from his pocket and take a sun shot. He watched while the blunt-featured, freckled Badham made a few rapid calculations, as composed and assured as if he were still sitting at his navigation table. 'According to my reckoning we're eighty miles off the Brest peninsula, perhaps eight or ten miles north of the latitude of Brest itself, and about a hundred and eighty miles due south of Land's End. Just a few miles to the south-west, actually.'

'You haven't got a course to steer there, have you?'

Badham laughed. 'You can have one if you want one.'

'I might take you up on that.'

Cartwright and McLean were still seasick, but the others were recovering, and Triggs had them watching the skyline for aircraft. Suddenly Walker pointed to a Wellington about a mile away heading south.

'A Wimpey!' he shouted. 'Must be one of the boys!'

'Could be at that,' said Badham.

'How about a rocket?' Devonshire's sharp Canadian accent contrasted with Badham's drawl.

'I think she's too far away,' said Triggs. 'We've only got two, you know. Better keep them till we can be pretty sure.'

'I wonder who it was,' said Walker wistfully.

'Well, let's see,' said Badham. 'Fraser and Bramwell were on with us last night. It can't be either of them. It might be Howell, or Dyer.'

'Yes, or Virgo, or Riding, or anyone from half a dozen other Wimpey squadrons,' said Triggs.

'I'll make a note of the time,' said the methodical Badham. 'When we get back we can check up.'

'I'll bet it was Virgo,' said Devonshire. The game of guessing who was in the disappearing Wimpey animated them all. Everyone perked up at the thought of having been close for a few moments to squadron colleagues.

The seas remained rough and towering and there was no relief for the seasick, but visibility improved, and soon after half-past eight that morning they saw what looked like a Beaufighter flying low some distance away.

'It's a Beaufighter all right,' said Devonshire.

'What's it doing flying so low? Can't be more than three hundred feet,' said Badham.

'I reckon it's searching for us,' said Triggs. He grabbed one of the distress rockets and watched the progress of the Beaufighter. Its track would take it about a quarter of a mile from the dinghy. Triggs waited, and when the Beaufighter was about eight hundred yards distant he ignited the rocket. The

Beaufighter continued on its course, passing about four hundred yards to the north, the R.A.F. roundels showing up clearly on the underside of the wings.

'They haven't seen us,' said McLean.

'There'll be another one along in a minute,' said Triggs. He was annoyed at wasting the rocket, but not at all disturbed. It certainly had seemed as though the Beau was looking for them. The Bay was a pretty big place and the search would be kept up until they were found.

During the morning they sighted a further ten aircraft, including a Whitley which flew so near that they risked their last pyrotechnic. They were still not seen. Triggs and Badham worked hard to keep up the spirits of the rest of the crew during this period. Their precise knowledge of their position was a great stimulus to everyone's morale. When Badham rigged a small sail and the dinghy appeared to be drifting eastwards towards land, the rest of the crew were greatly cheered. Triggs and Badham did their best to instil in the others their confidence that they would either be rescued or drift on to the coast of France.

After they had fired the second rocket they waved the flag whenever they saw an aircraft and dipped the fluorescine bag in the sea. These were the only methods remaining to them of attracting attention.

Triggs' and Badham's breezy assurance that they would soon be found was justified during the afternoon. Soon after half-past two they saw a Whitley with a Beaufighter escort obviously carrying out a thorough search. They waved the flag continually and trailed the fluorescine bag, and after about ten minutes the Whitley flew straight overhead, waggling its wings, while the Beaufighters peeled off and shot up the dinghy in line abreast. It was a thrilling sight and the finest medicine possible for the seasick men.

The Whitley made a circuit of the dinghy and then began a long, slow approach, culminating in the dropping of a spare dinghy. The dinghy fell upwind and they began paddling hard towards it without making any impression on the distance. The pilot of the Whitley, evidently realising that the spare dinghy was so far upwind as to be unattainable, now made a second approach and dropped a bag of supplies. This time the drop was more successfully timed and the bag fell within easy reach downwind. Triggs and his crew reversed the direction of their paddling and the bag was retrieved. They were pleased to find in the bag a Very pistol and several cartridges.

Things looked all right for the moment, but Triggs was beginning to wonder just how the air/sea rescue boys were going to reach them. If they weren't rescued today they might drift a long way from their known position during the night. Then the search would have to begin all over again.

His fears multiplied a few minutes later when the Whitley and the Beaufighters set course for home. They were alone for some time; but when they saw another Whitley in the distance half an hour later Triggs fired the Very pistol and the Whitley acknowledged the signal and circled overhead.

'Look!' shouted Walker, 'they're signalling something.' The Whitley was making a wide circuit of the dinghy, and someone was operating a signalling lamp. Cartwright, McLean and Devonshire spelt out the letters together.

'S-U-N-D-E-R-L-A-N-D. Sunderland! C-O-M-I-N-G. Sunderland coming!'

'When?' said Badham.

'If they meant tomorrow they'd have said so,' said Triggs. 'It must have taken off in the last few minutes or the other Whitley would have known about it.'

It was now late afternoon, and if a Sunderland had taken off it would just about have time to reach them and attempt a rescue before dark. There was no doubt the rescue people were doing everything they could to spare them another night in the dinghy; but Triggs was sceptical of the prospects of a Sunderland attempting to alight in the heavy seas.

'I'd better tell you men what I'm thinking,' he said. 'I don't think any Sunderland's going to land tonight. It's still pretty rough and I reckon they'll wait till tomorrow.'

'In that case, I guess *we'll* have to wait too,' said Devonshire.

'Too right,' said Badham.

Triggs' estimate of the arrival time of the Sunderland proved accurate: they sighted the Sunderland a few minutes before eight o'clock that evening. Triggs fired off another Very cartridge and the Sunderland acknowledged the signal and turned in their direction.

They watched anxiously while the Sunderland circled the dinghy. So far they had no indication of what was in the mind of the pilot. They imagined him weighing the possibilities. Was it worth risking a landing? Would the men still be there in the morning or might disaster overtake them? Would Jerry get there first? Was the swell as bad as it looked? Or might it be worse? Triggs knew from his own recent experience that the sea always seemed twice as rough when you were in it. He would never have guessed from the air last night that they would be thrown about as they were as soon as they ditched. He wanted to signal the pilot and tell him that there was a twelve-foot sea running and that attempting a landing looked dangerous in the extreme, but all he could do was gaze upwards dumbly. If he tried to signal with his arms he would probably be misunderstood, perhaps not even noticed.

The Sunderland banked into a wider circle until it was some two miles away from the dinghy.

'I think he's made the right decision,' said Triggs.

'You mean we've had it for tonight?' said McLean.

'They'll find us again in the morning,' said Triggs.

'Sure they will,' said Badham. He knew how the weather could close in for days on end in the Bay, even in August, but he kept it to himself.

Suddenly their ears were shattered by a series of explosions from the direction of the Sunderland. The dinghy rocked and shook under the influence of sledgehammer blows that seemed to come up from under the sea.

'Depth charges!' shouted Badham. 'They're going to have a go!'

'You're right,' said Triggs slowly. 'They'd never try to alight with depth charges up. They've jettisoned them.'

'You don't suppose they could have seen a U-boat, do you?' asked Devonshire.

Triggs watched the Sunderland closely. As he watched he saw it dripping like a tap. 'Petrol,' he said. 'He's jettisoning petrol. He's landing all right.'

They watched in deathly silence as the Sunderland began its landing run. Triggs, his own ditching horribly clear in his mind, was remembering details of those last few airborne moments that he thought he had forgotten, that he would prefer to have forgotten. It was a thousand times worse watching someone else do it. Like sitting in the back of a fast car. He could not rid himself of a sense of impending disaster.

It was ridiculous to feel like this. The Sunderland pilot knew what he was doing. Even if it was a calculated risk, at least it was calculated. It was a different matter landing with a specially stressed hull shaped to absorb the shock of the sea. In a few minutes they would all be aboard the Sunderland, shooting at the dinghy to sink it, setting course for home. Perhaps only one night late in Barnstaple after all.

The Sunderland was skimming along the surface of the sea into wind a mile distant, sometimes completely obscured by the swell. It was a long, low approach. Triggs clenched his fists as he felt the pilot holding off. He found that he was holding an imaginary stick and trying desperately hard to make the touch-down himself. The others were so intent on the Sunderland that they had not noticed.

The flying-boat had reached stalling speed and they watched it sink gently on to the sea. It slithered across the first wave, but the swell was deep and the Sunderland had lost little speed. It bounced into the next wave, bounded on and struck the third wave-top with its tail down and its nose in the air.

'Engines!' screamed Triggs. 'Engines!'

The delay until the sound of the engines reached them was agony. The Sunderland was sinking on to a fourth wave. A tremendous roar reached them as the Sunderland pilot used full motor to clear yet another surging, turgid swell-top. It was too late. The port float seemed to bury itself in the swell and drag the rest of the aircraft round with it in a great swinging arc, piling the starboard side of the Sunderland up on top of the port side in a grotesque illusion. The port side of the aircraft sank beneath the sea and the starboard wing groped fifty feet upwards to the sky.

'God Almighty,' breathed Triggs.

As he spoke he saw that the tip of the starboard wing was missing, and in the next moment there was a screaming sound as of an engine racing and the starboard inner motor streaked fire and then burst into flames. The men in the dinghy watched with appalled wonder as the great Sunderland, enormous in its death-throes, like a huge animal, righted itself for a second and then nosed forward with its tail pointing to the sky.

The sun was setting and the evening sky, dark and lowering, reflected the blazing aircraft grandly as the sun went down. The men in the dinghy, peering for signs of life on the sinking Sunderland, saw two pigeons flap away from the shattered hulk, flying low at first so that their wings swept the sea and then climbing until they were silhouetted against the darkening sky.

Unknown to Triggs and his crew, the men in the Sunderland, numbering twelve in all, had clambered out quickly on to the wing, where they fought to inflate their dinghies. Only one dinghy inflated, and as they began to pile into it a bulge appeared in the pneumatic outer ring and swelled up until the dinghy burst. From the air they had seen the dinghy that the Whitley had dropped some hours earlier. The pilot of the Sunderland told his men to try and reach that dinghy. One of them, Watson, a beach life-saver from Sydney, fought against the tumultuous seas and reached the dinghy exhausted. He was unable to carry out a plan to paddle the dinghy back to the others. One by one the remaining eleven men of the Sunderland drowned in the turbulent sea.

Within a few minutes the great flying-boat, constructed to land and take off on the sea and to lie at anchor in calm waters, foundered and sank. When it disappeared, Triggs and his crew saw the Whitley dinghy beyond where it had been, hardly more than a speck on the horizon. They assumed that the crew of the flying-boat were aboard.

As night fell and ended their first eventful day in the sea, the wind increased and the sea roughened and waves began to break into the dinghy again, keeping all six men baling incessantly. Then, just as they seemed to have the sea under control and were about to settle down as best they could for the night, Cartwright made a discovery.

'This doesn't look too good,' he said. 'Look here. There's water seeping in through the bottom. There must be a hole somewhere.'

'My oath there is,' said Badham, feeling the well of the dinghy until his fingers found the leak. 'Over here near the buoyancy chamber. Who's got the leak stoppers?'

'They're in the pack,' said Triggs. He produced one and Badham plugged the hole, padding it round with the flying-helmet he had been wearing when he left the aircraft.

'I'm putting my helmet here,' he said. 'This stopper's right up against the buoyancy chamber. I'm scared stiff it'll chafe its way through.'

Cold and wet and uncomfortable, disturbed at the prospect of a serious leak occurring, some of them still plagued with seasickness, they slept only fitfully, longing for morning. Tomorrow the search would be redoubled. There were two crews to look for now. This would surely be their last night in the sea.

Next morning the wind had dropped to twelve to fifteen knots, but the water was still rough and the dinghy tossed precariously on the switchback seas. Sometimes, lifted to the top of the swell, they caught a glimpse of the Whitley dinghy, too fleeting for full recognition.

'They're flying a flag, anyway,' said Triggs.

None of the Wellington crew felt hungry or thirsty and the thought of the dinghy rations was unappetising. The dampness from their clothes had seeped into their bones and they felt clammy and wretched. Perhaps they would feel like eating later. Meanwhile it was just as well to conserve what food they had.

'Do you think they'll be able to do anything today?' The question came from Cartwright.

Triggs fingered the ends of his moustache critically. 'I shouldn't think last night's effort will encourage them much. They won't try landing any more Sunderlands in a hurry. Not unless we get calm weather, anyway.'

'What else can they do?'

'I don't know, Arthur. I'm not an air/sea rescue expert. I don't think they'd send a Catalina down here. Too many Jerry fighters about. The same goes for a Walrus or a Sea Otter. I don't know about a high-speed launch. Pretty risky do, I'd say. Still, I daresay they might try it. What do you think, Col?'

'Well, they must know our position now, so they ought to be able to get something down here. Trouble is they'll be waiting for news of the Sunderland. They won't have a clue what's happened to it.'

'I reckon they'll guess quick enough,' said Triggs. 'The Sunderland must have radioed that it was landing to pick us up. After that – silence. It won't take an ops-room genius to work that one out.'

In the course of the morning they saw several aircraft in the distance, apparently searching, but they conserved their Very cartridges until the search should get closer. From midday onwards they saw nothing, and by four o'clock that afternoon their minds began to face up to the prospect of another night in the dinghy.

A few minutes after four o'clock Devonshire sighted a Beaufighter on the horizon. Triggs decided to risk a cartridge if the Beaufighter came within reasonable distance. It might be their last chance that day. When the Beaufighter was about two miles distant he fired the cartridge, and as the aircraft flew on its course he felt the same incredulous feeling that he felt on the shooting-range when he missed a clay pigeon. He reloaded the Very pistol and watched the progress of the Beaufighter. Firing the pistol was like gambling. Once you started, you lost your sense of proportion and went on when you ought to stop. As the aircraft turned towards them again and he felt they had a chance of being seen he fired a second time. The aircraft continued irritatingly on its course. Completely absorbed now in the game, he rammed another cartridge into the pistol and waited like a man who has placed a big bet and settles down in the stand to watch the race. He would get his losses back this time.

The Beaufighter was heading their way again and he waited until it was about a thousand yards distant, on a course that would miss the dinghy by perhaps half a mile. He fired the pistol. There was no reaction for a moment, and then the Beaufighter turned towards them and started to climb. Its crew had evidently seen the signal and were now looking for the dinghy. Just when Triggs and his crew thought that the Beaufighter must see them it turned and began circling half a mile upwind.

'They've seen the other dinghy,' shouted Badham.

'Good enough,' said Triggs.

The Beaufighter circled for some minutes and then set course for base. An hour passed and no more aircraft appeared. Then two Whitleys arrived on the scene. The first one dropped another bag of equipment, but the bag broke open on impact with the water and the supplies were soaked. This aircraft left almost at once. The second Whitley began circling at two hundred feet.

'Here comes another message,' said Cartwright.

The navigator of the Whitley was already operating the signalling lamp. His morse speed was slow and most of the men in the dinghy read it comfortably.

'D-E-S-T-R-O-Y-E-R O-N W-A-Y.'

'Destroyer!' shouted Devonshire. 'Can you imagine that! A destroyer laid on for us!'

'I wonder what time it left,' said Triggs.

'How long would it take?' asked McLean.

'Look out!' shouted Cartwright. 'Another message.'

This time they spelt out the message with sinking hearts.

'R-E-C-A-L-L-E-D T-O B-A-S-E. B-A-D W-E-A-T-H-E-R.'

'Bad weather,' said Badham. 'I thought the wind was changing. Clouds are lower too. I wonder how long we've got this for.'

'It shouldn't stop the destroyer,' said Devonshire.

'It may not stop them looking for us,' said Badham, 'but that's another matter from finding us.'

'Look at that Whitley,' said Cartwright suddenly. 'It's in a helluva hurry.'

As they looked up they saw the Whitley climbing swiftly

for the clouds with a roar of engines. Seconds later three German Arado fighters swept past the dinghy and gave chase. The Whitley disappeared into the clouds.

They breathed more freely. 'Looks like they made it,' said Triggs. 'If they can stay in that cloud they'll get away.'

Even as he spoke there was a muffled explosion in the distance, and as they gazed northwards they saw columns of black smoke rising from the sea.

No one in the dinghy spoke. Each man was trying to convince himself that the Whitley crew might have escaped, and each man knew in his heart that they hadn't had an earthly.

Badham voiced a thought which had occurred to all of them.

'Do you suppose the Arados saw us?'

'I expect so.'

'Suppose they come back to shoot us up? It's happened before.'

'We'll take our coats off and cover the dinghy,' said Triggs.

They removed their jackets and spread them over the yellow dinghy. The Royal Air Force blue and the deeper blue of the Australian uniform of Triggs and Badham merged with the blue of the sea. The Arados did not return.

The light began to fade with a misty cheerlessness, surrounding them with the ghosts of the day's memories. The wind changed to the south-west. Then, just as they were giving up their silent watch on the horizon for the destroyer, McLean saw a ship. He pointed excitedly to the east.

It was a French tunnyman, less than a quarter of a mile away.

'Sit tight,' ordered Triggs. 'It's a Frenchman. If they see us it means the bag.'

They watched breathlessly as the tunnyman hurried by. They were not seen. The thought that they were missing a chance of rescue which might not occur again, perhaps for several days and perhaps not at all, was a thought they brushed aside. They had ample evidence that determined air/sea rescue operations were in progress. It would be breaking faith with the men who were looking for them, some of whom perhaps had already lost their lives in the process, to accept safety from any other quarter.

They settled down for their second full night in the dinghy. The floor of the dinghy was cold and damp, and they spread their Mae Wests underneath them in an attempt to keep warm and dry. Discomfort and cramp, and the fear that the dinghy might spring another leak, prevented them from sleeping for more than short periods, but even an hour's sleep was immensely refreshing. When morning came, the wind was still in the south-west and the promised bad weather had arrived. The cloud was right down to sea-level and they were surrounded by a thin misty whiteness. Visibility was little more than a mile. Even so, shortly after dawn they recognised a Ju 88 heading out into the Atlantic. It was the only aircraft they saw all day.

They had now been in the dinghy for more than three days without food or water, and although everyone protested that he did not feel hungry, Triggs decided that they ought to eat. Their first meal consisted of a biscuit, a malted-milk tablet, one small square of chocolate and a mouthful of water. It wasn't until after the meal that they began to feel hungry.

'I don't want to depress anyone,' said Badham, 'but this sort of weather is liable to cling to the Bay for days. As long as we've got a wind anywhere between south-east and north-west we might as well try to use it.'

'A hundred and eighty miles?' said Triggs.

'People have drifted more than that,' said Badham. 'Besides, now we know that ships are looking for us, it'll be much healthier if we can get right away from the Brest peninsula. And it gives us something to do.'

'That's a point,' said Triggs. 'But how about the search? Shouldn't we stay put?'

'There won't be any search today,' said Badham. 'Perhaps not tomorrow either. With the wind where it is we shall drift in a northerly direction anyway. We may as well give the wind what assistance we can. When the search starts again they're bound to allow for our drift.'

They broke the telescopic mast in two and tied the flag between the two stubs. Triggs opened the first-aid kit and made makeshift stays and sheets out of bandages. The sea anchor was streamed to help them steer a straight course.

McLean, keeping a look-out for the other dinghy, saw something like a fin sticking out of the water a quarter of a mile away. He drew Triggs' attention to it.

Triggs recognised the fin quickly enough. It was a shark. All they had to scare it off with was the Very pistol. He had kept it loaded ready for emergencies, and he held it nervously, knowing that if the shark attacked them they would have little chance. The rest of the crew prepared to splash the water to frighten it away. After cruising quietly round the dinghy for fifteen minutes the shark disappeared.

About midday they all felt empty again, and they tried to quieten their hunger with a malted-milk tablet. The day dragged on and there was no sign of any change in the weather. The many incidents of the first two days had left them ill-adjusted to long hours of boredom, and they became impatient and sometimes ill-tempered and despondent. The prospect of drifting for several days was one they could not easily accept.

They rested little that night, and when they roused themselves on the morning of the fourth day the weather was much the same. Sea-mist and showers shrouded them all day and they saw nothing of the other dinghy. The wind was in the same direction and they drifted northwards, helped by the improvised sail, at about two knots. They had a meal similar to the one they had had on the previous day, and at dusk Triggs opened a tin of tomato juice from the emergency pack and handed it round.

'It's Friday night,' he said. 'Big night back in Barnstaple, remember? Have a swig and pretend it's beer.'

In the middle of the night Cartwright roused them suddenly.

'Look!' he shouted. 'We're in harbour! We've drifted into a harbour! Wake up!'

Triggs sat up in the dinghy and the whole crew began asking questions at once.

'Where? Where is it, Arthur?'

The sea was becalmed and the low cloud and mist had cleared. Even in the extreme darkness Triggs thought he could see for a hundred yards or so. There was no sign of any harbour.

'You wouldn't be pulling our legs, would you, Arthur?'

Cartwright blinked dazedly. It had been far more than a dream. He had sat upright in the dinghy and clearly seen two bollards on a quayside. As he sank back into the well of the dinghy he realised what had helped his hallucination. The two bollards turned out to be the heads of McLean and Devonshire on the far side of the dinghy.

None of them could sleep after this incident, and shortly afterwards torrential rain drenched and refreshed them and continued till daybreak. They sat in silence, licking their nullahed faces and preserving what they could of the rainfall. The wind had veered and was now blowing directly from the north.

'No more drifting home,' said Triggs.

'Never mind,' said Badham, 'this'll change the weather.'

The morning was clear except for a few clouds on the horizon. The whole of the western sky was blue. They waited expectantly for signs that the search had been resumed, but the long morning passed without incident. Each man scanned one-sixth of the horizon, and during the morning Badham spotted the other dinghy, a tiny speck about a thousand yards away which he thought at first might be a buoy.

'They're still there,' he said.

'Doesn't say much for our sailing,' said Triggs.

'Perhaps they've been sailing too.'

At midday they saw a Beaufighter, the first aircraft sighted for two and a half days. It seemed too much to hope that the first aircraft they saw would find them, but they fired off Very cartridges and the Beaufighter flew straight overhead, waggling its wings in greeting. It was the only one of four Beaufighters on search that morning to find the dinghy. This Beaufighter sent a sighting report and a second Beaufighter, searching an area nearby, appeared quickly on the scene. The first Beaufighter began signalling.

'T-R-Y T-O C-O-N-T-A-C-T O-T-H-E-R D-I-N-G-H-Y.'

'Try to contact other dinghy,' repeated Triggs. He said it as though they had been asked to paddle to New York. He waved his arms repeatedly at the Beaufighter to indicate that such an attempt was beyond them. This aircraft climbed to a thousand feet and set course for base.

The second Beaufighter now circled them and began signalling. They spelt out the message together as before.

'Contact other dinghy, one injured man aboard.' They still did not understand that the injured man was the sole occupant of the dinghy.

'Haul in the anchor,' said Triggs. Badham at once assumed the role of navigator and they paddled in turns. The distance was about a thousand yards. In three shifts of two they paddled right through the afternoon. Sometimes they lost sight of the dinghy, but first one Beaufighter and then another circled over the spot, and they kept a straight course.

In the middle of the afternoon two Hudsons appeared overhead, and the crew watched with dismay as one of the Hudsons dropped what appeared to be depth charges, which fell close to the dinghy. They waited anxiously for an eruption. But when the water subsided they saw what appeared to be a dinghy with two containers on each side. The whole gear was upside down, but they changed direction to paddle towards it and reached it within a few minutes. One by one they removed their clothes and jumped in the sea in an effort to right it, and after a tremendous struggle they succeeded. They emptied all the contents into their own dinghy, and then continued to paddle towards the Whitley dinghy.

Shortly afterwards the Hudsons and the remaining Beaufighter dipped in salute and flew off to the north, and they were left alone. Within a minute Devonshire spotted four more aircraft racing down towards them from the east, still two or three miles distant.

'What the devil are they?' said Triggs.

'F.W. 190s,' said Devonshire. 'Four of them. What do we do now?'

'Sit tight,' said Triggs. Perhaps they wouldn't be seen. But as he watched he was convinced that they had been seen already. The German fighters were diving down straight towards the two dinghies.

For the first time he felt fear gripping at his throat. He had often argued about the niceties of shooting at people in dinghies. It was something that you just wouldn't think of doing until you heard it had been done to your own chaps.

Even then he couldn't imagine that it was a thing he was capable of doing himself. Yet there were arguments in favour. He admitted that. If they got back safely to the U.K., they might be responsible for the death of thirty to forty men in a U-boat on their next trip. This aspect was unlikely to be lost on the Germans.

He still refused to give any order to abandon the dinghy. To jump in the water was undignified and panicky and might put ideas in the minds of the Germans.

The F.W. 190s were now low over the sea and hurtling towards the dinghies at four hundred miles an hour. When they were almost overhead they broke off in formation, and, as they sped past, Triggs had a momentary picture of helmeted Hun pilots waving to them. Waving to them! The men in the dinghy were too astounded and relieved to wave back.

They turned to watch the German fighters climb steeply and vanish among the white wispy clouds that had gathered during the day.

Triggs and his crew resumed the hard labour of paddling to reach the other dinghy. At six o'clock, after five hours' almost continuous paddling at the rate of two hundred yards an hour, they at last arrived within hailing distance of the Whitley dinghy. They saw one head only in the dinghy and looked in vain for others.

'Hullo there,' called Triggs. 'Are you all right?'

'I feel fine, thanks.'

One voice, saying it felt fine. Nothing about anyone else. Triggs and his crew gazed at each other dumbly. For almost exactly four days they had been ignorant of the tragedy that had occurred right in front of their eyes. Now they stopped paddling for a full minute, their minds grappling with the enormity of their ignorance.

Long before they drew alongside the Whitley dinghy they knew for certain that it contained only one man. No one dared to ask how many the crew of a Sunderland might be.

While Cartwright and McLean steadied the two dinghies, Triggs and Badham hauled the Sunderland survivor aboard.

'Hurrah for the open-air life,' said their new companion. Triggs and Badham pricked their ears up instantly. There was no mistaking that twang.

'You wouldn't be an Aussie by any chance, would you?'

'Watson's the name. All the way from Sydney.'

Watson's weak and exhausted condition was all too apparent despite his attempt at gaiety. They stripped him and gave him a thorough rub down to stimulate his circulation, clothed him in a sleeping-suit from the dinghy containers dropped by the Hudson, and gave him a meal consisting of a malted-milk tablet, two biscuits, some sweet chocolate and half a tin of tomato juice. Then they gave him a cigarette and told him to rest.

'I wonder what happened to those F.W. 190s,' said Watson.

'I wouldn't be surprised if they're sitting somewhere up on top of us waiting to pounce on search aircraft,' said Triggs. Shortly afterwards they saw a Beaufighter flying at deck-level heading straight for them. Triggs decided not to signal in case he should attract the German fighters, and then as the

Beaufighter turned away he saw two F.W. 190s in hot pursuit. But the Beaufighter had a good start and looked like escaping. Soon they saw the F.W. 190s break off and climb away.

The next aircraft they sighted was a Sunderland. The word threw a heavy silence across the drifting dinghy. The flying-boat passed five hundred feet overhead, but they did not signal it. They were tormented by the fear that the F.W. 190s would return, and they knew that if that happened the Sunderland would have no chance. Yet in the evening light it looked calm and unhurried and indestructible. It continued its course unmolested.

Watson was feeling much stronger following his meal, and the events of the day convinced them all that this would be their last night adrift. The sea was moderate, and for the first time since the ditching they had a good night's sleep.

The following morning, 17th August, their spirits were high. Something of the determination with which the rescue efforts were being pursued had somehow been transmitted to them.

The Sunderland they had seen the previous evening landed at base shortly after midnight. Four hours later Hudsons and Beaufighters and motor-launches were resuming the search.

The Hudsons and the Beaufighters appeared over the dinghy promptly at dawn. Triggs, sure that the German fighters would be back at dawn too, tried to warn the circling aircraft in an elaborate pantomime, but he was by no means certain that they understood. One of the Beaufighters circled and began signalling.

'I-T W-O-N-T B-E L-O-N-G N-O-W.' They chanted it together. 'It won't be long now!'

As if to remind them that their elation was premature, three Arado fighters circled some distance to the north. They did not realise the significance of this at first.

'My oath, if it isn't the destroyer!' Triggs shouted suddenly. Steaming straight at them out of the mist to the north he could see a ship. All eyes turned to follow his pointing finger. The dinghy rocked wildly as they craned their necks to see.

'You're a bit out in your recognition,' drawled Badham, 'but it's a British boat all right. A motor-launch, I reckon.'

'There's two more launches just behind!' shouted Walker.

'Three more,' corrected McLean.

The first motor-launch had almost reached them, and Triggs stood up in the dinghy to shout to its captain. He cupped his hands to his mouth and bellowed. 'Can you signal our chaps that there are Jerry fighters about?'

'Sure.'

They watched the crew of the motor-launch signalling, and the Hudsons sought shelter in cloud. But suddenly Triggs realised that Jerry was after a different fish.

'Look at those Arados!' he shouted. 'They've got a motor-launch with them!'

A German motor-launch, protected by a fighter umbrella, was bearing down on them fast. Triggs sat down again in the dinghy. The race was so gloriously exciting that he forgot for the moment that he and his crew were the prize.

'Here come the F.W. 190s!' shouted Triggs.

But the Beaufighters escorting the British motor-launch had seen them first. They dived on the F.W. 190s as the German aircraft prepared to attack the motor-launch. One F.W. 190 pulled up suddenly with smoke pouring from the cockpit. Triggs suddenly remembered that it wasn't a game after all.

The first British motor-launch was now alongside the dinghy, and one by one the Wimpey crew and the Sunderland survivor were taken aboard. The German motor-launch hovered in the distance, awaiting its chance. It was 0745 when one of the escorting Hudsons signalled 'Operation completed'.

The Hudson's signal was premature. As the four motor-launches assumed a close diamond formation and got under way on a northerly course for home, back came the F.W. 190s to attack them.

'Couldn't we man a gun?' shouted Triggs, as the German fighters swept into the attack.

The captain of H.M. Launch Q180 gave Triggs and his men an anti-aircraft gun to man, but the first attack was driven off by the Beaufighters and Hudsons before it came within range. The F.W. 190s peeled off and formed up again for a second attempt. This time, although the Beaufighters turned into the offensive as the German fighters dived towards the launches, the attack was pressed home with more determination.

'Now I know what it's like to be at the other end of this business,' shouted Triggs above the roar of the guns. All four motor-launches opened fire simultaneously, putting down a curtain of fire through which the F.W. 190s had to fly. Cannon and machine-gun bullets from the fighters lashed the sea around the launches.

'We've got him! We've got him!' the airmen shouted excitedly as one of the F.W. 190s swerved and pulled up shakily, smoke pouring from its exhaust. They watched as the second fighter rapidly overtook it, and then both aircraft broke off the action and hurtled on their way towards Brest. The damaged F.W. 190 staggered on uncertainly in the wake of its fellow, leaving a trail of smoke to mark its path.

'Why don't the Beaus get after him?' demanded Triggs.

'You'll see in a minute,' said the skipper of the launch.

'What do you mean? More fighters?'

'I'll be surprised if they don't chase us all the way. We don't want our air escort going after winged ducks. I've already signalled for more escort aircraft.'

Two minutes later an F.W. Condor and a Ju 88 were sighted. And in the distance, frustrated and envious, but still constituting a latent threat, waited the German motor-launch and the three Arados, watching like the jealous neighbours of a lottery winner.

The Condor shadowed them at a distance of some five miles, but the Ju 88, after two feint attacks, suddenly burst through the cloud above them and dived into the attack with guns firing.

'Dive-bombing!' yelled Triggs.

Whether the Ju 88 carried bombs or not they would never

know, for in that moment the German pilot looked over his shoulder, like a jockey who fears being overtaken, and gazed straight into the nose of a Beaufighter approaching from abeam. He pulled straight out of his dive as bullets ripped into his fuselage, and followed his F.W. 190 friends in a dash for Brest.

The Condor shadowed them for three hours, but they soon left the German motor-launch and the Arados behind, and the rest of the voyage was uneventful. They arrived off Land's End at three o'clock that afternoon and entered Newlyn Harbour at 1729, five and a half days after their take-off from Chivenor.

In spite of this long exposure, in the open sea and in bad weather, they showed no signs of nervous strain and suffered little reaction. Their total injuries amounted only to a few cuts and scratches and bruises. Their commanding officer sent them on sixteen days' leave, none the worse for their experience, reporting 'Morale high, all ready and willing to continue operational flying'.

And when the analysis of the incident came to be written, the Director-General of Aircraft Safety struck a Balance Sheet. He had to enter on the debit side the loss of the Sunderland with eleven of its crew, the Whitley with its crew of six, and Triggs' Wellington. Three aircraft and seventeen men. Then he turned the page over and wrote down the credit side. Six aircrew from the Wellington. One aircrew from the Sunderland. One Ju 88 probably destroyed. One F.W. 190 damaged and probably destroyed. Two hundred hours' flying experience of air/sea rescue operations. And lastly, and perhaps most significant of all, the maintenance of a high state of morale through having snatched an entire crew from within the grasp of the enemy after a hundred and twenty-four hours at sea.

THE LAST DETAIL

'One detail however was still missing, and not to be discovered for many
months. Towards the end of the year Professor Lindemann, now Lord
Cherwell, told me that the Germans had fitted their night fighters with
a new kind of Radar set. Little was known about it except that it was
called "Lichtenstein" and was designed for hunting our bombers. It was
imperative to find out more about it before the start of our air offensive. On the night of December 2, 1942, an aircraft . . . was presented
as a decoy . . .'

WINSTON S. CHURCHILL, *The Second World War*

PILOT Officer H. G. Jordan walked back to his quarters from
briefing, deep in thought. From force of habit he took the
path that led past the Sergeants' Mess, until so recently his
home. The rest of the crew had gone on ahead of him to tea,
and he had stayed behind to have a final word with the signals
officer about the trip. He stepped out briskly, partly to keep
the cold December evening air at bay and partly in the hope
that he might still be in time for tea.

The wind blew unimpeded across the airfield and into the
cluster of buildings which formed the administrative and
living accommodation of the station. Jordan turned up the
collar of his new overcoat, buttoning it up to the neck in
the regulation style. He wondered whether this biting

December wind came under the heading of 'inclement weather'.

It would be cold in the Wimpey tonight. There was no heating half-way down the fuselage where his special equipment was mounted. He wondered if they would ever be successful in locating and confirming the frequency of the new German radar. Certainly the Germans had been far too canny to risk their newly equipped aircraft on flights outside occupied Europe, so there was no chance of capturing the equipment. It seemed that these decoy flights were the only possible way. They had now flown seventeen times to targets in Germany inviting interception, and seventeen times they had been unmolested, while other aircraft were being shot down with uncanny facility by the newly equipped Hun fighters. It was almost as if Jerry knew that the old Wellington IC from 1474 Flight was up to no good.

But of course that was impossible. Even if there had been any leakage of information – and he didn't believe that for one moment – it would be impossible for a night fighter to distinguish between an aircraft carrying out a routine bombing sortie and an aircraft on a special flight of this nature. Besides, their main worry at first had been to ensure that the necessary information about frequencies was passed back to the U.K. before disaster overtook the decoy aircraft. Surely Jerry would look at the problem in the same way and determine to shoot them down before they could escape with the secret.

But the planners even had that eventuality taken care of. As soon as he received signals which he identified as likely to have emanated from the new German air-interception radar, he was to tell Bigoray, the wireless operator, and he would pass a coded message directly to base. Not a long message – just a prearranged code group which would tell the boffins all they wanted to know. Then, when he was sure, when he could say without any doubt in his mind, this is the transmission of the new German A.I. and the frequency is so-and-so, he would instruct Big to send a second coded group to base, and as far as the planners were concerned it didn't matter then what happened to the aircraft. As far as the planners were concerned.

That was what they wanted to know. The frequency. When they had that, they would devise some countermeasure for interfering with or nullifying that frequency. That was what they called the Radio War. It was important enough to have capital letters nowadays.

He passed the Sergeants' Mess and imagined the rest of the crew enjoying their tea, exchanging outrageous banter with the W.A.A.F. staff, and, in spite of their quick Canadian wit, generally getting rather the worst of it. He would be a few minutes late for tea in the Officers' Mess, and as a brand-new pilot officer it was not so easy to ask for favours. He thought with a fleeting nostalgia of the rather more raucous life of the Sergeants' Mess. He no longer had his Canadian crew with him to cajole the Mess staff into serving him with a hot cup of tea ten minutes after tea-time.

He was quite used to flying with Canadians now, and he thought they had got used to him. They treated him with a kind of jaunty respect, and he liked it. He guessed that they probably found him dull, serious, set in his life and ways. Well, war was a more serious business when you were a married man of thirty-three, nearly half-way through life, than when you were in the twenties. He knew without asking that they understood that.

Paulton was a good pilot and a very sound chap. Barry was an exceptional navigator, one of the best he'd known. They were both up for commissions. 'Peeny' Grant, the little front-gunner, was a wonderfully smart and efficient little fellow. The other two crew-members, Bigoray, the wireless operator, and Vachon, the tail-gunner, were both French Canadians, and he had found them steady and likeable. He knew that he had a first-class crew to fly him around. That was what it amounted to.

Tonight's trip would be just like the others. There would be the usual long periods of tension, they would take the same deliberate risks to attract attention, and they would be ignored. They would come home fatigued and frustrated. Then the long wait till the next trip. Even when they had to wait only a night or two it seemed a long time.

Tonight the main force of aircraft were bombing Frankfurt. They would link up with the main stream some hundred miles or so before the target. Then, just before they reached Frankfurt, they would turn north and stay on this new course for some minutes. Any fighter following the main bomber stream which had an image of them on its radar screen would surely turn and follow them, thinking that it was on to a straggler, an aircraft already in some kind of trouble and unable to reach the target.

He would be watching his equipment for signs of following aircraft all the time. Most of the indications would come from friendly bombers. But if anything followed them when they turned north just before Frankfurt, they could be almost sure that it was a German radar-equipped night fighter. Once they had established that, it was just a question of identifying the type of radar transmission being used and determining the frequency.

Then to beat it back home — having ensured that a modern night fighter was on their tail — in a clapped-out old Wellington which was so slow that they had to start out earlier than the main force in order to join the bomber stream of Stirlings and Wellington IIIs approaching Frankfurt! Who would be a special operator?

When he reached the Mess he was just in time to collect a plate containing two slices of bread, a rectangle of butter, a blob of pippy jam and a piece of pale fruit-cake. And a luke-warm cup of tea.

Take-off was not until two o'clock in the morning, and he resolved to get a few hours' rest before then. The trip across Belgium was a long one and they would not reach the neigh-bourhood of Frankfurt until half-past four. They wouldn't be back in England until half-past seven. Just in time for breakfast.

They took off at two minutes past two and set course for Frankfurt five minutes later. The night was a complete black-out, and they would not get the benefit of the moon until later. Not that the moon was likely to be their friend. A really bright night would mean the threat of trouble from cat's-eye fighters — not the sort of thing they wanted at all.

They crossed Belgium uneventfully and joined up with the

main bomber stream. Now was the time to look for an interception. As soon as the Germans thought they had identified the main area of attack they would start to deploy their night fighters. Blips on the radar screen were numerous now that they were in the main stream, and Jordan redoubled his vigilance.

Jordan's special receiver, constructed so as to pick up the questing radar radiations of other aircraft, now began to give indications which could not at once be recognised as emanating from friendly aircraft. He called Paulton.

'I've got something peculiar here. I don't suppose it's anything, but it might be. Something I've never seen before, anyway. I'll call you again in a minute.'

'Roger.'

Jordan felt within him the awakening of a profound excitement, the culmination of weeks of tension. He could not be sure — yet. But the more he studied the signals the more suspicious he became. His pencil raced across his log sheet, describing in detail every reaction of his equipment. All that he wrote would be studied and dissected when he got back.

He looked at his watch. 0425. In six minutes they were due to turn on to the northerly enticing leg away from Frankfurt. That would be the crucial moment. If these signals he was receiving emanated from Lichtenstein, the aircraft radiating them must almost certainly be following them or a nearby aircraft in the stream. When they turned away they would lose the protecting confusion of the stream. Unless he was way out in his calculations the fighter would turn and follow them and a combat would ensue.

It was not a part of their brief to engage enemy aircraft in combat if they could avoid it. Their task was to gather information and escape with it. But had they yet obtained enough data?

The conviction was growing in him every moment that the source of activity on his equipment was the new Lichtenstein. But for practical purposes it was still no more than a suspicion. The questing aircraft was some miles distant and its signals were weak. He spoke to Bigoray.

'Send the first coded group with the figure 492. That's it. 4-9-2. I'll write it down for you so there's no mistake. Don't forget – the first coded group. I'm not certain yet.'

Two minutes later Bigoray called him. 'That's O.K.,' he said. 'I've just received an acknowledgement.'

Meanwhile the signals from the questing aircraft grew progressively stronger. They would be turning north in two minutes. He called Paulton.

'I've just sent a message to base telling them that I'm receiving signals on a frequency of 492 megacycles which in all probability come from an A.I. Lichtenstein fighter,' he said. 'I've logged the characteristics of the signal, and there's no doubt that we've already got a good deal of gen. If we dive now to get clear of the stream, turn through 180 degrees and set course for home, we should manage to evade the fighter. On the other hand, if we carry on the investigation we shall almost certainly be caught and attacked.'

Paulton digested this slowly. He didn't like the idea of beating it if there was anything to be gained by carrying on.

On the other hand, there was no point in sticking their necks out for nothing. On the whole he guessed it was Jordie's decision. If Jordie wanted to carry on, it was O.K. by him. He answered Jordan.

'Well, it's your party . . .'

This was the answer Jordan had looked for. He was not the captain of the aircraft, but he was undoubtedly its *raison d'être*.

'In that case I think we'll keep going according to plan. We know the probable details but we may as well find out for certain while we're here.'

'Darn good,' said Vachon, squinting down his sights in the rear turret. 'Let me have a bash at him.'

They turned on to the northerly leg at 0431, and Jordan waited tensely for the effect of this manœuvre on the German fighter. His emotions were inextricably muddled as the impulses his set was registering faded and disappeared and then reappeared again a few moments later at about the same range. He called the crew.

'Don't look now,' he said, 'but I think we're being followed.'

He judged the range of the German fighter as about three miles. The northerly leg lasted eleven minutes and the distance closed surprisingly slowly.

'He's tucked in dead astern of us and about five hundred feet below us at the moment,' he said. 'Range approximately three miles. Keep a look out for him, Vash.'

'Sure thing.'

The range began to close more rapidly and Jordan warned the crew again. He could make only a rough estimation of distance, but by the time they turned on to the homeward leg at 0442 his receiver was becoming saturated and he computed the range at less than one mile.

'Astern and slightly to port,' he shouted in his inter-com. 'Two or three hundred feet below us. He's so close you must see him, you must see him . . .'

The saturation of Jordan's receiver culminated in that same moment in a burst of cannon fire as the enemy fighter closed to within shooting range. Vachon, trying desperately to pick out the lines of an aircraft, saw nothing until the fighter's gunfire disclosed its position. He swung his turret towards it and shouted, 'It's a Ju 88. Port quarter.' Before he could steady the turret and train his guns, Paulton had begun a series of violent corkscrew turns. Jordan, realising that there could be no further doubt that the signals he had been receiving came from the new Lichtenstein, turned to tell Bigoray to send the second coded group. As he turned he felt a stinging pain and shock in his left arm and knew that he had been hit.

'Get the second message out, Big. It's Lichtenstein all right. Frequency 492. Get that out at all costs.' Then he called Paulton. 'Lose height as quickly as you can in a spiral turn. We've got to shake off his A.I.'

'Roger.'

Vachon had found the Ju 88 and was pouring .303 bullets at it from the rear-turret guns. Jordan, his left arm limp at his side, continued to operate his equipment and to log the results. Another long burst of cannon fire from the Ju 88 was directed point blank at the rear turret, and Vachon, wounded in the shoulder, suddenly found his controls seizing up and locking and knew that the hydraulics had been punctured and that the turret was unserviceable.

Bigoray, trying desperately hard to clear his message before it was too late, could raise no reply from base.

Hardly had the Ju 88 broken away from its first attack when Jordan warned the crew that a second attack was developing from starboard. Paulton continued the spiral dive but the Ju 88 hung on. Vachon disconnected his hydraulic system and tried to rotate the turret by hand, keeping up a running commentary as the Ju 88 closed.

'He's coming in from the starboard quarter,' shouted Vachon. 'My turret's u/s, but I've still got him. Turn to starboard – now!'

Paulton yanked the Wimpey viciously to starboard but the Ju 88 held them in his sights long enough for a short burst. Jordan was hit in the jaw. He fell back into the well of the aircraft, but struggled to his feet again to watch for the direction of the next attack. Grant in the front turret put in a burst as the fighter broke away, and this evidently decided the Hun pilot to put the front turret out of action as well.

'He's coming in from the port beam,' said Jordan.

'I've got him,' shouted Vachon. He tried desperately to manipulate his turret so as to get in a burst, but the Ju 88 had fired and broken away before he had moved the turret more than a few inches. The front turret was badly hit and put out of action and Grant was wounded in the leg. The turret jammed and he couldn't get out.

'Are you all right, Peeny?' called Paulton.

'I think so. Trouble is the turret's jammed. I'm stuck.'

'See if you can free him, will you, Big?'

Bigoray, who was still trying to clear his message, went forward. Meanwhile, Jordan could tell from his equipment that the Ju 88 was about to try an attack from underneath. He called Vachon and Grant, but they were powerless to interfere and the aircraft was now defenceless.

'Stick the nose down, Ted,' called Jordan. 'Make him overshoot.'

Paulton held the nose down steeply for a moment and avoided the full cone of fire, but a stray shell caught Bigoray between the legs as he went forward to free Grant.

'I can't get at Peeny for the moment,' said Bigoray. He went back to his set and began transmitting his message again, saying nothing of his injuries. Barry then went forward and succeeded in getting Grant out of the turret.

Jordan was still noting the reactions of his equipment and he saw the Ju 88 break off to starboard and prepare for another attack from the starboard beam. Paulton kept up his spiral dive, but this time the fighter's aim was true, firing at point-blank deflection from close in, and a hail of cannon fire tore through the fabric of the fuselage by Jordan's equipment like falling masonry. This time Jordan was hit in the eye. It was a stupefying, sickening blow, like being hit in the eye with a cricket ball. Dazed and stunned, his head drenched with blood, he felt no distress or fear or insecurity, only a passionate revengeful anger. Somehow they must hit back.

The cold air rushed in through the gaping hole in the fuse-lage with a tremendous icy force, chilling Jordan but helping to restore clarity to his mind. He could not continue with the investigation much longer. He had no idea what physical damage he had suffered, but he was at least temporarily blinded, and if further observations were to be made he must have help. He called Barry to come back and help him, but his microphone and headphones were dead; he looked down and saw dimly that his inter-communication box had been shot away. He began to crawl forward through the fuselage to enlist Barry's help.

Navigation was impossible while the aircraft was still spiralling and corkscrewing, and Jordan brought Barry back and tried to explain to him how to continue operating the equipment. He wished now that he had taken more trouble to instruct Barry before. It was vitally important to lose no scrap of the valuable information that was being registered every second on his equipment. He tried hard to show Barry what to do, but by this time he was almost blind and he realised it was impossible and gave up the attempt.

There was still no respite from the continual attacks of the night fighter. Vachon had now freed himself from the jammed rear turret and, in spite of the wound in his shoulder, he installed himself in the astro-dome forward, from where he continued to give a running commentary on the manœu-vres of the fighter and to direct evasive action. This was so successful that the fighter made several abortive attacks, until in a further attack Vachon was hit again in the hand

and Barry went back and took over in the astro-dome.

It now seemed to Jordan that they had not even the slenderest chance of avoiding destruction. He fingered his precious notes. Whatever happened they must not fall into enemy hands. If the Germans knew that we had discovered the secret of Lichtenstein, and how we had discovered it, they would be doubly on their guard.

He picked up his pages of notes and tore them deliberately into hundreds of tiny pieces. Then he pushed them through the hole in the fuselage. Most of the pieces were blown back by the slipstream like confetti, but the confusion was such that they could never be pieced together.

Jordan watched grimly while Bigoray masticated the sheet of rice-paper on which the coded signals were printed. Now, if they crashed, no one would know that their mission had been any different from that of an ordinary bomber. They would pass for a crew that had dropped its bombs prematurely after getting into difficulties on the run in.

Paulton began to wonder when the Ju 88 would run out of ammunition. They had lost height from 14,000 feet down to 500, and he was at a loss to know what manœuvre to attempt next. However, owing to their proximity to the ground the Ju 88 was finding its choice of manœuvre more restricted, and now that the Wellington was flying so low its outline easily merged into the dark background. Jordan, resting in the fuselage, knew that if only they could shake the fighter off for a moment, its radar would not be effective at this height. He went forward and spoke to Paulton.

'We've got to shake this fellow off somehow,' he said. 'Try turning back towards the target.'

'Towards the target?'

'Yes. His A.I.'s no good to him at this height. If we can shake him off for a moment, that's the last place he'll think of looking for us.'

Paulton turned sharply back towards the target area. Barry, watching from the astro-dome, saw the Ju 88 pass nearly a thousand feet above them, on a different course, its pilot evidently mystified. They held their breath as the Ju 88 began to orbit, but soon they lost sight of it altogether. They felt like some horribly injured animal slinking away to die alone.

Barry went forward again from the astro-dome to pick up the threads of navigation, and shortly afterwards Paulton set course for home. It was little more than a gesture. He knew that the aircraft was riddled with holes and badly damaged, and he wondered how long he would be able to keep it under control. The starboard throttle was shot away and the engine was stuck at plus-three boost. The port throttle was jammed and inoperable. Both engines were running roughly and irregularly and he had no control over them. Flying the aircraft on an even keel was extremely difficult as the starboard aileron control had been almost completely shot away and the trimming tabs had no effect at all. The starboard petrol-tank had been holed and the gauge showed empty, and there must be a danger of fire. He had no idea of his airspeed as the indicators were reading zero. There was a gaping hole in the starboard side of the fuselage, big enough to implant the fear that the aircraft might break up. The hydraulic system had been punctured and the undercarriage and brakes and flaps would be useless. Making any kind of landing would be a most hazardous affair. All kinds of other troubles, fatal troubles, might develop in the course of the two and a half hours it would take them to get back. There were several wounded men on board. Both turrets were jammed and they would be a sitting target if intercepted again. It would be just the irony of fate if, after seventeen trips looking for a night fighter, they should meet two in one night.

On the other hand, there were points on the credit side. Miraculously, he and Barry had come unscathed through ten or twelve attacks by a cannon-firing fighter in which the aircraft had been hit innumerable times. No one had been fatally wounded. The engines had not apparently sustained a direct hit. A petrol-tank had been holed but the worst danger from fire must be over. They had enough petrol to get back. The important members of the crew for the homeward trip – pilot, navigator and wireless operator – were uninjured. (No one knew that Bigoray had been severely wounded when he went forward to extricate Grant from the nose turret.)

The attack had developed immediately after they turned on to the homeward leg. That was at 0442. It was now just after five o'clock. The whole attack could have lasted less than fifteen minutes.

Paulton decided to try and gain more height. He eased the stick back and was greatly encouraged when the aircraft answered. He climbed slowly to 5,000 feet and then levelled out.

Throughout the period of the attack Bigoray had been sending the precious message repeatedly, without receiving any acknowledgement. Apart from the few moments when he went forward, he had never left his set. He knew that the loss of height would react against the range of his transmitter, but he persevered in the hope that the message might be picked up. He finally received an acknowledgement at 0505, twenty-two minutes after the attack started.

After advising Paulton to turn towards the target area to escape the attentions of the fighter, Jordan went back into the fuselage. Here he lay for some time in a collapsed state. Reaction had set in, reaction to the cumulative effect on his nervous system of the excitement and concentration and tension and the three injuries he had received. The temporary collapse in his nervous resistance was accompanied by a nerve-shattering pain in his head. He realised that if he was to be of any further use as a crew member he must try to get a grip on himself. He knew they must be lumbering along in the direction of base, and he struggled to his feet, steadied himself, and went forward to talk to Paulton.

'How are we making out, Ted?'

'We're still airborne,' said Paulton. 'It looks like wc might make it with any luck. But what do we do when we get there? No throttle control, only one aileron, no undercarriage, no flaps, no brakes. I daren't risk a landing on a runway.'

'What do you plan to do, then?'

'I don't think I can get her down in any restricted space. I've been thinking about putting her down on the beach somewhere. I think that'll be about it. The beach.'

Jordan pictured some of the long stretches of beach on the East Coast. It seemed a good idea, and then he remembered the mines and barbed wire that covered most beaches.

'I think the beach is out, Ted. They mined all the beaches in 1939. They're still mined as far as I know.'

'Jeeze, you think of everything.'

Paulton was silent for a moment, turning over the possibilities in his mind.

'I could ditch her,' he said. 'I could ditch her off-shore. I'd have a long enough run for that. The whole English Channel. What about that?'

'That sounds like the answer.'

'Yes, I'll ditch her. With nothing to hit or overrun I could get her down all right, I guess. We'll cross the Channel the shortest way and ditch off the Kent coast. I'll put her down about half a mile off-shore. Then we get in the dinghy and paddle ashore. It's a natural.'

Yawing and unsteady, one engine at a dangerously high boost, the geodetic construction subjected to unlooked-for strain, the Wimpey plodded on across Belgium. Bigoray, anxious not to give away their position, maintained wireless silence. The last hazard before they reached the Channel was now the anti-aircraft barrage at Dunkirk.

The night was still dark and they were thankful for it as they crept towards the French coast ten miles north-east of Dunkirk. Then suddenly the sky was ablaze with dancing marionettes of light as the searchlights probed for them. Paulton executed a diving turn to starboard and the marionettes danced grotesquely, sightless and bewildered. As soon as they had crossed the coast Paulton came down low over the sea and one by one the searchlights behind them flickered and went out. The show was over.

When they were clear of the French coast and out of range of the guns Paulton eased the stick back again and the Wellington gained height steadily. He flattened out at 2,000 feet and called Bigoray.

'Better send out an S O S, Big. Barry will give you a position and so on. Tell them we've been damaged in attacks by an enemy aircraft and that we have wounded men on board. Tell them we're going to attempt a ditching somewhere off the Kent coast near Deal.'

Bigoray sent the S O S, and then repeated the last coded message on Lichtenstein in case it had not been correctly received the first time. The content of the S O S was his first intimation that Paulton intended to ditch, and he doubted whether he would have the mobility to struggle clear of a waterlogged and perhaps sinking aircraft.

They reached the English coast at 0720. Even on a dark December morning the lace fringe of sea and the sandy shore showed clearly against the dark inland shadows. Somewhere beneath that impenetrable blackness men and women were rousing themselves from a night's slumber and preparing behind blacked-out windows for the new day.

Paulton turned out to sea and tested the landing light to see if it might be possible to carry out a ditching in darkness with its help. The fierce white light gave wonderful illumination, but it threw fanciful and confusing shadows. A landing in darkness would be feasible, but it would be wiser to wait for dawn. He called the crew.

'I'm going to ditch as soon as it's daylight, fellers,' he said. 'Can't possibly get her down on a runway. Is there anyone who'd rather bale out over land before we ditch?'

Bigoray waited, and when no one else answered he flipped on his microphone. 'I guess I'd sooner jump, Ted. One of my legs has stiffened up a lot and I'm not sure that I'd be much good at getting out in a hurry.'

'What happened to your legs, Big?'

'Oh, I'm O.K. I'd just sooner bale out, that's all.'

'Have a look at him, will you, Jordie?'

Jordan could see that Bigoray had lost a lot of blood from the wounds in his legs. The aircraft was badly shot up and it might sink quickly. If Bigoray found he couldn't move they would have to stay behind to get him out. It might end in disaster. Against that, the escape hatch in the floor of the Wimpey was easy enough to make an exit from – all you had to do was let yourself gently down into it, keep your body stiff and erect and let go. As long as they could be sure that Bigoray didn't finish up in a tree or on a roof-top, baling out seemed the best thing for him. He reported this to Paulton.

'We'll try and drop him on the edge of a town,' said Paulton. 'Somewhere where he won't land on a roof-top but won't be so isolated that he'll be liable to bleed to death.' In the distance the town of Ramsgate was pushing up its myriad shoots through the soil of night. 'We'll drop him on the edge of Ramsgate.'

Jordan went back to help Bigoray with his parachute. He found the chute and examined it closely for bullet-holes, but it was undamaged. He helped Bigoray to fix the chute to his harness and then led the way to the escape hatch. He turned the catches anticlockwise and lifted the hatch clear. Dust in the bottom of the fuselage was whipped up by the influx of the slipstream and for a moment he was blinded again. When his vision cleared he looked down into the hatch and saw the sea deceptively near, leaden in the first light of dawn.

'I don't want to be too long on this,' Paulton said to Barry. 'The ship's been all right so far but it would be screwy to stay up here longer than we need. Will you give me a course to steer to drop Big? Then we'll get around to this ditching business.'

Barry worked out a wind and confirmed that there was a strong breeze blowing inshore. They would need to drop Bigoray about a quarter of a mile out to sea. He would then drift in over the outskirts of Ramsgate.

Paulton held the Wellington steady on course and Barry prepared to give Bigoray the signal to jump. Just as Barry was about to give the signal, Bigoray remembered something.

'I haven't clamped the key down,' he said.

'Can I do it?' asked Jordan.

'Must do it myself,' said Bigoray. In spite of his wounds he pushed past Jordan and dragged himself back to his set. There he clamped down the transmitter key. 'That'll mean they can get a bearing on you. Up to the time of the ditching, anyway. You'll see that no one touches it, won't you?'

174

Paulton wiped his hand across his brow impatiently and turned back out to sea. When they were about a mile offshore he turned on to the course Barry gave him and began another straight and level run.

Barry was timing the drop exactly and he gave the signal to the second. Jordan saw it and shouted at Bigoray to jump. Bigoray looked down, saw that he was still over the sea, and refused to go. Someone must have made a mistake. Even when it was explained to him that they were allowing for drift he was unconvinced.

Paulton turned out to sea again. 'Tell him he's got to go this time or never,' he said. After a minute or so he turned back on to the inland heading and Barry began timing the drop as before.

'Now!' shouted Barry, giving the signal.

Bigoray hesitated. He had no experience of parachute jumping and didn't know that one went instantly or not at all. He was doing the most unnatural thing in the world – jumping into space when no immediate danger threatened him where he was – and he just couldn't believe it was right to jump over water. He wanted to see for himself where he was, but he was facing the tail of the aircraft and could see nothing at all forward. He wanted more than anything to see how near they were to land.

While Bigoray vacillated, Jordan made up his mind. They couldn't afford to spend any more time flying round in circles. He reached down and grabbed Bigoray by the shoulders and pushed. Bigoray, surprised, turned to look over his shoulder at Jordan, lost his grip for a vital second, clawed desperately and disappeared through the hatch, his eyes eloquent of unholy

175

reproach. In spite of the shock of his unready exit he pulled the ripcord instantly and Jordan, looking backwards through the hatch, saw with intense relief the parachute billow open. He shuddered again as he recalled Bigoray's last astonished look. Bigoray landed safely in Ramsgate.

Paulton turned the aircraft once again and headed out to sea. Now for the ditching.

'Jettison escape hatches. Here we go.'

He lost height as rapidly as he could without gaining speed appreciably, and then from about three miles out to sea he began a long low flat approach towards the open beaches near Deal, easing the stick back gently at intervals to reduce speed. He still had no airspeed indicator and could only guess at the aircraft's speed from the feel of the remaining controls. When he thought he had reduced speed down to about a hundred knots he pulled the stick back into his belly and the Wellington sank slowly on to the water. Everyone was braced for the shock and the aircraft came tranquilly to rest about two hundred yards off the coast near Deal.

Vachon, standing up under the jettisoned astro-hatch, pulled the dinghy release and they scrambled out on to the wing.

The dinghy had inflated, but it was gurgling and bubbling like a soak-away. Water was pouring in through innumerable bullet-holes. Jordan jumped in and tried to plug the holes with his hands, and Barry followed, but the dinghy was filling rapidly and nothing they could do would staunch the influx of water. They abandoned the attempt and stepped back on to the half-submerged wing.

The others were scanning the shore in the hope of seeing signs of a rescue craft. From the air they had seen a number of rowing-boats pulled up high on the beach, but a long promontory now cut them off from this part of the shore. Straight ahead of them they could see what looked to be a Royal Marine station, with uniformed figures evidently preparing to launch some kind of craft. If the Wellington would float for two or three minutes they would be spared immersion in the icy sea.

Just when it seemed certain that the Royal Marines would be first on the scene, a rowing-boat appeared round the promontory and bore quickly down on them. The Marines were launching two motor-boats but the rowing-boat would beat them to it.

They were hailed by two swarthy fishermen in the rowing-boat.

'Ahoy there!'

They waved and shouted at the fishermen, and as the rowing-boat pulled alongside the sinking aircraft they stepped in one by one until the sea almost flowed in over the gunwales. Simultaneously, the two Royal Marine motor-boats appeared on the scene, arriving in a flurry of wash and rocking the overladen rowing-boat dangerously.

But the two Men of Kent hadn't put out in their rowing-boat to surrender the glory of rescue to the Marines. Determined to keep their rescue to themselves, they glared scornfully at the trim Royal Marine motor-boats.

'Take them thar boats away,' they said. 'We'ms doing this.'

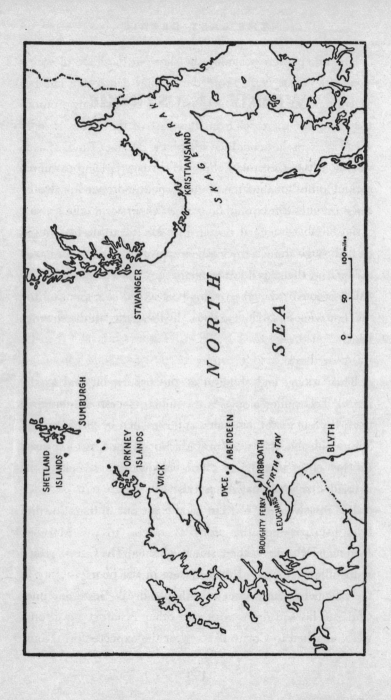

WINKIE AND STINKIE

THE months of December 1941 to February 1942 were nerve-racking times for the men of the torpedo-bomber squadrons. The pocket battleships *Scharnhorst* and *Gneisenau*, under heavy aerial bombardment at Brest, were known to be planning a dash through the Channel and northwards to a safe harbour in Norway, there to join the *Tirpitz* in threatening our North Atlantic convoy routes. A similar break-out was planned for the *Prinz Eugen* at St Nazaire. This was the atmosphere in which Squadron Leader W. H. Cliff found himself when he was posted as second in command to No. 42 Squadron, based at Leuchars in Fife, a few miles south of the Firth of Tay.

Cliff had been with a torpedo-bomber squadron in Singapore from 1938 until the summer of 1941, when he was invalided home with the ubiquitous tropical skin-disease, prickly heat. A few months after he left them, his squadron was wiped out in its first engagement. In the tense atmosphere of expectancy on 42 Squadron, he was out of the fire but still well in the frying-pan.

In mid-December the tension heightened. The German ships at Brest were expected to make use of the poor visibility in the Channel during winter to attempt a break-out at any time. Cliff and his squadron, with two other Beaufort squadrons, were detached to Cornwall to cover the expected break-out.

179

Days passed quickly at St Eval. There were wing-formation drills, discussions on tactics, and the usual false alarms. Then came an Intelligence report that the *Tirpitz* was making ready to put to sea from Trondheim. 42 Squadron were immediately ordered back to Leuchars. The other squadrons stayed at St Eval to threaten the *Scharnhorst* and *Gneisenau*.

Christmas 1941 came and went. Cliff was one of six crews detached to Sumburgh in the Shetlands to cover the *Tirpitz*. They flew patrols over German convoy routes off Norway and the Dutch coast. The North Sea was vast and icy-cold, steel-grey and spume-flecked. They flew through mist, rain, snow and sleet. Ice formed on the leading-edges of the wings.

Cliff's crew consisted of Flying Officer McDonald, navigator, and Pilot Officer Tessier and Sergeant Venn, Wop/A.Gs. When they were not flying there were the usual training routines, or the tense boredom of being stand-by crew. This meant a formal briefing, loading the aircraft with all the necessary gear – torpedo, ammunition, colours of the day, parachutes, Mae Wests, rations, carrier-pigeons – and long hours of uncertainty. Shadowy fears, without the stimulus of a known action. Games of solo for which accounts were kept but never paid. Too many cigarettes.

On 12th February 1942, Cliff's twenty-seventh birthday, the *Scharnhorst* and *Gneisenau* slipped quietly out of Brest. They were joined by the *Prinz Eugen*, and by a large screen of destroyers, minesweepers and flak ships. Under cover of atrocious weather, they passed rapidly into the English Channel.

Cliff and his crew, now back at Leuchars, were sent south

to Coltishall in Norfolk. Cliff led the squadron into action on the same day. They were one of the few squadrons to locate the enemy convoy. Low cloud, sleet and fog baffled and frustrated them, but Cliff followed a hunch and the attack was pressed home. They landed safely at North Coates in Lincolnshire, only to be told that the German ships, apparently unharmed, were steaming strongly for the shelter of Wilhelmshaven. The job would have to be done all over again.

The torpedo-bomber squadrons were now disposed in Scotland and the north of England to cover the coast of Denmark, the Skagerrak and the coast of Norway. Routine reconnaissance patrols of the approaches to Wilhelmshaven were established. Cliff and his crew went back to Leuchars, and a few days later were sent further north again to Sumburgh. Intelligence had wind of something.

February 23rd, eleven days after the action in the Channel, was a sunny winter's day, crisp and cold. Snow glistened on the tops of the Shetland hills. The day began with a breakfast of thick Scotch porridge, eggs and bacon, and strong black tea. Cliff was sipping his second cup of tea when the Tannoy blared.

'Squadron Leader Cliff wanted in the operations room. Squadron Leader Cliff wanted . . .'

A few minutes later Cliff was reading the advance warning order. One of the German capital ships was suspected of having slipped through the net around Wilhelmshaven and of being on its way to join the *Tirpitz* in Trondheim Fiord. The Beauforts at Sumburgh were to be prepared to attempt an interception.

A study of the map convinced Cliff that if the enemy ship were anywhere in the region of Trondheim, the Beauforts would not have the range to get there and back. The possibility of a forced landing in Sweden suggested itself. That meant the certain loss of the aircraft and the probable internment of the crews. An hour later the operation was cancelled and the detachment ordered back to Leuchars.

Then the Tannoy called for Cliff again. Intelligence reports now indicated that the German ship had not passed north of Kristiansand, if indeed it had yet completed the crossing of the Skagerrak. The detachment of six aircraft was therefore to carry out a search down the Norwegian coast from Stavanger to Kristiansand. If contact with the enemy ship was made, a report of its position, course and speed was to be wirelessed back to group headquarters *before* the attack. Afterwards, or if no contact was made, the Beauforts were to return to Leuchars. The operation was to take place next day.

Cliff worked out a plan of campaign and then called the rest of the crews to the operations room. He explained the situation and told them the plan.

'We shall take off and fly a south-easterly course to southern Norway on six independent but parallel courses, each fifteen miles apart. In other words, we shall be approaching the Norwegian coast on parallel courses from the north-west at an angle of about forty-five degrees. When we get within four or five miles of the coast, we sweep down due south for some twenty miles, and then turn west-south-west for Leuchars. We'll stagger the take-off times so that each aircraft makes its appointed landfall on the Norwegian coast at the same time. That way, in about six or seven minutes' reconnaissance we shall cover a hundred and twenty miles of enemy coastline.

'The sudden appearance of six aircraft off the Norwegian coast at different points will tend to confuse the enemy defences and thus increase our chances of getting away. If there really is a German capital ship there, we can expect many more enemy fighters than usual to be deployed in the area.

'The search areas overlap slightly, but it's better to cover a hundred and twenty miles thoroughly than spread the search over too wide an area. In any case, group headquarters are sure the enemy ship is very little north of Kristiansand, if at all.

'The area of the search takes into account the fact that we can't reach the Norwegian coast in daylight today, so that the operation will have to be delayed until tomorrow.'

Cliff chose for himself the southernmost lane covering Kristiansand South and the Skagerrak. Next day visibility was still perfect. The take-off was delayed while a further Intelligence report was awaited, but no more news came through. Cliff, with the longest distance to fly, took off first at 1400 hours.

Across the North Sea they flew through scattered snow-storms, but the weather was generally clear. There was a following wind and they made good time, covering the three hundred and fifty miles to the southernmost tip of Norway in well under two hours. They flew low, a hundred feet above the sea, watching the coast of Norway expand into focus, backed by a range of snow-clad mountains. The sky was now obscured by cloud, but surface visibility was still good. There was no sign of any ship.

Straight ahead they saw the lighthouse off Kristiansand. They flew along parallel to the coast about four miles out to sea. Soon the lighthouse lay off their port beam. The rocky coast swung away to the north-east. No sense in pressing on in that direction. They had been off the coast about fifteen minutes, for rather more than the safe limit if they were to avoid interception. If they turned back for Leuchars now they would still be another ten minutes in sight of the coast.

Cliff felt something tugging him out into the Skagerrak. It was the old hunch again. But more than that, he wanted his search to cover the area beyond all reasonable doubt. Intelligence had said yesterday that the German ship was no further north than Kristiansand. Might it not still be crossing the Skagerrak?

The suspicion was enough. They would turn south for five minutes or so. It was worth the risk. The other boys would take care of the rest of the area. There was just this nagging doubt about the Skagerrak.

He stayed on the southerly course for ten minutes. The north coast of Denmark appeared in the distance, dark grey and hostile. There was no sign of any shipping. At 1605 they set course for Leuchars.

Soon they were clear of the Skagerrak and out in the North Sea again. The snow-clad mountains of Norway merged into the cloud-base. They climbed to 500 feet and levelled out. Cliff began to relax. That tight feeling in the stomach-muscles was easing. He plugged in the automatic pilot. McDonald, the navigator, brought out a flask of hot tea. Cliff looked at his watch. Half an hour since they set course for Leuchars. One more operation was nearly over.

It happened with stupefying suddenness. One moment they were sipping their tea. Thirty seconds later they were in the water.

There had been the sound of a thousand milk-cans rattling at once, and smoke and flame had poured from the port engine. They were diving into the sea at 160 miles an hour. Cliff had whipped 'George' out and struggled with the controls. 400 feet, 300 feet, 200 feet, 100 feet – and the next thing they knew they were flung into the icy-cold North Sea.

Everything was suddenly silent. Cliff felt the chill water attacking his limbs. Then he saw the yellow dinghy ahead of him, the two gunners already aboard. As he swam towards the dinghy he saw McDonald away to his right, heading in the same direction. Miraculously they all seemed to have escaped.

But what in hell had happened?

He vaguely remembered that they had hit the water port wing first. That must have put out the fire. The whole aircraft had disintegrated. In doing so it had thrown up the dinghy.

His right arm was numb. Tessier and Venn helped him up beside them into the dinghy. Then they pulled in McDonald. They were all stunned into dumbness. There were a hundred questions demanding answers, but no one asked them.

What had hit them? Tessier, in the turret, had seen no sign of enemy aircraft. Had the port engine simply blown up? Cliff had noticed nothing unusual in the instrument readings. Baffled and dazed, they took some minutes to recover the normal processes of thought.

Cliff noticed that Venn was clutching one of the pigeon-baskets. The pigeon seemed to have weathered the ditching.

'How on earth did you get hold of that?' asked Cliff.

'As soon as I heard the bang and felt we were diving,' said Venn, 'I sent S O S and our call-sign on the radio, clamped the key down, grabbed the two pigeon-baskets, and braced myself for the crash. When we hit, the water flooded past me and I found I was floating near the aft escape hatch. I still had hold of one pigeon-basket, but the other one had broken open and I couldn't see any sign of the pigeon. I think it must have drowned.'

'Jolly good work, anyway,' said Cliff. He darted an admiring glance at Venn. It was a wonderful example of quick thinking.

'How about the S O S? Do you think it was picked up?'

'It should have been. I doubt if anyone had time to get a bearing on us, though. It was only seconds and we were in the water.'

'How far from base, Mac?'

'About a hundred and fifty miles, I reckon.'

The situation looked pretty desperate. Although the sea was calm, the temperature was only just above freezing. Soon it began to snow. The pigeon was about their only hope. They had no food, as all the food containers were stowed in the aircraft, and no one had had time to grab them. All they had between them was a packet of malted-milk tablets, two bars of chocolate and a few pellets of chewing-gum. Cliff commandeered the lot with the idea of instituting a rationing system; but he knew the principal threat was exposure. They would freeze to death long before they died of hunger or thirst.

There were two glove-type canvas paddles in the dinghy, and Cliff set up a watch of ten minutes on and ten minutes off for paddling. He had a small pocket-compass, and after consultation with McDonald he set the first two men to work. He had no hope that they would make any real progress, but thought the exercise might help to keep their circulation going. He absolutely forbade anyone to sleep. Somewhere he had heard that if you went to sleep under these conditions you never woke up.

Then he turned his attention to the pigeon.

There had been two pigeons when they started, Winkie and Stinkie. Now that one had presumably been drowned, they would need to be doubly careful to get a message securely attached to the second pigeon and send it on its way.

Cliff took the pigeon-basket from Venn. 'Is it Winkie or Stinkie?' he asked.

'Stinkie.'

'Come on, Stinkie,' said Cliff, 'here's your chance to make a name for yourself.'

They found a scrap of paper and a pencil, and McDonald wrote down their estimated position in latitude and longitude and rolled the paper into a cartridge. Then they took the pigeon out of the pannier, holding it firmly and with the utmost care, and rammed the cartridge into the special container affixed to the ring on Stinkie's leg. They made a note of Stinkie's registration number, and then released him.

They had been so afraid that Stinkie would escape before they could affix the message, and so sure that the bird's only thought would be to return to its loft, that they gaped in astonishment as it perched itself contentedly on the side of the dinghy and showed every sign of staying there permanently.

Cliff took the pigeon in his hands and launched it as best he could. But Stinkie had had enough flying for one day. He completed a circuit of the dinghy and then came in to land on his former perch.

Cliff and his crew yelled and shouted, waved their arms and swore. Sometimes the bird flapped its wings and took off momentarily to avoid a lunge from one of the crew. But always it settled down again on the edge of the dinghy.

Cliff laughed with the others, but all the time he was thinking of the bleak prospect facing them if Stinkie failed them.

'We've got to get him airborne, chaps,' he said. 'Come on, wave him off and don't let him alight on the dinghy again.'

This time they nearly overturned the dinghy in their efforts to get Stinkie airborne. At last he took off again, and after two unsteady circuits of the dinghy he obediently set course for home. They watched him disappear into the darkening sky.

'How long will he take?' asked Tessier.

'Pigeons fly at about forty miles an hour,' said McDonald. 'And they make good use of winds and up-currents. I should think three to four hours and he'll be home.'

'Where's his loft?'

'I think Winkie and Stinkie come from a loft at Broughty Ferry. That's just north of the Tay, near Dundee. About the same distance from us as Leuchars. He'll be all right.'

A few minutes later, as the daylight began to fade, Cliff remembered something. 'Wasn't there something about pigeons not flying at night?' he asked.

They remembered that there was.

Night fell, and with it the temperature. There were occasional snow flurries, and sometimes the moon watched them, its every feature distinct in the crystal night air. Cliff somehow kept his crew alert, manning a watch and paddling. Imagination played tricks with them. Water gurgling by the dinghy was surf breaking on the shore. The wind was the noise of searching aircraft. The stars were parachute flares. Dawn brought stark reality – a vast expanse of empty, heaving ocean, wave troughs which limited visibility to a few hundred yards, and a sky obscured by fleecy grey snow-clouds.

They still pinned their hopes on Stinkie. Although he had probably been forced to alight on the sea at nightfall, he would be airborne again by now.

The previous evening, the five Beauforts engaged on the sweep with Cliff and his crew had landed back at Leuchars at varying

times between six-thirty and seven. Cliff had been the first
to leave, but his leg of the sweep had been the longest, and
it was not until eight o'clock that night that hope of his return
was abandoned. Beaufort M of 42 Squadron was reported
missing.

In the operations room at Leuchars the only clue they had
to help them plan a search was Cliff's probable track. They
knew that he had been making for Kristiansand. They knew
that the crews had been briefed to search for ten minutes
only. They knew, from messages received, that Cliff had set
course for base. What they did not know was the time Cliff
had spent sweeping the Skagerrak, and, most important of
all, the fact that he had pressed on south across the Skagerrak
in the vain hope of sighting the German ship.

They drew a line from Kristiansand to Leuchars direct.
This represented Cliff's probably homeward course. They sent
a Catalina to search along this track. It searched all night in
vain. Cliff and his crew were many miles to the south.

At first light next morning a second rescue aircraft, a
Hudson, took up the search. Again it searched along a line
joining Leuchars to Kristiansand, up to a distance of one
hundred and fifty miles out to sea. Again without result.

Meanwhile, on a small farm at Broughty Ferry, some
twenty-five miles north of Leuchars, Mr James Ross, master-
plumber, an ardent member of the National Pigeon Service,
carried out his morning inspection of his pigeon-loft. In the
back of the loft, its feathers so clogged with oil that he
wondered how it could have flown there, was an exhausted,

bedraggled-looking bird which he took at first for a stray. On closer examination it proved to be one of his own.

Mr Ross looked eagerly at the ring on the pigeon's leg. He was disappointed to see that it was empty. But something of the length of the pigeon's flight could be guessed from its exhausted condition. A hundred miles, he thought, maybe more. He went back into the farmhouse and picked up the telephone.

'Give me R.A.F. Leuchars,' he said, and added as an after-thought, 'Priority call.' A few moments later he was talking to the controller at Leuchars.

'James Ross, Broughty Ferry, here,' he said. 'One of my pigeons has come back this morning all wet and oil-stained. One of those you were using. Registration number 1038. There's no message on her, I'm afraid.'

'I think I know where that's come from,' said the controller eagerly. 'Let's have that number again.'

'1038.'

'Hang on a moment, will you? I'll check up on that.'

The controller checked the squadron pigeon-records and confirmed what he had suspected and hoped – that No. 1038 was one of Squadron Leader Cliff's pair.

'This is wonderful news,' said the controller. 'No sign of the other one, I suppose – No. 1042?'

'No. Were they together?'

'Yes.'

'That's very peculiar,' said Mr Ross. 'They're fine birds, both of them.'

'Hang on,' said the controller. 'I'll fetch the station navigation officer. Between us we ought to be able to work out something.'

The station navigation officer took over the telephone. Maps were spread out in front of him.

'You say there's no sign of a message on this pigeon?'

'No.'

'How far do you think it's flown?'

'It's hard to say without knowing the conditions. It's covered in oil and that makes it look worse than perhaps it really is. I thought at first it must have covered a hundred miles or more, but now I think about it, I don't see how it can have flown more than forty or fifty miles. She wouldn't fly at night, and I went up to the loft about an hour and ten minutes after dawn. So she can't have been in the air much more than an hour. She won't have covered more than about fifty miles.'

'Right. This'll be a tremendous help. We'll draw a circle of fifty miles radius round Broughty Ferry and concentrate the search in that.'

For the next hour, seven Beauforts from Cliff's squadron, with Hudsons of Nos. 320 and 489 Squadrons, based at Dyce and Arbroath, combed the area without result. The ops-room staff at Leuchars were bitterly disappointed. They were back where they started.

'Looks like they've had it,' said the navigation officer.

'I'm afraid so,' said the controller. 'Probably had it when they ditched. Only the pigeon got away.'

'I'll have another word with that Broughty Ferry chap,' said

192

the navigation officer. 'He may be able to suggest something.'

Mr Ross spoke slowly and deliberately on the telephone, but his mind worked fast.

'You know,' he said, 'it's funny that any bird so covered in oil and muck as this one could fly at all. I can't make it out.'

'I heard about it being covered in oil,' said the navigation officer. 'Where in heaven's name would a pigeon get oil from?'

'Possibly from the wreck,' suggested Mr Ross.

'I don't think it's very likely. Are there any oil depots near you?'

'I don't think so.'

'How about oil-tankers?' The navigation officer was convinced instantly. 'God, that's it – a tanker! Suppose they released the pigeon when they ditched, and when it got dark it spent the night on a passing tanker? That could easily double the length of its flight – an hour before dark last night and another hour this morning. They may be much further away than we think.'

'It's possible – but how can you find out about the tanker?'

'I'll try Rosyth Shipping Control. They should know.'

Within a minute the navigation officer was talking to Rosyth.

'R.A.F. Ops Room Leuchars here. Did you have an oiltanker going north last night?'

'Yes, we did. What do you want to know?'

'Can you give me its dawn position?'

'I think so.' There was a short pause. 'Here it is. 56.25 North, 02.05 West.'

'Thanks a lot.'

The two men, navigation officer and controller, rushed into the main plotting-room to fix the dawn position of the tanker. It was due east of Broughty Ferry, just inside the fifty-mile circle in which the unsuccessful search had been made.

They back-tracked the tanker to plot its position at dusk the previous night, and as they did so the Station Commander came in with news of a third-class bearing which an Army signals unit had taken on a short S O S transmission picked up at 1635 the previous day. This was assumed to have come from Cliff's aircraft. The bearing was of little value by itself, but it was a useful check, and, more important, it gave them the probable time of ditching, and therefore the time when the pigeon might be assumed to have started its flight. If the bird had escaped from the aircraft at the time of ditching, just after 1635, it would have had less than an hour and a half's daylight left. It might perhaps have covered up to seventy miles.

After explaining the situation to the Station Commander, they back-tracked the flight of the pigeon from the dusk position of the tanker to seventy miles out in the North Sea towards Kristiansand. Rather than make any precise estimate of track, they drew an arc of seventy miles radius from the tanker in the general direction of southern Norway. Then they laid off the Army signal unit bearing until it crossed this arc.

'That intersection is far south of where they should have been if they'd turned for home on time,' said the navigation officer.

'So it is,' agreed the Station Commander, 'and the whole thing is built up on supposition, conjecture – guesswork, if you like. But since all else has failed, I think it's worth a try. Which squadron has aircraft available?'

'The Dutch squadron, sir. Some of them are searching now. We could divert them to this position.'

The Station Commander picked up the telephone.

Out in the North Sea, Cliff and his crew were drifting slowly and imperceptibly towards Scotland. Everyone felt ineffably tired, but somehow they all managed to keep awake. They were finding that battledress plus fleecy-lined flying-jackets and flying-boots was inadequate protection against the fierce cold. At Cliff's suggestion they took off their flying-boots so as to dry their socks in the tepid warmth of the February sun: Cliff thought this might lessen the danger of frostbite.

The dinghy dipped and swayed. Occasionally an aircraft, obviously on patrol, flew past low on the horizon. They were not hungry or thirsty. As the pallid sun warmed them they felt drowsy and languid. They were too tired now to paddle. One by one they relaxed a little and dozed.

It was still only 1115 that morning when the Royal Netherlands Air Force Hudson spotted them, half an hour after this aircraft had received instructions on the new area of search from Leuchars control. The dinghy was in exactly the position calculated by the navigation officer at Leuchars. The Hudson crew saw the men in the dinghy quite plainly, lethargic at first, and then animated as they realised they had been seen. The Hudson dropped a bag of supplies containing rum, chocolate, water and cigarettes, and radioed the position of the dinghy back to Leuchars. An hour later an air/sea rescue Walrus appeared and touched down a hundred yards away. The pilot taxied right up to the dinghy and called out to them:

'Are you the crew of Wellington P for Peter of No. 504 Squadron?'

'No,' said Cliff, 'we're Beaufort M for Mother of 42.'

'Terribly sorry, old boy,' said the Walrus pilot, turning into wind to take off again, 'but you're the wrong crew.'

For the next two hours they were a perplexed and somewhat disgruntled crew. But, in the meantime, four high-speed launches had been despatched to pick them up, two from Blyth and two from Aberdeen, the dinghy being about equidistant from the two bases. One of the launches from Blyth arrived first, picking up Cliff and his crew at 1415, twenty-one hours forty minutes after the crash. They were landed at Blyth at 1730 that evening. They were all suffering from exposure and frostbite and might well not have survived another night.

When they eventually got back to Leuchars they were met by the Station Commander, the controller, the navigation officer – and Mr James Ross. They had already heard that one of their pigeons had provided the vital clue in locating the dinghy.

'Why didn't you put a message in the container?' asked the Station Commander.

'We did,' said Cliff. 'Didn't Stinkie still have it?'

'No,' said the controller.

'Never mind,' said the navigation officer, 'we had a lot of fun working it out.'

'Just a moment,' said Mr Ross. 'You mentioned Stinkie – did you release him all right?'

'Yes. He was a bit reluctant to go, but he went in the end, thank God.'

'How about Winkie?'

'I'm afraid we lost Winkie,' said Cliff. 'The crash was terribly sudden and she went down with the ship.'

Mr Ross held up the pigeon he was carrying for all to see.

'Went down with the ship, eh?' he said. 'She must have come up again. We haven't seen a sign of Stinkie yet. *This is Winkie.*'

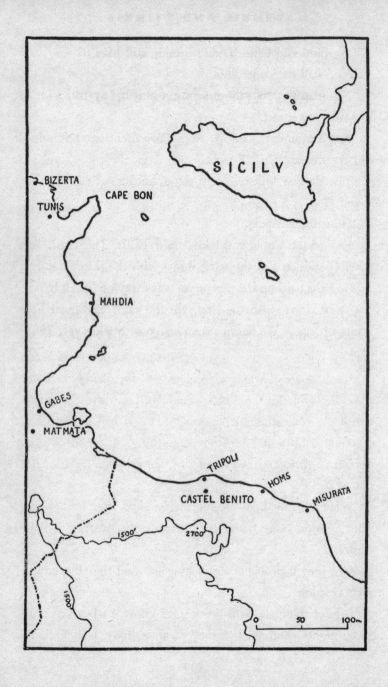

MEDITERRANEAN CRUISE

WARRANT Officer Micky Vertican put his head between the flaps of the tent, his face screwed up in a smile.

'Ops tonight, lads,' he said. 'We're having a crack at them tonight whatever happens.'

'What about the weather?'

'What time's take-off?'

'When do we eat?'

Vertican grinned. There wasn't much wrong with crew morale, even after a fortnight's lay-off. It was a fortnight to the day since, impatient with the inactivity forced on them by the shortage of serviceable Halifaxes, they had scrounged a Wellington from the Maintenance Unit and sneaked off to bomb the retreating Afrika Korps. They'd had permission, of course. Still, it had been something of an adventure. Vertican's air force, they'd called it. They'd got a terrific kick out of it.

'What's made them change their minds after four days?' The question came from Don Curnow, the Australian flight engineer.

'Oh, they'll probably scrub it again,' said the tail-gunner, Jock Gordon.

'I don't think so,' said Vertican. 'I know it's been a scrub three nights running, but they mean to have a go tonight.

They say the weather's still duff, but if we don't drop something on Jerry by tonight the bird may have flown.'

'Maybe we could go twice,' suggested Curnow.

Vertican laughed. He certainly had a keen crew. They were always thinking up ways of getting in an extra trip. Seventeen operational sorties had cooled them down a little, but not much.

'How about the new chaps?' asked Jock Gordon. 'Are they coming?'

Vertican nodded. 'Yes, same crew.'

'A sprog wireless operator and a sprog second pilot?' said Curnow.

'That's it,' said Vertican. 'But they're good lads and they've got to start sometime. By the way, Jock, will you let Taffy know? Briefing six o'clock.'

'O.K.'

Vertican watched Jock Gordon disappear through the flap of the tent. In a way he supposed he'd been giving an order, but it was good to see it acted on so readily. That was the secret of good crew work. Other crews could natter away on the R/T, smoke in the aircraft and all the rest. If it suited them, it wasn't his business. But they didn't do it after a trip with him. People had a capacity for taking serious things seriously where he came from. They said Yorkshire people were dour, but their dourness was as much innate discipline as anything. One day the discipline he'd always insisted on might pay a dividend.

At briefing Vertican joined up with his navigator, Flying Officer Timmy Tempest, his mid-upper gunner, Sergeant

Taffy Smith – somehow he hardly ever saw Taffy except when they were flying – and the two new boys, Sergeant 'Ace' Allard, second pilot, and Sergeant Ben Ward, wireless operator. Allard was a strong six-footer, Ward a square-jawed open-faced Londoner. Vertican liked the look of both of them.

The briefing officer cut in on his thoughts. 'Tonight the target will be the main roads converging on Tunis from Bizerta and from the west and south. Make a good do of it, because this may be our last chance to help push what's left of the Afrika Korps into the sea.' Vertican listened intently. They had been champing at the bit for long enough – here was their chance to be in at the death. 'You can't go straight across the bay to Tunis because you may get fired on by our chaps – they're up there in strength, and they're apt to be a bit trigger-happy about aircraft approaching from the sea. So fly along the coast to a turning-point approximately due south of Tunis at Matmata, and then turn north for the target area. The met people don't think you'll see much on this leg, so you may have to turn on your estimated time of arrival at Matmata, but the weather will be better around Tunis and you'll be able to pick out the main roads. It's up to you to find your own targets, but we know there's a good deal of transport and several German columns making their way along these roads. You'll have the usual load – eleven five-hundred pounders – so make them all count. The bomb-line is clearly marked on this map. Make sure you all know where it is. Cameras will be carried by J Jig and F Fox.'

Vertican pricked up his ears. He was used to carrying a camera – he couldn't remember when he'd last done an operation without one – and he still regarded it as something of a compliment. But it meant straight and level flying for nearly two minutes after the bombing run – he'd have to explain that to the new boys.

When the briefing officer had finished, the met man said his piece. The weather was still likely to be bad for most of the way. They might encounter electrical storms, and there would certainly be a good deal of low cloud, possibly some rain. Winds were northerly. They could expect abnormally high air temperatures up to ten thousand feet.

Vertican watched while Tempest noted the wind speeds and directions at the various heights. Then the signals briefing followed for the wireless operators. He went across to see that Ward was getting all the help he wanted. On the way he walked right into the A.O.C. The great man caught his eye, and Vertican stopped.

'Improperly dressed, Vertican.' There was a twinkle in his eye, and Vertican decided not to play dim.

'I'll put it up tomorrow, sir.'

'Congratulations, anyway.' The A.O.C. shook his hand. 'Good work, Vertican. Keep it up.'

He'd heard about his D.F.C. only that morning – it was pleasant to be congratulated personally by the A.O.C. Well, it was one of those things. He was more than half-way through his second tour, and he supposed he hadn't done too badly.

They took off that night from their airfield south of Misurata at 2255. They were due over the target area at approximately 0215. They climbed steadily until they reached 11,000 feet, through cloud at first, and then in clear enough air, although a heavy layer of cloud above them made the night as dark as Vertican could remember. The heat, too, was freakish. He had never known it to be so hot at this height. He supposed it was something to do with the ceiling of cloud pressing down above them. He wondered if it would affect the engine temperatures.

Their track took them only a mile or so north of Castel Benito airfield, but they saw nothing. Navigation was entirely by dead reckoning. To get a drift they dropped incendiaries, and when at last they saw one explode through a gap in the cloud, the tail-gunner trained his guns on the flame and worked out a drift for the navigator. The northerly wind seemed about right. They saw nothing at all of the coastline, so turned north dead on their E.T.A. Matmata at 0055. They kept a close watch on the starboard side for the Gulf of Gabes and the town of Gabes itself, but still saw nothing but blackness. The wireless operator tried to get a loop bearing on Tripoli, but the signals were very weak and magnetic interference almost blotted them out. It was dead-reckoning navigation with a vengeance.

There was nothing for it but to press on and hope the met man was right about the cloud thinning out around Tunis. The heat was oppressive, and they loosened their collars and battledresses, sweating freely and wishing they hadn't changed out of khaki drill. For long periods the inter-com was silent. J for Jig ploughed steadily on.

A rushing sound of sea-shells in his ears told Vertican that someone's microphone was alive. A moment later he heard Curnow's Australian drawl, quiet but urgent.

'I don't like the look of this oil-temperature gauge,' he heard Curnow say. 'The starboard inner. I think the engine's crook.'

'What does the exhaust look like?'

'It's giving that white flame you get with a glycol leak. I don't like it.'

A dozen thoughts flashed across Vertican's mind. An over-heating engine and a glycol leak – that meant feathering the engine. He wondered if he could make Tunis safely on three. Once the bombs were gone they would be able to maintain height all right. But already the starboard inner was losing power. The slow but steady loss of height told him that.

He eased the throttle gently back, cut the engine and feathered the propeller. Their rate of descent increased at once. What was the matter with her? She ought to maintain height on three. It must be the extreme heat rarefying the air – perhaps a down-draught from the cloud layer above them. There was no chance of making Tunis. The first thing to do was get rid of the bomb-load.

'How far are we from the bomb-line, Timmy?'

'About thirty-five miles, I should say.'

'And from the coast to starboard?'

'About the same. Perhaps forty miles. No more.'

'Give me a course for the coast, will you? The shortest way to the sea.'

Vertican watched the altimeter creep gently down to below ten thousand feet. They had plenty of height, anyway, and within a few minutes they would be over the sea. He daren't risk dropping the stuff here with the brownjobs underneath. Ten to one they'd fall in open country but he couldn't take the chance.

Tempest came up on the inter-com. 'E.T.A. at the coast-line 0145. We should cross the coast somewhere near Mahdia. Can you get me a loop bearing, Ben?'

'I'll try, sir. The static's very bad, though.'

Soon afterwards Vertican heard Ward pass an approximate bearing from Tripoli to the navigator. Timmy seemed satisfied. Vertican wondered how thick the cloud was below him. He was anxious to see the sea before dropping the bombs. He didn't much like the idea of dropping them on E.T.A.

'0145, Micky,' he heard the navigator say. 'We should be just about crossing the coast now.'

'Keep your eyes peeled, chaps,' said Vertican. They were still losing height at about fifty feet a minute, and there was more chance of one of the three good engines overheating while they had a full load to pull. There was still nothing visible below.

'Got any incendiaries left, rear-gunner?'

'Yes, I think so.'

'Drop one, will you?'

205

A few moments later Jock called him to say he'd dropped an incendiary. Timmy watched anxiously from the nose, timing the drop. Just when he thought they'd drawn a blank, there was a splash of light beneath them and they knew that they were still over land.

'There was a break in the cloud there, anyway,' said Timmy.

'Did you see any sign of the coast?'

'Not a thing.'

Thank God he had confidence in Timmy. They must surely be very near the coast now.

'Try another incendiary, Jock.'

The process was repeated, and once again Timmy reported a sudden splash of light. He was still unable to get a glimpse of the sea.

Two minutes later Vertican spoke again on the inter-com.

'Have you still got some incendiaries left, Jock?'

'Yes, one or two.'

'Have another go.'

This time they waited and waited until long past the moment when the flash should have come.

'Drop another one to make sure,' said Vertican.

'Roger.'

Again there was no flash. With a sigh of relief, Vertican pressed the jettison button and at once felt the aircraft shake itself free of its load.

The next step was to get a course for base from the navigator. They still had three engines and plenty of height – there was nothing to stop them taking the shortest route home. The alternative was to turn back to the coastline and follow the coast all the way, but that would nearly double the distance, and since they couldn't see the coastline it was doubtful whether there would be any advantage in it. There might be forward landing-strips that way but they wouldn't be likely to find a flare path. No, the obvious answer was to cut across the bay and go straight in to Misurata. If they had any difficulty they could always cut the trip short by changing course for Castel Benito.

A moment later Timmy gave him a course for base. He turned on to it, peering beneath him as he banked the aircraft for a glimpse of the sea, and looking away to his extreme right for some indication of the Tunisian coastline, all in vain. There was nothing for it but to settle down to a featureless sea crossing.

Even now, nearly nine thousand feet above the Mediterranean, the aircraft was unbearably hot. Vertican wondered how the other chaps had got on. He hoped they'd had better luck than he had. The met people had been right about the freak weather conditions. He watched his instruments carefully for signs of overheating or loss of power in the three remaining engines. With an empty bomb-bay, there would be no difficulty in making base provided they had no more engine trouble.

Curnow's voice came up on the inter-com, clipped and breathy. 'I don't like the look of the port inner, Skipper,' he said. 'The temperature's going up and the exhaust looks about the same as the starboard inner did.'

'Hell,' said Vertican. He didn't need to be told now that something was wrong on the port side – he could feel it on the controls. He throttled the engine gently back. It wasn't just the overheating that worried him. That combined with the glycol leak could finish in the engine blowing up.

'It's no good, Micky,' said Curnow. 'The temperature's still going up. You'll have to feather her.'

Vertican closed the throttle slowly until the engine cut, looking out to see the blades turn first jerkily and then come to rest with the inevitability of a roulette wheel. He thought, and then there were two. He flicked on his microphone switch.

'There's nothing to worry about, chaps. She's quite capable of getting us back on two. But I think we'll take every precaution we can, all the same. Give me a course for Castel Benito, will you, navigator? And let the wireless operator have a position and an E.T.A. as soon as you can. Wireless operator, send out a message now to Tripoli telling them we're on two engines. You'd better make it an S O S. Send them a position and an E.T.A. when you get it from the navigator. Gunners, come out of the turrets and take up ditching positions. Will you all acknowledge that?'

While the others were calling him, Vertican watched the altitude needle going down like a deflated balloon. She shouldn't be losing height like this. The only possible explanation was the heat. It didn't take any advanced mathematics to calculate that at their present rate of descent they would run out of altitude before they ran out of sea.

'The old crate's blowing like the top weight in the Grand National,' he said. 'We shall have to jettison everything we can. Get the guns and ammunition overboard, Jock and Taffy, and anything else you can lay your hands on. It's a hundred to one against running into a Jerry fighter now. If you can find any fittings that look as though a good hard tug will loosen them, get rid of them.'

In the tail and mid-upper turrets, Jock and Taffy wrestled with the guns. Soon they reported that they had been jettisoned, together with thousands of rounds of ammunition.

'How about the Elsan, Skip?'

'Overboard,' said Vertican. 'I daresay we all need it, but – overboard.'

'How about parachutes?'

Vertican hesitated for no longer than it took his eye to focus again on the altitude needle. What he saw settled it. 'Overboard,' he said. Ward, tapping out his S O S, and not switched in to the inter-com, saw his precious parachute wrenched from its stowage and snatched greedily through the escape hatch by the slipstream.

'E.T.A. Castel Benito 0355,' said Timmy. Vertican looked at his watch. Ten past two. An hour and three-quarters to go. He called the wireless operator.

'Did you get your S O S through, Ben?'

'I've sent it out three times,' said Ward, 'but I can't get an answer. I'll keep on trying.'

'Is the radio all right?'

'The radio's all right, but the static is pretty bad – there must be electric storms about. Still, we ought to hear them.'

'Keep on trying, lad.' The boy's first op, and he had to bash out an S O S. And then he couldn't get it through.

By this time J for Jig had settled down at 1,000 feet and looked like holding her own. Vertican began to feel a bit easier. If only the two good engines kept going they would make it yet. The night was still a black opaqueness that defied the eye. Vertican judged that the blanket of low cloud was now not far beneath them, but they couldn't get a pinpoint even if they went down under it, so all they could do was sit tight and wait for E.T.A.

Three o'clock came, and then half-past three, and still the Halifax chugged steadily on, nothing being said on the inter-com for long periods, each man either at his job or at his ditching station. Soon after half-past three Vertican began to look for signs of the coast. Conditions were still the same, not a break to be seen, not a fleeting glimpse of the sea, not a light, not a glow, nothing.

The wireless operator came up on the inter-com. 'Loop bearing Tripoli 176 degrees at 0345 hours,' he said. 'Seems like a reliable one.'

'Thanks,' said Tempest, 'that's a help. Can you get me another one in about ten minutes?'

'Roger.'

When 0355 came, Vertican called up the navigator.

'Well, that's it,' he said. 'We ought to have seen something by now. How do you feel about it? Shall I go down and have a look?'

'We haven't had a pinpoint since we left,' said Timmy. 'That loop bearing wasn't bad but it doesn't tell us how near we are. The met people gave us a northerly wind but it might have slackened. I think we'd better keep on for a bit. Any chance of that bearing, Ben?'

'I can't hear a thing at the moment,' said Ward. 'The static's terrible. The Tripoli beacon packs up at four o'clock, and I think it must have gone off the air.'

Just our luck, thought Vertican. This was the moment when they had to keep their nerve and trust in dead-reckoning navigation. He knew there was high ground behind Castel Benito, high ground which was already the graveyard of many a bomber crew, but they had to hold their course as long as they dare.

'How about that high ground, Timmy? We're only just over a thousand feet.'

'We're all right yet,' said Timmy. 'There's certainly high ground up to two thousand seven hundred feet forty miles south of Castel Benito, but we can't possibly be anywhere near it yet.'

Vertican felt more uneasy now than at any stage of the flight. He thought of the incendiaries. At least they could try that trick again.

'Jock, push out another incendiary, will you?'

Jock, sitting at his ditching station in the fuselage, answered at once.

'I'll see if I can find one.'

He groped and rummaged about in the darkened fuselage, wishing that he hadn't thrown his torch overboard.

'There's none in the rack,' he reported after a few moments, 'and I can't find any lying about. We must have dropped the last one over Tunis.'

Vertican held his course, beads of sweat forming under his flying-helmet and trickling down his face. His inclination was to turn straight on to a reciprocal course, but he had to give Timmy a chance. On a night of freak conditions they hadn't seen the ground or the sea for over five hours – they couldn't expect to hit Castel Benito right on E.T.A. But, on the same reasoning, they could easily be far enough out to run into that high ground. He looked at his watch. Ten past four. He would give it five more minutes.

The next five minutes were the longest Vertican had ever known. He kept his eyes narrowed, vainly trying to pierce the blackness. He was sorely tempted to cut the period short, even if only by half a minute. But he waited the full five minutes before calling Timmy.

'Here we go, Timmy,' he said, 'I'm turning on to reciprocal. We must have crossed the coast some time ago.'

'I'm afraid we must have done,' said Timmy. 'How about going down underneath this cloud for a look?'

'I think we'll head out to sea for a bit first. If we go down we may not be able to climb up again.'

'How are we off for petrol?'

'Plenty of petrol. Only two engines to consume it.'

'It'll be dawn in about half an hour,' said Timmy. 'Can we stooge around till then?'

'Comfortably.' Just to be sure, he rechecked his petrol gauges. He began to feel more at ease. They had enough petrol for perhaps another two hours. That gave them a safe margin unless they were a very long way out in their reckoning.

For the next twenty minutes they flew due north, out to sea, waiting for first light. Then Timmy came up on the inter-com.

'The sea!' he said. 'I'm sure I caught a glimpse of the sea! Through a gap in the clouds. Yes, that's it sure enough! We're over the sea!'

Vertican turned once again on to a reciprocal track and waited for a course to steer for Castel Benito. At the very worst they could not be more than ten or fifteen minutes' flying from the coast. With daylight their worries would be over.

Curnow's voice, urgent and insistent, interrupted his thoughts. 'The port outer,' he said. 'It's going just like the others.' Vertican was all alertness at once. 'Temperature's going right up,' said Curnow. 'Glycol leak, too, by the look of the exhaust. You'll have to cut it, Skip, you'll have to cut it.'

Vertican could already feel the loss of power, the slewing of the aircraft and the sluggishness of the controls. He throttled back both engines, put the nose down into a gentle glide, and called the crew.

'Jettison escape hatches. Collect the emergency rations. Ditching stations. This is it.'

As they came out of the cloud layer, Vertican saw dimly beneath him the grey white-capped sea. There was no sign of land. He kept the Halifax on the same heading – every mile they made towards land now was one less to travel later – and watched the sea come quickly closer, until he could make out details of the swell. He had no difficulty in judging their height. With a quick look at the open hatchway above him, and a last warning word on the inter-com, he aimed J for Jig in a flat breasting dive into the sea.

His first impression after they struck was that the aircraft was diving straight for the bottom. Water completely enveloped the nose. Then, recoiling like a rubber ball, the Halifax seemed to bounce back out of the water in the direction from which it had come, stand poised for a moment with its tail in the air, and then plunge forward like a half-submerged submarine. Suddenly Vertican was sitting in water up to his waist. He wrenched himself free of his harness and climbed up through the escape hatch.

As he emerged into the open he was surprised to find that it was still almost dark. He saw at once with intense relief that the dinghy had inflated and that some of the crew were already in it. The others were scrambling down from the fuse-lage on to the wing. He followed them cautiously, balancing for a moment precariously on the top of the fuselage and then swinging first one leg and then the other down on to the wing. He was the last to reach the dinghy, which seemed hopelessly overcrowded already. Somehow the others regrouped themselves. Curnow held out his hand to him, and he stepped in. He did not notice at once that the dinghy had shipped a good deal of water.

The first elation of escape had hardly been savoured when the whole crew felt a surge of panic at the prospect of the aircraft sinking and dragging the dinghy down with it. Curnow took the curved knife from its stowage in the dinghy and cut the cord that tied them to the Halifax like a child to its mother. Then he seized one of the canvas hand-paddles and began paddling furiously away from the Halifax, throwing the second paddle to Jock Gordon on the opposite side of the dinghy. Desperately they fought to put a safe distance between themselves and the sinking aircraft, Curnow and Gordon with the grotesque canvas gloves and the others with their bare hands. In a few moments the Halifax disappeared from view as they sank a full twenty feet in the swell, then as they rose on the other side they saw the aircraft still frighteningly close.

Partly by their own frenzied efforts, partly with the aid of wind and sea, they eventually found themselves clear of any danger from the sinking aircraft. But the moment their minds were relieved of terror and the concentration of effort, they became acutely conscious of the roughness of the sea. One by one they hung their heads over the side of the dinghy as sickness came and went and came again, leaving in its train only languor and apathy. After nearly an hour and a half they watched without emotion while J for

Jig slid deeper and deeper and finally disappeared into the sea.

Weakened and exhausted to the point of collapse by seasickness and shock, they drifted helplessly all day, soaked to the skin by the water the dinghy had shipped when it inflated, yet lacking the energy to make any effort to bale it out. Their proximity to each other sapped what strength they had and made movement of any kind laborious. Their bodies were thrown together like corpses in a mass grave.

Towards evening, Vertican recovered sufficiently to erect the telescopic mast from the dinghy equipment and fly the red distress-flag. Some of the others were well enough to sit quietly, regaining their strength. Taffy, always the most liable to sickness, remained sprawled across the bottom of the waterlogged dinghy, too sick and weak to care, constantly slipping back into the well of the dinghy in spite of rough handling to make him sit up.

Still feeling sickly and depressed, they showed no interest in food or drink that day, huddling together when night fell and sleeping fitfully, two of them keeping awake in turn so as to maintain some kind of a look-out. These two sat on the air-chamber and relieved the congestion to some extent in the well. During the night Curnow roused them excitedly with news of an aircraft, and they hurriedly prepared distress rockets as the sound of engines seemed to be almost overhead. They fired off two signals but could not tell if they were seen, the aircraft droning on without any change in the note of its engines. Darkness and depression surged around them again as the rockets disintegrated and the sound of engines died away.

They all seemed to rouse themselves about the same time next morning, refreshed by sleep and optimistic with the coming of daylight. They set to work with a will to bale out the dinghy, and what moisture they were unable to mop up soon evaporated. Vertican began to take stock of the position. For food and water they had the rations stowed in the dinghy and a small quantity of emergency rations from the aircraft. As part of the dinghy equipment they had a length of rope, a rope ladder, the distress rockets, the telescopic mast and distress flag, the dinghy knife, first-aid equipment, the canvas paddles, and a fluorescine bag for colouring the water so as to mark their position or attract attention from the air.

Vertican outlined his plan of campaign. 'We'll start off with the strictest possible rationing,' he said, 'instead of eating a lot to start with and having to cut down later. If we get used to a small amount of food and water now, we'll be able to last out longer.' Everyone seemed happy with this idea and Vertican went on: 'I've collected all the rations and water and stowed them behind me. It's not a case of distrusting anybody, it's just a matter of having what little we've got under one control.

'We've got thirty half-pint tins of water and two water-bottles which we'll keep for emergency. We'll have half a pint of water between us in the morning before the sun comes up, and another half-pint at night. That's a seventh of a pint each per day. That way our water will last us . . . well, over a fortnight, anyway. We shan't be here that long, of course, but it's just as well to take a pessimistic view. We've got plenty of vitamin tablets, so we'll have one each three times a day, and a piece of chocolate every morning. We've also got a little chewing-gum and barley sugar which we'll dole out now and then as a change of diet.

'We'll have a proper watch system going at night, so as not to miss any chance of rescue, and we'll try to work out some way of helping the dinghy along in the direction we want to go. How far do you think we are off-shore, Timmy?'

'When we ditched I should have said not more than about twenty miles,' said Tempest, 'but I've changed my mind since then. Did you notice how we drifted yesterday? Right up to the time the old kite sank we drifted away from it to the north. I didn't take any notice of it at the time, but it suddenly hit me last night. The wind must have changed completely while we were flying. Instead of having a northerly wind it was blowing dead against us from the south.'

'I begin to see the light,' said Vertican. 'That's why we never reached Tripoli.'

'Then we might be a hundred miles out in the Med?' suggested Ward.

'Not as much as that, I hope,' said Tempest, 'but quite possibly sixty or seventy.'

'What's the wind doing today?' asked Curnow.

'Northerly,' said Tempest, pointing to the ripples on the sea. 'If this keeps up we should get somewhere.'

'There's a fluorescine bag in our equipment,' said Vertican. 'We can use that to check our drift.'

'I wonder if we can do anything in the way of making a sail,' said Tempest. His eyes alighted on the telescopic mast. 'Suppose we broke this mast in two and fitted something up that way?'

Vertican unfitted the tubular aluminium mast and twisted it back and forth until it snapped easily in two. Then he tied the distress flag at either end between the two pieces of tube and handed one piece to Tempest. They sat together in the well of the dinghy holding the sail into wind. It flapped and billowed to the cheers of the rest of the crew. For the first time their spirits rose.

'What's the chance of air/sea rescue catching up with us?' asked Curnow.

Vertican hesitated. There was no sense in encouraging false hopes, and still less in being unduly depressing. He gave his honest opinion.

'I can't see that they're likely to come into it. Not unless Ben's S O S was picked up, and that doesn't seem likely. They'll almost certainly conclude that we were shot down over the target.

'Even supposing the first S O S was picked up, we flew back and forth so much afterwards that we must have thrown them completely off the scent.

'We're much more likely to see the air/sea rescue boys after we've been spotted from the air. And there's two ways of looking at that. We were briefed to bomb the last of the

Afrika Korps. We may have been actually on the last op in Tunisia. If that's the case there probably won't be much flying for a few days, and there's not much chance of being seen. On the other hand, air/sea rescue will have nothing in the world to do but look for *us*.'

Vertican organised the seven of them on a two-hour watch system covering the whole twenty-four hours, two of them to hold the sail in the daytime whenever the wind was favourable, and two to keep a look-out at night. Another thing he decided to do was keep a log. Turning out his pockets, he found that the only suitable piece of paper he had was his 'goolie' chit. He read the English translation grimly.

'To All Arab Peoples — Greetings and Peace be upon you. The bearer of this letter is an Officer of the British Government and a friend of all Arabs. Treat him well, guard him from harm, give him food and drink, help him to return to the nearest British soldiers and you will be rewarded. Peace and the Mercy of God upon you.'

Curnow, watching Vertican closely, recognised the printed strip of linen.

'My oath,' he said, 'here's a man got his goolie chit. And I left mine behind. How fat can you get?'

'I've got mine,' said Ward quietly, tapping his pocket.

'It's not *your* goolies I'm worried about,' said Curnow.

Vertican made the first entry in the top left-hand corner of the chit in bold print. *'First Day. 0445, ditched. Southerly wind. All feeling sickly and depressed. No meals or water. Heard aircraft at night. Fired off two marine signals. No results.'*

Vertican read the entry to the crew. It gave him a great

feeling of satisfaction. They were getting organised. Everyone seemed to derive comfort from it. That night they had their first drink of water.

On the third day the wind blew again from the land, driving them out to sea. It was very hot and they were plagued incessantly by flies. All who had kept them on at the time of the ditching wore their wireless helmets; the others donned yellow skull-caps provided in the dinghy equipment. The thought that the progress they had made on the second day was slipping away every hour oppressed them. There was no point in using the improvised sail, and they rested all day. Some of them were already showing a thick growth of beard and this helped to protect them from the sun. Their noses were reddened and raw. When they drank their water ration that evening it tasted warm and metallic, hardly slaking their thirst. That night it rained sufficiently to dampen and chill them but not enough to enable them to trap any water. They smoked their last cigarettes.

There was a brisk northerly wind awaiting them when they awoke next morning, and they found that with the help of the sail they were making good headway, Tempest computing the day's progress at about ten miles. But fear that the wind would veer round again next day obsessed them, and the absence of any sight or sound of searching aircraft gave them a growing sense of grievance. They did not talk of rescue. The monotony of the motion of the sea, the silence save for the lap-lap-lap of water under the dinghy, the absence of any hope of shade, and the dogged persistence of the flies, all

nagged at their patience. They began to get on each other's
nerves. The cramped space in the dinghy caused frequent
outbursts of bad temper. Boredom engulfed them. They
became keenly aware that their only chance of survival lay in
drifting to the North African shore. Doubt as to their precise
position throughout the flight doubled the doubt as to their
position now. That night each man prayed silently for something to give him hope on the morrow.

The wind dropped in the night and although on the fifth
day it stayed in the north it was scarcely strong enough to
ripple the sea. They drifted no more than two miles all day.
The shortage of water was beginning to tell; lips and throats
became parched and dry and conversation was limited to
essentials. Vertican prayed hard for their continued loyalty
and courage. Allard and Ward had been magnificent, and he
had almost forgotten that this was their first trip with him.
The members of his own regular crew he had never doubted
for a moment. If he was worried about anyone it was Taffy,
who had had by far the worst bout of seasickness and who
had never fully recovered. For some hours he thought he had
noticed a deterioration in Taffy's physical and mental resistance. Taffy's temperament had always puzzled him. A kind of
odd man out he had always been, living apart from the rest
of the crew with his own particular chums, never mucking
in with the crew on leave or stand-down, yet with it all
Vertican wouldn't be without him in the air. A queer one,
was Taffy. He had an unpredictable obstinacy which was at
once his weakness and his strength. As Vertican watched him

now he saw his eyes glaze over. Taffy seemed to be trying to say something. Vertican realised that he was half-delirious. He feared almost as much for the effect on the rest of the crew as for Taffy.

'Taffy,' he said, half-shouting until he thought every syllable would stick in his throat. 'Taffy, pull yourself together, do you hear? I won't have any nonsense, you know that, don't you? Pull yourself together! Do you hear me?'

Vertican was amazed at the effect his outburst had. He watched fascinated as Taffy seemed to shake off his delirium and return to normality. Taffy seemed hardly aware that anything had happened. The others were breathing more freely. Thank God, thought Vertican, thank God. He had an instinctive feeling that they had all passed through a crisis.

That night their prayers were answered. It was Tempest who saw it first — the ghost of a light at a great distance to the south, which seemed to flash on and off at intervals of a few seconds. They lost it almost at once as the dinghy sank with the swell, but a moment later they saw it again as the dinghy rode the sea.

'What do you reckon it is,' asked Curnow. 'A ship?'

'Maybe it's some kind of a beacon,' suggested Gordon.

'If it were a ship it would be moving,' said Vertican. 'It looks static to me. Look, there it is again. It doesn't seem to have moved at all.'

'It's a long way away,' said Allard. 'It might be a ship.'

'It might be anchored, anyway,' suggested Ward.

'What ship in the Mediterranean would advertise its

presence like that?' asked Vertican. 'No, it's some kind of a lighthouse, and it's just about as far away as it could possibly be by the look of it. How far do you think, Timmy?'

'I don't know, Micky. Forty or fifty miles, perhaps, if it's a lighthouse.' He paused a moment, weighing carefully what he wanted to say. 'But I don't think it *is* a lighthouse.' He could feel attention riveted on him, but he could not keep the excitement out of his voice, try as he would. 'They operate a searchlight some nights to illumine the approaches to Tripoli Harbour. Anti-sub precautions. That's what it is.'

Tripoli! The whole crew echoed the word. After five days of drifting with only the vaguest idea of their position and chances of reaching land, the recognition of a landmark affected them deeply. They watched the light in wonderment, like children at a firework display. Not one of them took his eyes off it for some hours, fearing that if he looked away his eyes might never find it again. Eventually the light was extinguished and they fell asleep.

It was not until next day that it occurred to them to doubt Tempest's interpretation of the source of the light. They were impatient for night to fall again, so that their fears could be confirmed or confounded. Vertican was under pressure that day to increase the rations, but he resisted grimly. Now that they had seen evidence of land he was even more determined to reach it.

'This is how I see it,' he told them. 'We know now exactly where we are in relation to the coast. That's assuming that Timmy's interpretation of the light is right – and I should think it probably is. What we can only guess is how far away we are. Timmy thinks we're about forty miles. Suppose we've covered thirty miles already. That means we've got at least another week in here. If we don't make good progress in the next two or three days I shall be cutting down the water ration, not increasing it. Agreed?'

There was no more talk of increasing the rations, but Vertican searched his mind for some means of overcoming the days of boredom which threatened them. Then suddenly it came to him, and he wondered why someone hadn't thought of it before. The sea! They would swim in the sea!

He had no trouble in persuading Curnow, Tempest, Gordon and Allard to take a dip, and Ward, who was a poor swimmer, clung to the side of the dinghy and immersed himself for some time. But Taffy was immovable. Vertican decided not to press the point too far. He was determined that Taffy should go in, especially when he found how refreshed they all felt, but he guessed that Taffy would go in in his own good time.

Later that day Curnow cut a piece of tin from an empty water-can and shaped it into a hook, fastening it to the end of the length of rope to make a fishing-line. He cast around in his mind for some form of bait. Eventually he took the chewing-gum from his mouth, stuck it on the hook and lowered the rope over the side until the hook lay at a depth of eight or ten feet. He watched the hook for nearly two hours, seeing no movement of any kind. Then, after cursing all the fish in the Mediterranean, he hauled the rope slowly back into the dinghy. He took the chewing-gum from the hook, dried it carefully, and popped it back into his mouth.

They saw porpoises playing in the distance, and Curnow grabbed Timmy's revolver and fired a couple of shots at them. All the other guns had been jettisoned. Then Allard fired a shot. Vertican did not stop them. The cartridges were valueless, the sport amused them, and the porpoises were unharmed.

In spite of the incidents of the day – the swim, the fishing, the porpoises – it seemed intolerably long. Darkness found them staring fixedly south, frightened now night had come lest they should be disappointed. But just on nine o'clock the light was clearly visible again, nearer than the night before, it seemed, and they slept well that night, immensely reassured.

The seventh day brought a fair northerly breeze, and Vertican had them swimming twice, in the morning and early afternoon. Taffy went in both times without a word, clinging to the side of the dinghy. They trailed the fluorescine bag for some time, plotting their course and computing their drift. There was no doubt that they were making headway. Later in the afternoon to their great delight they saw seagulls, and for a moment the birds wheeled noisily above the dinghy. It was the first sound they had heard other than the wind and the sea and their own voices since the unknown aircraft had flown over on their first night in the dinghy.

Curnow gazed up at the wheeling gulls. 'Sorry to disappoint you birds,' he said, 'but I'm afraid we've got no titbits here. Or maybe it's carrion you're after. Which gives me an idea.' Without taking his eyes off the gulls he felt in

226

the well of the dinghy for the revolver. 'I hate to do this to a reception party but . . .' He aimed the gun carefully. '. . . maybe it'll be your turn later.' A moment later their ears were shattered by the explosion. The gulls screamed still louder and wheeled in wider circles, making out to sea. Curnow fired the last two bullets in the revolver at the retreating gulls, and something that was as near as they could get to a cheer rose from the dinghy as a gull side-slipped and settled on the water.

'Winged him,' said Curnow. He took off his clothes and let himself carefully over the side of the dinghy, striking out at once for the injured gull. Vertican measured the distance with his eye. It looked close enough, but it might be as much as a hundred yards. He wondered if Curnow had the strength to make it. Of all of them Curnow had seemed the least affected by the rigours of the past few days, keeping up his Aussie bravado in a way which had been a tonic to all of them. Curnow swam well and he soon closed the distance. Then, just as his outstretched hand seemed about to close over its prey, the gull took off from the water with a great flapping of wings.

It was too much for the men in the dinghy. They threw their heads back and laughed for the first time for seven days. Vertican looked at them for a moment uncertainly, scared that it might be the laughter of hysteria. It was some moments before he realised why they had laughed. The whole incident had been like being at the pictures, with Curnow the hero. Then at the last moment Curnow had been changed into a comic, a Charlie Chaplin whose heroics never came off.

For a moment Vertican had forgotten about Curnow. He looked round to see the Australian making his way back with difficulty, showing obvious signs of distress. He seized one of the canvas paddles and thrust the other one in Jock Gordon's outstretched hand.

'Paddle with all you've got,' he said. 'Don's in trouble.'

They made a little progress in the right direction, and Curnow, encouraged, kept going. At length they reached him, grabbed hold of him and hauled him aboard. He, Gordon and Vertican himself were exhausted. No more of this sort of thing, thought Vertican. They were weaker than he had realised.

That night they heard an aircraft again, the first one for exactly a week, and it seemed to fly almost directly over-head. They fired a distress rocket, but it took so long to extract the rocket from the watertight container and fire it that once again it seemed to burst under the aircraft where it was most unlikely to be seen by the crew. But they saw the searchlight again and this revived their drooping spirits.

On the eighth day Vertican was conscious that they were all perceptibly weaker. Their throats were completely dried up and the inside of their lips stuck to their gums. They talked only when absolutely necessary, and chewing was so difficult that it took nearly an hour to masticate a small piece of chocolate. They swam twice but had the greatest difficulty in dragging themselves back into the dinghy. Vertican watched them critically. Hope engendered by the light they saw each night had kept their spirits high, and a strong northerly wind which blew all day encouraged Vertican to stick to the same rationing plan. But he was beginning to wonder just how far away the coast might be, just how far away the light could have been when they first saw it. They must have drifted twenty-five or thirty miles in the last three days, and if their calculations were right they could be no more than twenty or twenty-five miles off shore. How far was it possible to see a light in the Mediterranean? He had once seen the island of Pantelleria at a distance of eighty miles flying practically on the deck. It might be possible to see a searchlight at night for over a hundred miles.

The sun went down with a breathtaking brilliance, rivalling anything Vertican had seen. Then, just as the sun touched the water, Gordon, sitting on the edge of the dinghy gazing towards the south, gave a shout.

'Look there,' he said, his voice hardly more than a croak. 'Don't you see it? Roof-tops, that's what it is! Roof-tops!'

Vertican caught a glimpse of something white flashing above the sea on the horizon. He turned to Tempest.

'Could it be Tripoli?'

'That's about the direction.'

Vertican peered again into the distance. The light had changed. His eyes swept the horizon for the white roofs of Tripoli in vain.

'I've lost them,' he said. 'Where are they?'

No one answered. They stared silently into the distance until the sun went down and a star lit up like a street-lamp in the sky. None of them was sure that he had seen anything. They waited for the searchlight that night in vain.

Just before dawn they heard an aircraft again and fired a distress signal, without reply. When daylight came they looked in vain for the coastline. They dipped the fluorescine bag and saw they were drifting parallel with the coast in an easterly direction. They drifted like this until midday, hardly daring to hope that the wind would ever change. But at midday it veered to the north, and Curnow and Gordon had to be dissuaded from attempting to jump in the sea and tow the dinghy towards land. This ninth day was the hottest they had had, and Vertican persevered with the swimming, though they had such difficulty in regaining the dinghy that he resolved that this should be the last time. That night they saw the searchlight to the south-west, unmistakably nearer. Curnow pointed beyond it to a cluster of lights which he said he could see clearly between the flashes. Some of the others saw them too, or thought they saw them. Vertican, noticing that they were being driven more and more along the coast away from Tripoli, said nothing. To be washed up on a featureless shore, exhausted and at the mercy of isolated tribes who might or might not be friendly, could be out of the frying-pan into the fire.

It was Curnow who first saw it next morning – a layer of cloud so low that it might almost be the coastline. They watched it suspiciously, unwilling to expose themselves to the risk of disappointment.

'It *must* be land,' said Curnow at last. 'What else could it be?'

'One's eyes can play queer tricks,' said Vertican. 'After ten days bunched up like this it's easy to start imagining things. It looks like land, all right. What do you think, Timmy?'

'According to my reckoning we've drifted a good seventy miles now,' said Tempest. 'I've been expecting to sight land for two or three days. I'd say it's land all right.'

'Land!' Curnow shouted the word exultantly, expressing for all of them the pent-up emotion that the enunciation of the word released. 'Land! We're going to make it!'

Vertican tried hard to put a brake on their excitement, fearful that there might be a fatal reaction to any disappointment now, but as the day progressed and the outlines sharpened there seemed no sense in denying themselves the pleasure of discovery any longer. Stretched before them, straight and unending and not sending the tiniest little promontory down to meet them, lay Africa.

The wind stayed in the west throughout the morning, blowing them still further along the coast, and at midday it veered to the south-west, pegging them back until by nightfall they had almost lost sight of land. As Vertican had feared, they became an easy prey to despondency and apprehension. But Tempest was reassuring. 'We've got the prevailing wind on our side,' he said. 'Sooner or later it'll blow from the north again.'

They awoke on the eleventh morning to find a strong northerly wind blowing them inshore. One by one, in spite of their weakened state and the motion of the sea, they stood up in the dinghy, heartened indescribably by what they saw, keeping an unbroken watch on Africa. They could make out the features of the coastline clearly now. Nothing but sand dunes and desolation.

'Look,' shouted Curnow suddenly, 'there's someone hiding behind that sand dune over there!' They followed his pointing finger with a mixture of eagerness and trepidation, seeing the barest sign of movement as a figure disappeared from view.

'Looked like an Arab,' said Gordon.

'Where there's life there's water,' said Tempest.

'Do you think we can stretch two goolie chits to cover seven?' asked Curnow.

'One-track-mind, Don,' said Ward. 'Always thinking of your goolies.'

'Too right,' said Curnow.

A few moments later the Arab reappeared, this time with a companion.

'There he is,' shouted Curnow. 'Two of them now. He must have gone to fetch his mate.'

The dinghy was now being tossed about in the swell less than a quarter of a mile from shore. Curnow and Gordon, impatient to reach land, jumped into the sea and began towing the dinghy shorewards. In a few minutes they shouted that they had touched bottom. They half-swam, half-dragged the dinghy into shallow water, by which time the others had joined them in the sea, splashing the last few yards to the beach, where Curnow and Gordon collapsed with exhaustion and the others stumbled and fell into the sand. Vertican, dragging the dinghy in with Tempest, collapsed beside Curnow, and seeing that the Australian lay face down in the sand like a drowned man, he pushed at his shoulder until he had turned him over on his back like a turtle. That was the last thing he knew for some minutes, until he was aware of someone standing watching them not more than twenty yards away.

The two Arabs, emboldened by the weak and exhausted appearance of their invaders, had come out of their hiding-place.

'*Sayeda Effendi*,' said Vertican. '*Ingleezi. Moya. Moya.*' He pulled the goolie chit out of his pocket. '*Sa-deck.*'

The two Arabs disappeared at once, and the crew lay for the moment on the sand, hardly caring who their discoverers might be, letting the sea-water lap at their feet. After a few minutes one of the Arabs returned with a large porous pitcher of water. They dropped in their purifying tablets and emptied the pitcher between them in a few seconds. Then the second Arab returned with another pitcher of water and a basket of eggs. Squatting on their haunches; they picnicked on the sand, drinking the second pitcher of water although they had run out of purifying tablets. Then they pierced the egg-shells and sucked in the raw eggs. Taffy alone saw anything to resent in the food.

'I only like mine boiled,' he said.

Vertican couldn't believe his ears. Eleven days in a dinghy, and he wanted his egg boiled!

'Don't be a fool, Taffy,' he said, as sharply as he could manage. 'Swallow it before you offend them.'

'I tell you I want it boiled,' repeated Taffy. He turned to the Arabs, gesticulating and demanding his egg boiled in the most impossible Arabic. Vertican was sure there would be trouble.

But evidently the Arabs not only understood him, but were ready to humour him, for one of them lit a fire from nowhere, took an empty water-tin, filled it with sea-water, and a few minutes later presented Taffy with a lightly boiled egg. Hell, thought Vertican. I can see what it is about Taffy now.

By this time a number of Arabs had collected, one of them bringing a pony, which none of them had the strength to mount. Partly under their own steam and partly helped by the Arabs, they made their way to a small hutted village about four hundred yards inshore. They could hardly put one foot in front of the other. It was uncanny to be on firm ground again.

They were taken to the biggest hut in the village, where they were received with great friendliness by the chief. In no time a crowd of Arabs collected around them. They did not see any women. There was no mistaking the kindliness of the Arabs. Vertican watched fascinated while tea was made, the Arab using two pots and pouring the tea back and forth from one pot to the other, boiling it up again each time, and tasting its strength carefully. Vertican noticed that the Arabs drank with an intake of breath, making a great sucking noise. He did the same and was gratified when the others followed suit gravely. Then came a meal of bread, dates, eggs and water. Vertican understood from one of the Arabs that the local Sudanese Defence Force had been sent for, and when they came he delivered up his goolie chit and received assurance that the nearest British post would be informed within a few hours.

The crew of J for Jig slept that night in the same hut, huddled together with their hosts, while chickens scratched about between them and goats sniffed outside. About twenty of them were thrown together in the small unventilated hut. The crew were soon aware that they had other living companions besides human beings and animals. Sleep eventually came to some of them, but in the early hours of the morning Vertican, Tempest, Ward and Gordon found themselves still awake, feeling very sick and imagining the motion of the dinghy. Struggling to their feet carefully so as not to disturb anyone, they picked their way across sleeping bodies to the hut entrance and passed out into the cool night air.

'Look,' said Jock Gordon, 'the dinghy. They must have dragged it up here from the beach.'

One by one they climbed in, stretched themselves out in the well of the dinghy, and slept soundly till dawn.

WHITLEYS AND HAMPDENS
ON HAMM

THE posting signal had come right at the end of his fortnight's leave.

'904231 Sergeant (Air Observer) J. F. Haffenden,' it read, 'report to No. 78 Squadron R.A.F. Middleton St George 8th July 1941.' A railway warrant was enclosed.

This, to Haffenden, was the end of a long road. He had held a flying licence with the Civil Air Guard before the war, and in October 1940 he had joined up, having been accepted by the R.A.F. for training as a pilot. Then he had made a sorry mess of it. Based at a Midlands airfield, he had been sent one morning on a solo cross country in a Miles Magister, an aircraft he had normally felt competent to fly. But it was contact flying, and he had run into worsening weather. After flying blind for a time, expecting the weather to clear, he had caused his instructors infinite trouble by flying straight through the Derby balloon barrage. He had ended up crashing into the side of a hill a few miles north of the town. No one sympathised – rather the reverse. Almost at once he was taken off the pilot's course and transferred to training as a navigator.

No one was keener to get on to operational flying, in any capacity, than Haffenden. Rejection was a setback, but it didn't put him off. He was the bearer of one of the oldest of all Sussex names and he meant to live up to it. For his navigation course he was sent to Kinloss and he set about his new studies with enthusiasm. He passed out the top of his course.

That had been barely a fortnight ago. He was sent home on posting, back from Scotland to southern England, close to London, where he would be rejoining his newly-wed wife. Now the posting notice had come and, to make his way in time from Orpington to Middleton St George, he would need to catch a train at four-thirty in the morning. There was little time to prepare. Early on the morning of 8th July, a taxi took him to the station in plenty of time, and he dumped his kit-bag near the top of the platform to save time for his change at Waterloo. Not surprisingly, at that time of the morning there was no one about.

It was still dark when the train came in. The black-out was in force, and the carriages too were blacked out and dimly lit. The train seemed to be empty. He got in the front compartment, just behind the driver, and hoisted his kit-bag on the rack before stretching himself out full length in the empty carriage.

Suddenly a voice spoke: it was the train driver. 'Like to come up in the cabin with me?'

Haffenden sat up. He was tired, but also lonely. The carriage seat, however he spread himself on it, was none too comfortable. And it would be fascinating to travel with the driver.

'Yes, I would.'

'Come along, then.'

Haffenden sat silently beside the driver. This was a new experience. He felt exhilarated as the train sped forward into the night. Blue flashes from the distance signalled the progress of other trains. Ahead of them, he knew, lay the amorphous vastness of London. Already it was gathering about him. In the occasional electric flashes he glimpsed tall skeletons climbing up to the sky. The war was here all right, in London, far more real than anything he had seen before, far closer than he'd imagined it in 1941, far closer than it had yet approached him in nearly two years of service.

'Been over Berlin?' asked the driver.

They all asked that.

'No,' said Haffenden. 'I haven't.'

'Hamburg?'

Haffenden shook his head.

'How about the marshalling yards at Hamm? You chaps have given them a bashing, eh? Every time Jerry drops one on the railway, I think of what he's copping at Hamm.'

'I'm afraid I haven't been over Germany at all yet.'

The driver turned and looked up at Haffenden speculatively. Haffenden felt like a fraud. He would have to explain.

'Just finished my OTU – my training. I'm off to a Bomber squadron today. Whitleys near Darlington.'

The driver looked at him again, rather sharply this time. Haffenden coloured deeply. He had said more than perhaps he should have done. Careless Talk. There weren't any notices in drivers' cabins to remind one.

At Waterloo the driver shook Haffenden by the hand. He had forgiven him by now for not bombing Berlin. 'Don't forget, lad – we don't care what we have to take so long as you chaps are giving it to them. Give Jerry a taste of his own medicine – that's what I say. Well, good luck, lad.'

'Thanks – and thanks for the ride.'

Haffenden caught his train at King's Cross comfortably enough. He had no trouble getting a seat. The journey to Darlington took about three hours, and he changed to the local line for Middleton St George. The R.A.F. van was already there to meet the train, and Haffenden asked to be dropped at the Sergeants' Mess. He was given a room in a large block nearby, where he dumped his kit-bag. Then he hurried along to the Squadron offices, and after a few minutes' waiting he was taken in to the Commanding Officer.

'So you're Haffenden,' said the CO. 'Yes, I know about you.' It was a pleasant change to be expected, to have someone know your name. 'You did well at your OTU, I hear. Good show. You can go with McQuitty. That means you'll be on tonight.'

Haffenden felt his stomach turn over. Tonight. Already. Excitement welled up inside him, stifling his breathing. He was glad the CO went on talking.

'McQuitty's a good chap. He's an Australian. He's about half-way through his tour.' (He and his crew had done fourteen trips.) 'His navigator's sick, so you can take over. We've got to put on a maximum effort tonight.'

'I see.'

'Now you'd better get cracking. You've got a lot to do before briefing. Go and find McQuitty, get some lunch, and then draw all your equipment. Briefing is at five o'clock. I'll see you then.'

'Thank you, sir.'

It must be after one o'clock already. And he had a thousand things to do. He met McQuitty, the Australian, and the rest of his crew, all except the second pilot, who was in the Officers' Mess. All the others were sergeants. He swallowed a quick lunch before beginning a tour of offices and departments and stores, to collect maps, navigation instruments, wireless helmet, parachute and harness – and a Mae West attached to a fleecy-lined jacket, a combination he had not seen before. He continued to walk back and forth from one department to another, signing forms and collecting equipment, and by the time he reached the briefing room he was exhausted. There was nothing about the life of a flying man quite so exhausting as the drawing of equipment – unless it was handing it in.

Haffenden learned a lot more at the briefing. There was a cynical reaction from the assembled crews – the target was a familiar one, the railway yards at Hamm. Even Haffenden's train driver could have told them.

Hamm was in the centre of the Ruhr railway yards – the viaduct linking Hamm and Hanover had still not been severed after many years – but Whitleys and Hampdens of various squadrons would do their best – or worst – tonight. Haffenden, having been up all night already, still managed to concentrate during the briefing, where he joined the other navigators and pencilled in the track to the target on his maps. He had one clear retrospective vision of the train driver he had met that morning, so recently, and yet so long ago.

Finally dinner in the Mess, and then down to the airfield. The trip started badly. On arriving at the Whitley, Haffenden's inter-com equipment, essential throughout the flight, proved unserviceable. It wasn't his fault. Delay followed while a dispersal van collected a replacement. They ended up taking off well after the other aircraft. It was maximum effort all right: from Middleton St George, twelve Whitleys were detailed for the raid, and there were over seventy planes, Whitleys and Hampdens, in all.

Whitley T4209 was already late, but Haffenden believed, even so, that much of this operation would be a long, feature-less slog. Flak was desultory and searchlights could be dodged. There was a full moon, which would help night fighters, but the gunners, Forster and Clow, would be alert. It was not long, though, before he began to change his mind.

Ignoring dummy fires, and proceeding on good pinpoints to Hamm, he could now see straight ahead that the target area was clearly marked by very heavy medium and high flak. The Whitleys were all between 8,000 and 10,000 feet, with the Hampdens higher, perhaps 12,000 to 14,000. He knew they were late on E.T.A., and it looked very much as though they would get the worst of the resistance that had been stirred up.

Haffenden's initial reaction was that this was his first bombing run and he wanted to make a good job of it, and he began to give his pilot the correct procedure — 'Left-left, steady,' and so on — and, whatever McQuitty thought of it, he appeared to be carrying out orders as given. It was with great satisfaction that, combining with McQuitty, he manoeuvred to attack the primary target. They were at 10,000 feet, it was a clear night, and he could already see hits registering on the railway lines. Then everything happened at once.

One of the Hampdens above them must have dropped a premature flare. It illuminated the whole picture, and in the same moment, as it seemed, Whitley T4209 was in the thick of the shell-bursts, and the perspex bombing window from which Haffenden was viewing the target disintegrated in his face. Then a succession of explosions – near misses of shell-bursts, and direct hits – told him that the defenders were concentrating their fire on his own Whitley. Next Sergeant Forster was shouting from the turret to McQuitty that the port engine was on fire. Haffenden, fearing a conflagration, jettisoned the remaining bombs, telling McQuitty that he was doing so. He tested the bombing panel to make sure they'd gone, then realised that he was losing his physical grip. They were diving at a steep angle, out of control.

His parachute! He remembered that it was somewhere under the navigation table, up front behind the pilot, hopelessly out of reach. No chance of getting it now. His reaction was mainly one of fury. The beams of the searchlights were blinding him. If only he could somehow fire at them to silence them. He struggled to place the ammunition pans on top of the Lewis guns above his head, determined to have a go at those guns before they crashed.

Meanwhile McQuitty had doused the port engine with the automatic fire extinguisher, and under his hands the

Whitley gradually fought its way back on an even keel. He saw Pilot Officer Scott, the second pilot, move forward under the nose, and he seated himself alongside McQuitty and set course for home.

Haffenden could see at once that McQuitty was having great difficulty in keeping the Whitley in level flight. Perspiring freely from his efforts, he was holding the wheel against the dead engine, and, typical Australian, he managed a wry smile. Among other things the pitot head had blown off, giving no indication of speed of climb or dive. Haffenden decided that their only hope was to abandon a return to Yorkshire and set course for the nearest coastline, Norfolk. But he didn't know how long the Whitley or McQuitty could last.

Already the remaining engine was showing signs of high temperature and high oil pressure, and presently it began intermittent coughing. They were losing height all the time. The next hazard, thought Haffenden, was crossing the Dutch coast. The direct route meant that they would inevitably pass somewhere near Texel, and at least they managed to avoid any more searchlight belts, but the moon was full and there were bound to be fighters around.

They were not long to be left in doubt. Forster's voice came up loud and clear. 'Messerschmitt 110! Trailing us. Behind and slightly above.' There followed two long bursts of machine-gun fire. As the fighter bore down on them, Forster gave instructions to McQuitty on taking avoiding action. Then, as the intruder dived towards sea, they heard Forster's excited voice: 'I think I got the bastard!'

All the time they were losing height, and they lost still more while they were manoeuvring to avoid the fighter, drawing from Scott, the second pilot, sitting down in the nose, the plaintive cry that 'the sea was getting mighty close'. McQuitty immediately sent him back to the fuselage, ordering him straight away to 'Prepare the dinghy for ditching.'

He wasn't a moment too soon. Before he could get back to the fuselage there was an almighty 'bang' and the starboard engine blew up. They had already descended to about three hundred feet, alarming Scott, and now they dived precipitately into the sea. They hit the water point-blank.

Luckily the lights stayed on. Haffenden crawled back under water to the fuselage, which was already waist-high in water, and found Clow and Scott struggling to untie the knots holding the dinghy to the fuselage. His operational training came into practice now because he was the only one with a knife. He shouted to them to get quickly to the rear-gunner's hatch, and he dragged the dinghy pack back to them. Then he helped pass the pack up through the hatch, above which Scott and Clow were waiting. Haffenden noticed that blood poured past him in a continual stream from above. Clow had earlier been at his radio, sending an S O S, when they crashed, and, being thrown forward, he had badly gashed his eye. Meanwhile McQuitty had emerged safely from his emergency exit above the pilot's seat, worked his way down the fuselage, and was standing on the tail-plane.

What they needed now was the moon. It had been with

245

them over Texel, but suddenly it had disappeared. There were thunderstorms about, that much they knew, and the sky was now obscured, but they could see well enough to launch the dinghy. Haffenden remembers McQuitty standing there like a statue – could he swim? In fact, could any of them swim? Haffenden wasn't unduly worried: over a short distance he had been a schoolboy champion. Fortunately it didn't matter as long as they had the dinghy.

Scott and Forster, working on the air bottles, were getting ready to inflate the dinghy. They had launched it, and one man actually got in it. But dismay followed, turning rapidly to panic. At some point – either when they were experiencing heavy fire over Hamm, or when the Messerschmitt attacked them over Texel – the dinghy must have been in the firing line. It had been holed. As soon as the first man got in it, it turned turtle.

Meanwhile, although the landing lights were still glowing, slowly the tail-plane sank. The lights turned greener as the plane lost buoyancy, finally disappearing entirely. The position was, Haffenden reflected, not good. Scott was in immediate difficulties. Clinging to the useless and waterlogged dinghy, he was trying to inflate his Mae West. He had been married only a week previously, and it emerged that he could hardly swim a stroke.

Haffenden opted for action. They must be half across the North Sea, with the English coast still far away and out of sight, but he thought he saw a landing light of some kind. Probably a light-ship. He had already found the breath to inflate his Mae West, but now he disconnected it, and his Irving Jacket too, vowing to swim to get help if he could. Even with their Mae Wests, in these merciless seas, these chaps weren't going to last. So telling them to hang on, that he was going to try and make it, he took off all the rest of his clothes and struck out.

Shouts of encouragement were muted, but he swam towards the light, low on the horizon, apparently attainable. But it was getting no closer. He didn't know how long he swam, he supposed fifteen minutes, but he seemed to make little headway, and eventually he realised that the light he had seen was a star.

He returned towards the spot where he had left his friends. In the darkness he discovered his own Irving Jacket, floating by itself. The smell of petrol confirmed where he was, somewhere close to the wreck, but there were no signs of life. All the others must have given up their struggles, overcome by the boisterous seas. The loneliness he felt at that moment was indescribable.

Thoughts of the last despairing panic they must have felt must be shut from his mind. Those poor chaps. Don't think about it. He was alive. The night was still very dark. Without moon or stars he could not orientate himself. All he could do was paddle about and wait for dawn.

They had set course for the bulge of Norfolk, abandoning all hope of reaching their Yorkshire base. Norfolk would do. With the dawn he would get some idea. Meanwhile he just went on paddling. The sodden life-jacket, and the Mae

West, gave him little buoyancy, becoming so much dead weight. But he kept his hold on the life-jacket, in case he needed it.

Otherwise he just lay naked in the water. He noticed that his wrist-watch had stopped at four-thirty. He reckoned he must have hit the water about four-fifteen. The hours passed interminably. Then at long last he sensed dawn was breaking. The first rays of light were unmistakeably seeping into the sky. Keeping the dawn light slightly behind and over his right shoulder, he adjusted his direction and started to swim.

He still retained his Irving Jacket. It was something to hold on to. But it was more of a hindrance than a help. Eventually, with some misgivings, he let it go.

Maintaining a steady crawl stroke he suddenly felt strong. He told himself that if he just kept on and on, somehow or other he would make the coast, small chance though it must be. He told himself that the old Whitley, crippled as it was, with unknown air speed, only one engine, and damaged instruments, must have lasted more than half-way. It might be twenty miles. He would just keep on.

Another two hours, perhaps more, with no horizon to aim for beyond his own imagination, and a single seagull alighted on the water. There it sat, eyeing him speculatively, but giving him renewed hope. Surely he could not be so far from land now.

He loved that seagull. All he had concentrated on during the last few hours was represented in that bird. Eventually it flew off.

What did that mean? Was he seeing things? Faintly on the horizon he thought he saw a destroyer, or smoke from a destroyer: someone had come to look for him. Good old Clow! He must have got the S O S out. The Navy were on the look-out. With the rising of the sun he thought he could see low hills to the west. But there were no towering cliffs, just the merest hint of a shoreline. And he wasn't even certain of that. From sea level, buffeted by the swell, he could see very little. Though still hoping rescue might be at hand, he suddenly felt unequal to the struggle ahead. Violent cramp had assailed his legs. He was swimming now with his arms only. Totally demoralised, he began to feel it was useless to go on. In a crazy moment, he tried to drown himself.

He couldn't do it. Even by swallowing water he couldn't do it. He tried swallowing great gulps; he tried to give up, to let the sea have its will, but, in spite of himself, he retained a stubborn buoyancy. The whole episode had a reverse effect. It renewed his resolve.

He resumed swimming, and tried to increase his speed, but the pain in his legs was excruciating. Thoughts of the low hills of the coastline, which he was sure were now in sight, perhaps only two miles away, somehow left him incapable of further effort. Contemplating his plight made him aware of his exhaustion: any further effort seemed impossible.

He could no longer tell whether or not he had decided to stop. He felt himself giving up. He began to sink, feeling himself being carried along involuntarily by the irresistible swell of the sea. He let the waters swirl over his head.

Then, to his amazement, his feet touched bottom. He could not believe it. He was overjoyed. A few deep breaths first, and then he rested awhile, massaging his numbed legs for what must be the final effort. Eventually, in a state of exaltation, he started to wade and crawl through the surf. As he did so he remembered his crew-mates. They might somehow have lingered near the wreck; there might be some hope of finding them, and he had to get help in case they were alive.

Viewing the beach from a distance, he thought it was deserted. But presently, apprehensions of what he might find on the beach began to torture his mind. The beaches were mined! Anti-invasion measures meant that the beaches on the east coast would be bristling with mines. He had survived all the terrors of the air-strike and the sea, only to be blown up.

As he approached the beach, he realised he had to take some action. He could not just lie there until someone found him. Deserted as the beach was, there was someone perhaps two miles away who might in time be made aware of his presence. In the distance, across the mined expanse of sand, he could see a Coastguard hut.

There was no alternative. He set off across the beach, expecting every moment to be his last. But something happened to take his mind off the danger: he had disturbed a bird sanctuary, and the birds proceeded to attack him with relish. His naked flesh was their target. Hundreds of sea-birds began to attack him, all over his body and under his arms, the smell of the bare flesh driving them frantic. To try to keep them away he was forced to stoop at every step, grabbing handfuls of sand and throwing it over alternate shoulders in an effort to deter them.

With the most amazing luck, he made it to the hut unscathed. As he walked in through the back door, he surprised the Coastguard, who was just pouring tea out of a Thermos flask. Haffenden interrupted him. 'I could do with some of that.'

He had had no rest since getting up early to travel by train to Yorkshire at four-thirty the previous morning, to be told he was on operations that night. He could certainly do with a cup of tea.

The Coastguard soon got the message. In a few minutes he had telephoned the air station at nearby Bircham Newton, and passed a message on to Middleton St George. Then he telephoned home, asking his son to come out and to bring a boat, since the Coastguard hut was sited beyond Burnham Deepdale, on an island which constituted the limit of the coastline. Breakfast – eggs and bacon – was laid on at the Coastguard's home, and the Coastguard provided Haffenden with clothes: a shirt, grey flannels, and gum-boots.

A car was sent from the air station to collect Haffenden, bringing more clothes. They had tried to estimate his size and build, and they had come up with a coat too small and trousers too long, boots about three sizes too large, and a cap that came over his ears! But it was the best they could do at short notice, and this was how Haffenden, the new R.A.F. hero, appeared before the amazed villagers at the Coastguard's House at Burnham Deepdale.

At Bircham Newton he made his report to the Operations Room, and a sympathetic Group Captain sent his car to take him to the Sergeants' Mess, to have breakfast. When Haffenden arrived, he presented a droll figure, no sergeant's tapes, no half-wing on his battle-dress, and a uniform fitting nowhere.

The cook, a Sergeant W.A.A.F., raised her eyes at the 'sprog' in ill-fitting uniform who dared to ask for breakfast in mid-morning, pouring a torrent of scorn upon him. But after he had lost his temper, and explained why he was there, her attitude towards him changed rather suddenly. She was an angel to him from then on. Thus he sat down to a second breakfast that day.

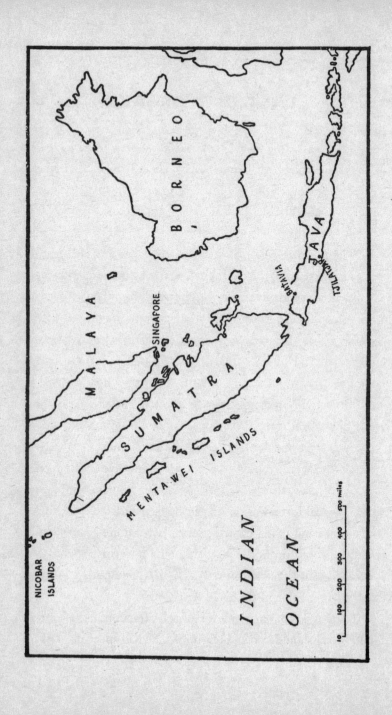

LAST OUT OF JAVA

Ever since they had steamed down the Clyde sixteen weeks earlier, the news from the Far East had grown steadily worse. One by one British, Dutch and American possessions had been attacked and in some cases overrun, until it seemed that the troopship *Dunera* was steaming towards a disintegrating world. But most of the troops believed, obstinately and pathetically, in a last stand which would turn the tide, believed in the tales of Japanese stupidity and myopia, believed that as soon as the Allies got into their stride the Japs would be contained and quickly defeated. They believed these things because they wanted to believe them, as they had believed in the 'no war' predictions, the overthrow of Hitler from within, the 'bluebirds over the white cliffs of Dover, tomorrow, just you wait and see'. Some of the older men, particularly those who were trained to think for themselves, saw deeper than this, saw that a well-organised and purposeful three-dimensional force was cutting through the cardboard edifices of empire and that a panic-stricken last-minute realisation of danger would do nothing to arrest its progress. Such a one was Sergeant Percival Tottle, R.A.F.V.R., equipment assistant and former pilot in the Civil Air Guard.

Tottle was a big man in every way. A fraction under six feet tall, broad-shouldered and big-boned, he had spent most of his

255

thirty-seven years in Plymouth, Devon. With the outbreak of war, the family business had fallen on lean times, and a compassionate posting near home to help a sick father had prejudiced his chances of commissioning. But he was not a man to cry over spilt milk, neither was he the type to complain that he was wasted as an equipment assistant. Whatever work he was given to do he carried out to the best of his ability; and more than this, he invariably sought responsibility, or was sought after to shoulder it. He was recommended for transfer to a new branch; but when the apparent result of the recommendation was a posting overseas in his old, he did not use the story to foster distrust in the Service, either in himself or in others, as some men might have done. Instead, he laughed his resonant laugh and shrugged his broad shoulders, and loyally accepted the modest part he was called upon to play. In fact, he showed himself to possess perhaps the most valuable asset of the wartime Serviceman – the instincts of the true sportsman. Such instincts might perhaps have been expected of a man whose prowess on the rugger and soccer fields had brought recognition before the war and again in the Service.

When they left Scotland their destination had been Singapore. Now, with Malaya almost overrun, Singapore untenable, and Sumatra already chaotic under the threat of invasion, rumour had it that the British and Dutch armies and air forces were to regroup on Java and start a counter-offensive that would drive the Japanese back beyond Indo-China. When Tottle saw in the distance the crowded quayside of Batavia, littered with troops, guns, transport and stores, he wondered whether the rumours might not have some substance. Then, as the ship drew nearer and he saw the quayside for what it was – an indiscriminate hotch-potch of shipping and a wilderness of dumped vehicles – he became sceptical. His doubts increased as the *Dunera* berthed alongside a large passenger liner which he identified as the *Duchess of Bedford*. He learnt that the ship had come straight from Singapore. The decks were lined with women and children. It seemed to Tottle that without exception they were crying. Anger and shame and a sense of his own impotence welled up within him. There was no sign of recovery here. The very air was charged with the voltage of panic.

Tottle wondered if there would be any R.A.F. movements staff on the quayside. The *Dunera* was an Army trooper, and the R.A.F. men on board were all members of small drafts. He was the only N.C.O. on his draft. To keep himself busy he had taken charge of purely R.A.F. administrative matters on the voyage, and he had been detailed by the O.C. troops to disembark first with an Army captain and check off the R.A.F. men as they left the ship.

There was no sign of any R.A.F. port organisation. He disembarked and stood at the foot of the gangway, checking names and numbers. Then the R.A.F. kit-bags were unloaded, and he had these stacked and then rechecked the lists to see that each man's kit-bags were there. The heat and humidity were overpowering and the men were bathed in sweat.

A long line of lorries was pulled up alongside the quay, swallowing the men as they came through checking. When Tottle had his airmen ready, he found that there were only six trucks left in the line, until such time as some of the earlier trucks returned. He got three truckloads of airmen away, and then had the kit-bags loaded on to the last three trucks, having instructed the men who had gone ahead to begin the unloading at the other end. He had previously got confirmation from an Army transport officer that they were all bound for the same camp.

Tottle now found himself awaiting transport with twenty-three other airmen, all that remained of the R.A.F. complement of the *Dunera*. Around them on the quayside, unkempt bedraggled men of indeterminate Service were being disgorged by other ships. Then two trucks arrived, on one of which the Army transport officer was riding on the running-board.

'Here you are, Sergeant,' said the transport officer, 'get your men aboard.'

One of the trucks was empty, but there were five airmen and four soldiers in the other. Tottle got in the second truck and discovered that the men they had joined were the last remnant of a shipload of evacuees from Singapore. There was a short session of question and answer between the two sets of men, and then the men fresh from home began to catch the general infection of apathy and despair.

After driving slowly and tortuously for three-quarters of an hour they reached the lush vegetation of open country, and shortly afterwards the trucks turned off the road and through an archway into the camp.

Tottle had never had any thought other than that they would join the rest of the men from the *Dunera* when they reached their destination. There were about two hundred men already in the camp: but there wasn't a single man from the *Dunera*. Tottle spoke to the truck-drivers.

'Where did you take the rest of our chaps?'

'We haven't been anywhere else but here. We only arrived yesterday. This is our first job. We brought this lot down this afternoon, and then you.'

'Where did the other chaps go? Where did they take our kit?'

'No idea.'

'Are you sure you were supposed to bring us here?'

'Yes. We asked the transport officer where to, and he definitely said Cornelius Barracks.'

'And this is Cornelius Barracks?'

'Yes.'

The men piled out, listless and bewildered. They hardly noticed the noise of the trucks whining into gear and rumbling away.

Tottle orientated himself briefly. On either side of the main archway was a line of low, flat administrative offices. Straight ahead stretched the parade-ground, a tarmac repository of heat. Bordering the square on three sides stood some thirty to forty rectangular brick huts, each hut capable of holding perhaps thirty beds. The camp must be capable of holding a thousand men under normal conditions, perhaps many more in an emergency. At least there was plenty of room.

Slowly the men digested their new situation. There was

nothing organised for them, no camp permanent staff, no one giving orders. They would have to fend for themselves.

They began to investigate the camp. The huts on the left were already crowded with the men who had arrived ahead of them. They moved towards the empty huts on the right. The first huts were bare; no beds, no bedding, no lockers — nothing. They moved on to the next hut, and the next, and so on throughout the camp. Every hut was the same.

The men felt thirsty, but there was no water. They felt hungry, but there was no food; no sign even of a cook-house.

Most of the men who had arrived before Tottle were a remnant of the force that was to have held the so-called Gibraltar of the Far East; their bodies were exhausted and their minds bludgeoned by defeat. Decimated by enemy action, their ranks had been further thinned by malaria, dysentery and jaundice. Utterly demoralised by the swiftness of events in Malaya, they now found themselves leaderless and disorganised, separated from their kit, immobilised and undisciplined and deserted. They had broken up into little groups and dumped what personal treasures they still clung to in the huts. Perhaps tomorrow someone would come out from Batavia to succour them: tonight they would go to Batavia themselves and get what sustenance they could.

By midday next day Cornelius Barracks was beginning to look like a gypsy encampment. On the concrete floors of the huts, men who had spent the night in Batavia slept it off fitfully. Some had acquired blankets. Oddments of clothes and food littered the floors. Half-empty bottles of Dutch gin mingled with the clutter of bodies. Empty beer bottles lay on the parade-ground like a challenge. Little piles of untended bric-a-brac in the huts testified to the continued absence of many. These and other sights met the morning gaze of Sergeant Tottle as he paced the camp.

Tottle had been so close to Service life for so long that its stolid strengths were one of the bulwarks on which he leaned. For most of his thirty-seven years he had watched the Navy at close quarters, lived and worked in their backyard. For the past three years, and for his reserve service before that, he had adapted himself readily to the petty disciplines which many found so irksome. The spectacle of a body of men rushing towards dissolution and anarchy was particularly abhorrent to him. It struck at something that was a part of his life and being.

The situation was no fault of the men. Tottle had no doubt that if the camp could be properly officered, equipped, watered and victualled, discipline could be quickly restored. Something had to be done at once for the men.

The previous day, Tottle had seen a warrant officer and two flight sergeants standing together, evidently discussing their plight. He had not joined them as these men had been so obviously fugitives from Malaya; he had felt that for the moment they might prefer their own company. In addition, he had had his own men to see to. Later, when his men were settled, he had looked for them, only to find that they had gone out of camp. But now he sought out the warrant officer. As the senior rank in the camp it was the warrant officer's duty to restore order.

He found him slumped on the floor in one of the huts, sleeping heavily. Tottle bent down and shook him. The warrant officer opened his eyes and gazed at him glassily.

'Sorry to barge in,' said Tottle, 'but do you know what's happening about this place?'

'How the hell should I know?'

'Well, what about the men here?'

'What about them?'

'What are we going to do with them?'

'They're nothing to do with me, chum. There's only twelve of my men here. I'll look after them.'

Tottle felt near to despair. On all sides he was meeting this utter physical and mental exhaustion, which, coupled with the enervating heat, had quenched the spirit of the men and reduced them to a supine indifference. He tried again.

'But somebody's got to do something about feeding this lot. The place is a shambles already. Some of them were out looting last night. You won't stop them unless you get them organised.'

'Look, chum, I told you – they're not my pidgin. Somebody must have sent them here so somebody's got their tabs on them. I've got enough to do looking after my own men without taking on this lot. I've brought them all the way from Singapore and I'm sticking to them.'

'What are you going to do?'

'I don't know yet. But one thing I can tell you. We're not staying in this dump. We're getting out.'

'Where are you going?'

'That's *my* worry.'

'And what about the rest of the men here?'

'I can't help about them. Let those who brought them here look after them. I'm off.'

Later that morning Tottle saw him go. The two flight sergeants and ten airmen went with him. Tottle was now the only N.C.O. left in the camp.

For the rest of that morning Tottle watched and waited – and wondered. Things had probably gone too far already. An attempt at enforcing discipline by one N.C.O., without orders from above, without support from below, without the backing of an administrative group to supply the necessities of life, would surely be met by ridicule. Yet he knew where his duty lay. He knew, too, where his inclination lay. Sooner or later he would have to have a shot at bringing these fellows into line. And the sooner the better.

They were a miscellaneous lot. Most of them were airmen, but there were forty to fifty Army men and a sprinkling of seamen. Most were from the U.K., but there were some Australians. Together they might survive. Individually only the fittest and most resourceful could hope to win through. That was why an attempt to hold them together was worthwhile.

He saw it this way. If they could stick together now they might still amount to over two hundred men. Such a number could hardly be ignored by the British authorities – if they could be found – or by the Dutch, or even by the Javanese. Batavia was a modern Europeanised town, an important port, certain to be well stocked with food and all kinds of materials. Somewhere near, there must be some sort of a headquarters.

In any case, a proper approach to the Dutch and Javanese businessmen in Batavia, backed by the good behaviour of the troops and the appearance of authority, would surely procure the bare necessities of existence. If there was any hope of a stand being made in Java, this reservoir of men must be kept together. If it was a question of evacuation, the authorities would consider a disciplined force of over two hundred men where they might repudiate a remnant of twenty or thirty plus scores of undisciplined stragglers difficult to round up. And then there was the aspect of the local population: looting and rampaging in Batavia would soon inflame the Javanese into open and perhaps active hostility. And if the worst came to the worst, and the Japs came in, the men in the camp would have infinitely more chance of being treated fairly, perhaps even of being left alone, if they were in numbers and it was apparent to the Japs that they were well organised and could be easily documented and guarded where they were.

The first thing to do was to call a parade and explain to the men what he intended to do and what he expected of them. He had no idea what their reactions to the idea of a parade might be. He sensed that most of them had been free from routine Service discipline for many weeks, perhaps months. They were desperate men. They might quite possibly knife him. He thought there was a very good chance that they would.

He suddenly felt an awful loneliness, a profound isolation. It would be like trying to advance waist-deep against a heavy surf. If you were not careful, the first buffeting swept you off your feet and flung you high and dry on the shore.

He needed an ally. Not that the task he had set himself could be shared. But he needed support. If he had the support of one man – one of *them*, as well as the handful of men from his ship – he might at least make the others think.

He chose a leading seaman. Partly because he liked the look of him, but mostly because he thought it might be decisive to have the Navy on his side. Respect for the seaman was their common inheritance: even the lowest rating went to sea. Somehow he felt that people didn't much like the idea of letting the Navy down.

Tottle went round the huts on one side of the camp and the leading seaman went round on the other. They announced that the whole camp would parade on the parade-ground at four o'clock sharp. No one would be excused. The announcement was greeted with oaths and ribaldry and catcalls. No one stirred.

Tottle retired to a discreet point of vantage and awaited events. It was a quarter to four. He had decided that the shorter the period between the announcement and the parade the better. Fifteen minutes was plenty to get everyone together. And it suggested urgency.

He was relying on their curiosity. He was relying on their boredom. He was relying on their helplessness. He was relying on their apathy. He thought they would come unless there was a strong lead from elsewhere.

At two minutes to four Tottle's heart leapt and then fell into his boots as the first slouching figures wandered out on to the parade-ground. The men stood about in groups and made no attempt to form up. At one minute to four Tottle strode towards the square. Even if there were only thirty to forty men there, he would be on time. His step gained in firmness as he braced himself for the part he had to play. Men started to pour from the huts nearest the parade-ground. Tottle, a magnificent, purposeful figure amongst an aimless mob, reached the square and drew a great breath into his lungs.

'On parade!'

The men formed up grudgingly, resentfully, some throwing wisecracks and some obscenities. But they formed up. Moreover, they showed a welcome orderliness by segregating themselves into the three Services, R.A.F., Army and Navy. Tottle numbered them off. There were 167 R.A.F. men, 41 Army and 14 Navy. 222 men in all. He had no means of compiling a nominal role, so he looked for a simple formula to memorise the numbers. Remembering 222 was easy – all the twos. The Army and Navy totals were reversions of the same figures – 41 and 14. Add these two together and substract the total from 222 and you had the R.A.F. figure.

Now to address the men.

'As the senior rank present in the camp, it's my duty to assume command. I'm doing that for the common good – mine as well as yours. I want to get out of here the same as you do. If we stick together as an organised body we'll get somewhere. If we degenerate into an undisciplined mob we'll be finished off by the Javanese before the Japs even get here.

'The first thing I want clearly understood is that if I'm going to run this camp I'm going to have discipline. I'm going to have three parades a day, I'm going to have guards posted on the gate, I'm going to detail working-parties for everything that's wanted. If anybody doesn't like the idea of that, they'd better get out now. And I mean *now*. This'll be their last chance. Anyone who stays and doesn't toe the line after this will go to the guard room.'

'Like hell we will.'

'What guard room?'

'I'll make a guard room.' No one moved. Tottle waited until the general muttering died down and then he continued: 'Tomorrow morning I shall go into Batavia. I shall buy what food and stores we need under local purchase.' He had no notion of how he was going to achieve this, but he knew it must be done. 'Then I shall send a working-party in to collect the goods.

'I shall try to make contact with the nearest headquarters on your behalf. I shall try to get you away from here.

'And another thing. As long as I'm running this camp, you'll keep it clean . . .'

'What with?'

'If necessary on your hands and knees. I shall inspect each hut daily. And you'll keep yourselves clean, too.'

'There's no water.'

'There's a *dhobi ghat*. Each hut will report at the *dhobi ghat* as detailed, the first hut at 0700, the second at 0730, and so on throughout the morning. Each man will have an oil-can full of water. There's only one can, so you'll take it in turns.'

'How about soap?'

'I'll get you some soap. And while we're on the subject of water, remember that the *dhobi ghat* is the only water we've got. It mustn't be polluted. I've found some pots and we'll boil all the water we need for cooking and drinking.

'Next to the *dhobi ghat* is a line of six toilets. It will be each man's responsibility to flush the toilet after use by throwing a can of water down it. The can will be left full outside the toilets. When you've used it, go and refill it. Then it will be ready for the next man.

'By keeping ourselves and the camp clean we'll avoid sickness – malaria, dysentery and so on. We've got no doctors here.

'There'll be three parades a day, 0630, 1200 and 1800. Every man not detailed for a working-party or picket will attend.

'There will be a picket of five men on the gate, two inside and two out and one resting in the first office. We'll call that the guard room. The picket will change once a day. The men will be detailed on the morning parade.

'There'll be no more all-night parties in Batavia. Forty men will be allowed out each evening. That'll give you about one night out a week. You'll be back by midnight. The forty men will be numbered off each day on the 1800 hours parade and marched out of camp. It's up to you to get to know when it's your turn.

'I think that's about all. Any questions?'

'What about some pay, Chiefy?'

'We'll stick with you, Chiefy.'

'When do we eat, Chiefy?'

They were with him.

Tottle spent the rest of the day repairing an old bicycle he had found in the administrative block. The frame was bent

and the wheels buckled, but he straightened everything sufficiently to make the bicycle work. Next morning he cycled
into Batavia, a preposterous figure astride a rickety machine
several sizes too small for him.

He began with the more prosperous-looking shops in the
main street. In some places he talked to Dutchmen, in others
to Javanese. Few of them understood a word he said. Or
perhaps they didn't want to understand. When he met so much
as a glimmer of recognition, he stayed. His story was that he
was fully authorised to purchase food and stores for a party
of men stationed at Cornelius Barracks; his instructions were
that he was to sign chits wherever he made a purchase, and
the goods would be paid for later by the authorities. Some
refused to serve him, and there was a frigidness in their manner
which made him seek elsewhere. Others who refused at first
looked sympathetic. These he told that if they gave him what
he wanted they would get their money eventually: but if they
hung on to their goods, the Japs would come and confiscate
them and in the end they would get nothing. It was an argument suited to the atmosphere in Batavia and it appealed to
some. By the end of the morning he had signed chits for bread,
rice, tea, tinned milk, fruit, jam, eggs, vegetables, salt, meat,
charcoal for cooking, and various other items such as cutlery,
disinfectant, and glauber salts. He cycled back to the camp,
and then marched a working-party into the town to collect
the goods.

When they saw that Tottle was getting results, the men in
the camp thawed out towards him still further. At the six

o'clock parade that night Tottle found that he still had two hundred and twenty-two men.

For the next week Tottle continued making daily purchases in Batavia. He began to get to know his way about the town. He kept a sharp look-out for other Servicemen, but saw none. The tradespeople he dealt with got to know him and he found less difficulty in getting what he wanted. On one occasion he managed to obtain twelve tins of ham.

He was much impressed by the general air of cleanliness and prosperity in Batavia. Sometimes, during his visits to town, the streets were cleared because of air raids, and the efficiency with which this was carried out astonished him. There was no panic among the Javanese.

Tottle installed himself in the office next to the archway by the main guard room, and supervised the camp from there. From the moment when he called the first parade at six-thirty in the morning until midnight, when he checked the men back from their evening out, he never rested, although he delegated responsibility as much as he could. For all the various tasks of cooking, cleaning, and fetching and carrying, he continued to detail men on the routine parades.

The meat was generally of very poor quality and most of it was either stewed or boiled into soup. Sometimes it was mixed with rice. Meat, bread and vegetables were not always obtainable, however, and most meals consisted only of eggs, fruit and tea. One teaspoonful of salt was issued to each man as a personal daily ration, in addition to what was used in the cooking. The glauber salts were issued on the basis of one dose per man per fortnight.

Tottle spent as much time as he could with the men, always being on hand during washing periods in case of trouble. On one occasion he caught one of the Army men washing his hands in the *dhobi ghat*. He called him over.

'When's your night out?'

'Tonight.'

'It *was* tonight. You'll report to me at seven o'clock, eight o'clock and nine o'clock.'

The Army man reported at seven o'clock and eight o'clock, taut and rebellious. At nine o'clock he apologised.

'I'm sorry, Chiefy. I realise you can't have people doing things like that. I just didn't think. I'm sorry.'

Tottle grinned and sent the man to bed.

On one of the first parades Tottle noticed a swarthy look about some of the men. Then he saw what it was.

'Some of you men seem to have lost the habit of shaving.'

'No razor,' said one.

Next day Tottle bought fifty razors and a thousand razor blades in town. After that he insisted on every man shaving regularly. In any case, once they had the implements they needed little encouragement. Tottle was proud of the cleanliness of the huts, but the absence of beds and bedding was a constant niggle. He feared that if he was unable to make contact with some responsible body and provide proper equipment and rations within another day or so, the men might become increasingly difficult to manage. Sometimes he felt overwhelmed by the awful responsibility that rested on his shoulders. Amongst over two hundred men there surely must be some who resented his rough-and-ready discipline and felt they could do better on their own. The thought determined him to keep the discipline as rigid as ever. He detailed as many men as he could for small routine jobs – anything to occupy their minds. He allowed only ten of the huts to be occupied, so that there must be over twenty men in each hut. If the men were allowed to split up into small groups, it would be possible for half a dozen bad types to get together and cause trouble: in a hut of over twenty men the good sense of the majority would prevail.

On the eighth morning in Batavia, Tottle was astonished to see an R.A.F. van parked in the main street, with a warrant officer sitting in the front cabin. He thought, here's where I get rid of my men. He hurried across to the van.

'Where the hell are *you* from?'

The warrant officer seemed not in the least surprised to see Tottle, and spoke phlegmatically. 'I'm opening up a new maintenance unit,' he said.

'Maintenance unit?' Tottle thought he must be dreaming.

'Yes,' said the warrant officer, warming to his point. 'In another day or two I'll have my shelves and bins in and then I'll be all set for a trial layout.'

Tottle had a lightning glimpse of a thousand empire-builders tidying their shelves and bins while the Japs encircled them. He saw that the warrant officer was living in a world that had crashed long ago.

272

'Where are you getting your instructions from?'

'Air Headquarters.'

The phrase slipped out so easily, but the sound of it made Tottle's heart leap. Again he saw the chance to hand over his men.

'Where's that?'

'Don't you know it?'

'No.'

Tottle listened in a kind of daze as the warrant officer directed him to air headquarters. It seemed to Tottle that he had been in Batavia for weeks. He could hardly credit that an R.A.F. headquarters had existed here at the same time. It made nonsense of his own struggle. Without another word he jumped on his bicycle and pedalled off.

He found the headquarters building and burst in unceremoniously. There were two airmen sitting in an outer office.

'Who's in charge here?'

'In charge?'

'Is there an officer here?'

'There's a flight lieutenant.'

'Where's his office?'

The airmen pointed over their shoulders with their thumbs. Tottle strode on and rapped on the door.

'He's out at the moment, Sergeant,' called one of the airmen.

Tottle sat down as composedly as he could to await the officer's arrival. Every minute that he bottled up his story increased his determination to tell it in full. It was two hours before the officer could see him.

'My name's Tottle, sir,' he began. 'I've got two hundred and twenty-two men at Cornelius Barracks. I'd like to hand them over to some responsible authority.'

'Cornelius Barracks? Where's that?'

'South-west of the town, sir.'

'What do you want me to do?'

'Take these men off my hands, sir. We're up there with no rations, no beds, no bedding, nothing. Something's got to be done quickly.'

'I can't do anything for you. I've got thousands and thousands to see to. You'll have to fend for yourselves.'

Tottle felt as though he had been struck in the face. He had thought that once he found air headquarters all would be plain sailing. The camp would be taken over and properly organised. The keen edge of his disappointment sharpened his tongue.

'Fend for ourselves? We've been doing that for eight days. I'm not going back there unless I've got rations and bedding for those men, or a promise to get them transferred somewhere else right away.'

'You'll do what you're told. And if I have any trouble with you I'll slap you on a charge. Do you think you're the only ones? I tell you I've got thousands of officers and men in the same boat.'

'Then send some of the officers out to Cornelius Barracks. The men out there are nothing to do with me. I'm handing them over to you.'

The flight lieutenant's manner became threatening. '*You'll do as you're told,*' he said.

'What about sending out some officers?'

The flight lieutenant eyed him a moment.

'Wait here.' He left the room, and Tottle sat down. About twenty minutes later the officer returned.

'Assume the rank of warrant officer. Carry on as best you can.' He handed Tottle a warrant officer's badge, already attached to a khaki wristband. 'Keep your men out of trouble and report here every day or so. We're doing what we can.'

Tottle realised that he still had to fight.

'Look, sir, leaving aside the question of rank for a moment, I want rations for those men. I want bedding. I want clothing too, urgently – there isn't a single man with a change of clothes. I want proper instructions. I want officers and N.C.Os. to run the camp. I want pay for the men. I'm not going back there without them.'

The flight lieutenant met Tottle's eye. Harassed as he was, he knew that nothing less than everything he could do would be enough for Tottle.

'I'll try and send you some rations. I don't know about clothing, but I'll see what I can do. I can't do anything about bedding. You're in charge. That's final.'

'Come and see the camp for yourself,' pleaded Tottle. 'No one else can be living like that. An officer ought to see it. Besides, it would help me with the men.'

'I'll try and come out there.'

'And how about pay?'

'Have you got a nominal roll? Have they got pay books?'

This was the last straw.

'Look, sir, leaving aside the question of nominal rolls and pay books, *let's give them some bloody money.*'

Once again the flight lieutenant eyed Tottle critically. If he had a spare N.C.O. in the place, thought Tottle, he'd have me locked up. But I think he knows I mean it.

'I'll send the flight-sergeant out with some pay as soon as I can,' said the officer. 'It won't be a lot.'

'It doesn't matter as long as they get something. And what do I tell them about the future?'

'You can't tell them what you don't know — what *we* don't know. That's all. You'd better get back to the camp.'

'One more thing, sir. What happened to the rest of the men from the *Dunera*?'

'I haven't the faintest idea.'

Tottle saluted and made his way back. He was bitterly disappointed with the result of his visit to air headquarters, but at least someone knew where they were. He would call at headquarters regularly for instructions. Somehow the men would be evacuated. He had no doubt that it would come to that, especially now he had had a glimpse of the confusion that existed higher up. Already Japanese bombers were paying regular visits to Batavia, dropping their bombs unchallenged. Rumour was rife that soon Batavia would be encircled and isolated from the south. Tottle calmed himself by phrasing the questions that he would ask the flight lieutenant next time.

The following morning there was a delivery of three days' rations, and by eking this out with the purchases he made in Batavia, Tottle contrived to make them last a week. But no equipment, bedding or clothing came, although a day later an accounts flight-sergeant arrived to pay the men. Tottle lined the whole camp up in three ranks, and the men filed slowly past him, collecting their pay. There were no documents and no signatures. Every man was given forty guilders – about five pounds. Tottle asked the flight-sergeant to pay the men.

'Not me,' said the flight-sergeant. 'I'll have nothing to do with this murderous lot.'

Only then did Tottle realise to the full what a desperate picture they must present to an outsider. Although the camp was clean, lack of almost all proper amenities, coupled with the depressed state in which most of the men had arrived there, produced an impression to the casual visitor far removed from the truth. The men looked like a mob of desperadoes. Tottle shrugged and paid the men himself.

When he reached the last man he counted out thirty-five guilders, five guilders short, and nothing left for himself. He turned to the flight-sergeant.

'I shall want another forty-five guilders.'

'That's all they gave me.'

'Look, this man's five guilders short. And I've got nothing.'

'You should have taken yours first.'

Yes, thought Tottle, I thought that would be your attitude.

'How much money have you got on you?'

The flight-sergeant shifted uneasily. Tottle was a big man. There was an airman standing watching expectantly, waiting for his five guilders. He was in a strange camp and a long way from safety. Some of the men had looked as though they might cheerfully slit his throat. The best he could do was to hedge.

'That's all they gave me. I can't give you any more.'

'You can put the books right when you get back,' said Tottle. 'You'll get it back all right. Come on. Forty-five guilders.'

The flight-sergeant had a good deal more than forty-five guilders on him. If he resisted he might lose the lot.

'All right.' He shelled out the forty-five guilders.

When the flight-sergeant had gone, Tottle paraded the men again.

'Now,' he said, 'we've all got forty guilders. That may have to last us a long time. A fortnight, a month – perhaps longer. We don't know what the next move may be. That money might just save you. Look after it.

'If you go broke, it won't be any use going to anyone else. We've all got the same. I've got the same as you. It won't be any use coming to me.

'But one thing you can do is buy yourselves some soap. If I catch any man without soap after his night out in town, he'll lose his privileges.'

The biggest headache now was the problem of clothing and footwear. With the idea of saving wear and tear on their shoes and socks, Tottle gave orders that the men were to go barefoot when in the huts. Keeping clothing clean was another difficulty, but Tottle got hold of two more empty oil-drums, and these were used solely for the washing of clothing. In the heat of the afternoon their clothes dried quickly. Priority in the washing queue was given to the forty men on evening out, so that they should look as presentable as possible in Batavia. The best clothing was handed round from man to man as the turn came round for an evening out of camp.

On his daily inspection of the huts Tottle examined each man's footwear. Nearly every boot and shoe on the camp was worn through. Tottle managed to get several large strips of cardboard from the traders in Batavia, and these were cut to the size and shape of the individual shoe. It was surprising how long the cardboard lasted.

The mending of shorts and shirts presented yet another problem. Tottle brought reels of cotton and needles back from Batavia, but their clothes were rotten with sweat and the effects of frequent washing, and the cotton tore the fraying material still further. One day he noticed that the Javanese stitched their clothing with a kind of raffia. He mentioned this to one of the traders, and was given two bales of what seemed to be a sort of dried weed, each strand about four feet long. At the same time the trader gave him six large needles. In their first attempts at sewing they broke three needles; but they soon got the hang of it.

During the second week Tottle was pounding the streets of Batavia in search of food when he stepped rather suddenly off the pavement and was very nearly knocked down by a passing van. The van, driven by a Dutch woman, proved to be one of several being operated by the Dutch equivalent of the W.V.S., and as a result of this chance meeting two vans called at the camp morning and afternoon with iced coffee and a variety of small comforts, including cigarettes. They also brought packs of playing-cards, chess sets, and dominoes, all of which proved extremely popular and did much to help relieve the general boredom. The arrival of the van always got a big cheer. Tottle was asked out to dine several times by the Dutch ladies, but always declined.

Japanese bombers were now raiding Batavia regularly, and although the camp itself was not attacked, Tottle felt more and more anxious. On his visits to air headquarters he pressed hard for the evacuation of his men. The patched-up bicycle had finally given up the struggle and he had acquired a three-ton truck. He had noticed numerous trucks apparently abandoned by the roadside, and he discovered that people were taking trucks from the quayside and running them until the petrol gave out. Tottle made for the quayside and found to his great delight that there were still a few trucks left. The quayside had been heavily bombed, but the trucks had escaped. He commandeered a serviceable-looking truck and managed to get a petrol supply by signing yet another chit in the town. By this time his doctrine that the Japs would soon come and take everything anyway was all too widely accepted.

More than two weeks after their arrival in Batavia, the flight lieutenant from A.H.Q. visited Cornelius Barracks. Nothing much could happen on the camp without Tottle knowing about it, and the news was brought to him as he sat in his office. An airman burst in breathlessly.

'Don't collapse, Chiefy!'

'Why, what's happened?'

'There's an officer on the camp.'

Tottle strode out of his office and caught up with the flight lieutenant. He thought he had never seen anyone look so harassed and ill.

'I'm very glad to see you here, sir,' said Tottle.

'I came as soon as I could. How are you coping?'

'Not too badly, sir. Have you got any news for us?'

'Not much, I'm afraid. As far as getting you away is concerned, it's a question of being ready for a move at short notice, but there's absolutely nothing definite yet.'

'I see. Well, we're all set for a quick move here, sir. Will you inspect the camp?'

'Yes, of course.'

Tottle showed the flight lieutenant round the camp and explained how it was being run, going into everything in detail. The officer was frankly astounded.

'This is wonderful. Wonderful. You're doing an exceptionally good job. I congratulate you.'

'Thank you, sir.'

'I'm very impressed by what I've seen.'

'You won't mind me stressing the question of food, then,' said Tottle. 'I scrounge what I can in town, but it's a pretty poor diet.'

'I'm afraid there's very little I can do at the moment. Carry on getting your food on the chit system, and have the men constantly ready for a sudden move.'

'Very good, sir.'

It was several days after the flight lieutenant's visit when a messenger arrived with instructions for Tottle to report to air headquarters at once. Tottle hurried off into town.

'I can take a hundred and fifty men off your hands,' the flight lieutenant told Tottle. 'Get them ready for transfer to Llan Travallis Barracks right away.'

'Right, sir.' One hundred and fifty men. That left seventy-two. It wasn't bad for a start.

'Any transport for them, sir?'

'No. Can't you use your truck?'

'It's terribly hard to get petrol now, sir, and I'd have to do several trips to clear a hundred and fifty men.'

'Well, I leave it to you. March them there if you like.' He explained the route. 'You'd better get them started right away.'

'What time do they have to be there by?'

'2200 hours.'

'Couldn't I march them there this evening? It'll be cooler then.'

'As long as you get them there by 2200 hours I don't mind.'

'Where are they bound for, sir?'

'Tjilatjap. Southern Java. That's for *your* information only. They should be able to get away to Australia from there.'

So the evacuation had come at last. Tottle had never doubted that it would.

When he got back to the camp he confined everyone to their huts and started a rumour that he was awaiting final instructions. This kept the men quiet. Then at six o'clock he called the usual parade.

He had given a lot of thought to how he would select the

men who were to go, and he had decided that the simplest and most arbitrary way would be the best. When he paraded the men, he numbered them off from 1 to 150, dismissed the rest, and marched the lucky ones to Llan Travallis Barracks straight away.

When he reached Llan Travallis, Tottle marched his men into the camp, stood them at ease, and went to find someone to hand them over to. He was directed to a flight-sergeant.

'I've got one hundred and fifty men for you here, Flight,' said Tottle. 'A.H.Q.'s instructions.'

The flight-sergeant's expression was boorishly resentful, and he answered as Tottle knew he would answer.

'First I've heard about it.'

'Those are the instructions.'

'I don't know what they'll say.'

'Who?'

'Well, the Camp Commandant.'

'I don't care what anyone says. I told you – my instructions are from A.H.Q.'

'Well, I suppose it's all right, then.'

The flight-sergeant was edging away.

'Don't you want to check them?'

'Not if you say they're all right.'

Tottle was determined to hand the men over properly. He'd been responsible for them for some time now and he couldn't bear to think of their becoming a rabble.

'You've got a hundred and fifty disciplined men there,' he said. 'You'll take them over properly.' He steered the flight-sergeant to the parade-ground and made him take the men over and dismiss them.

Tottle was unprepared for the men's reaction. Someone called for three cheers for him, and as they cheered he fought desperately against a lump in his throat. Then he turned and waved to them and walked quickly out of the camp, the cheers of the men – *his* men – still ringing in his ears.

Tottle had a feeling that he was due for a hot reception back at Cornelius Barracks. He was anxious to get back there as quickly as possible, yet he felt he must have something to tell the men who had been left behind. He called at A.H.Q. on his way back. The outer office was empty and he walked across to the flight lieutenant's office, knocked, and went in.

The flight lieutenant was still there all right – lying on the floor, asleep. Tottle went to go out of the room again, but the officer stirred.

'I'm sorry I woke you up, sir,' said Tottle.

'That's all right,' grinned the officer. 'Just a cat nap.'

'I'm dead-beat myself,' said Tottle, 'but you're worse.'

'First spot of sleep I've had in two days. But I'm fresh again now.' The officer looked at his watch. 'I must have slept for nearly three hours. Just flopped down where I stood. Did you get the men away all right?'

'Yes. They're all at Llan Travallis. What I really came for was some instructions regarding the rest of them.'

'How many have you got left?'

'Seventy-two, sir.'

'As many as that?'

'I haven't lost a man, sir.'

'Carry on and use your own discretion for a day or so. We're doing all we can.'

'Very good, sir.'

When Tottle eventually got back to the camp he found the place almost in revolt. He was assailed on all sides. Why had *they* been left behind? What had *they* done? How long would they be stuck there? Where was the boat sailing from?

There was no doubt now in the men's minds that an evacuation was in progress. Demoralising news had been brought back from every night out in Batavia. Air-raid warnings were frequent although air raids were desultory. They were gripped by the fear that they were being abandoned, trapped. Tottle saw his toughest work still ahead of him.

He paraded the remainder of the men and addressed them forcibly. He was still there himself. He'd be the last to leave. He didn't like being left behind any more than they did. He had a wife and two children at home. But if discipline broke down now it might mean the end of everybody's chance. They simply had to hold on and not lose their heads.

As the days passed, with agonising slowness, Tottle walked the tight-rope of his own discipline. Somehow he still managed to wheedle food out of the Javanese traders. The regular nightly rainfall kept the water-level steady in the *dhobi ghat*. The days passed in an atmosphere of a volcano about to erupt. The heat was oppressive. Their clothing wore away to rags. Still Tottle kept the routine of the camp alive. Parades three times a day.

Washing by huts in the morning. Working-parties to collect food and keep the camp clean. The inevitable guard on the main gate.

Much time had passed, and he still had seventy-two men.

In the morning a message came from A.H.Q. He was to report there at once. This was it.

The flight lieutenant was still there, and he gave Tottle instructions for the evacuation of the last of his men. Could Tottle bring them into Batavia in his truck? Tottle said no: he couldn't possibly get seventy-two men in the back of a three-ton truck, and his petrol supply was uncertain. Then the flight lieutenant would send transport half-way to the camp. The men must march the rest.

Tottle was busy at once drawing conclusions. The trucks had just so much petrol to get to their destination and no more. That was why they couldn't drive right up to the camp. It looked like a long ride. All the way to Tjilatjap, perhaps. It would be a desperately uncomfortable journey, standing in the back of a three-tonner, but at the end of it would be freedom – freedom not only from the clutches of the enemy but from the appalling responsibility he had borne in these past weeks.

The flight lieutenant was still talking. Something he was saying brought Tottle painfully back to earth.

'. . . volunteers. I want you to get volunteers to stay behind and destroy valuable equipment at the docks and at various other sites, mostly requisitioned schools and stores. Get about six men. Detail them if necessary. All right?'

So it wasn't over yet. They wanted volunteers to stay behind.

Well, one thing he knew for certain. He wasn't detailing anybody. It wasn't that sort of job.

'I'm not detailing anybody, sir. If I can get one volunteer, I'll stay with him. But I'm not detailing anyone.'

For once the flight lieutenant didn't argue. Perhaps he thought the same way.

Tottle went back to the camp with a heavy heart. The moment of relief had come and he could not rejoice. He knew now with utter certainty that his fate would be to stay behind. The course he had steered for all these weeks could not be altered now.

He paraded the men for the last time. He told them that they were being evacuated and that the trucks were coming to meet them half-way. Then he asked for the volunteers.

'Volunteers are wanted to stay behind for demolition work,' he said. 'They may not get away.' He had to put the case to them, and yet he had resolved not to be over-persuasive. For the first time the power that he had wielded frightened him. He must not dissuade anyone, and he must not inspire them. He must speak with restraint, and yet he must not discourage. It was a new relationship between him and the men that the past weeks had not prepared them for. He was passing the onus of decision to them.

'I'm not persuading anyone,' he said. 'It's up to you. All I'll say is this. If anyone will stay, I'll stay with him.'

There was no movement at first, and then two Australian seamen stepped forward together.

'Are you really prepared to stay, Chiefy?' said one.

'That's what I said.'

'Well, we've been here a long time, so I reckon a while longer won't hurt us. We'll stick with you.'

There was no further movement amongst the men, and Tottle dismissed them quickly, vaguely embarrassed. Half an hour later he had formed them up again and was marching them to the rendezvous. When the men were safely aboard the trucks and on their way south, Tottle turned slowly back to the camp. He found the two Australians waiting for him. It was late afternoon and he suddenly felt overwhelmingly tired. The Australians produced a bottle of Dutch gin and he sat down with them. It was too late to start the demolitions today. They would drive into town first thing in the morning. He produced the list of buildings and the Australians produced more Dutch gin. They studied the list until the place-names became jumbled and blurred.

Tottle discovered that the seamen's names were Smiler Nulsen and Tom Halliday. They were the toughest pair of characters he'd ever met. If he had to be left behind on Java, he couldn't have picked two better chaps to be with.

'How did you come to be here, anyway?' he asked them.

'We missed our ship.'

'Jumped it, I suppose,' said Tottle.

They laughed and poured him another gin. 'Let's launch another one,' said Nulsen.

At seven-thirty next morning the three men drove out of Cornelius Barracks and into Batavia. They spent a depressing two hours at the docks, finding hardly anything left to destroy, and then they began to look for the rest of the places on the flight lieutenant's demolition list. They searched schools and warehouses and found little worth the trouble of destruction. At one warehouse they found a stack of Army clothing, and they quickly disposed of the rags they were wearing and kitted themselves out afresh. Then they slashed the rest of the clothing with their jack-knives. At the fourth building, a school, they found traces of an Australian squadron that had been housed there. They destroyed a number of personal items and a stack of Mae Wests. Three of the Mae Wests were thrown into the back of the truck; they might come in handy on a crowded ship.

They searched building after building, ignoring the frequent air raids, disgusted to find that the valuable equipment they were risking their lives to deny to the Japs had already been looted, if indeed it had ever existed except on paper. And yet, as the heat of the afternoon came and Tottle's list shrank, their hopes mounted. They had never expected to finish so soon. Perhaps even yet they might catch up with the others.

Tottle ticked the tenth place off his list and drove steadily through the town. The last building was a school. For all they had found so far, they might have given it a miss. Tottle knew the school well enough – a solid, red-bricked building in the suburbs, Germanic in conception, lying back from the road. They might as well finish the job now.

They heard the sirens again as they reached the Freiburg School. The three men tried to force their way in through the main doors, but these were stoutly built and resisted their pressure. They hurried round to the back of the building, broke a window and climbed in. The school was empty.

The Australians went to search the furthest wing of the school. Tottle climbed out of the window and strode round to the front of the building to start up the truck.

The drone and whine of the bombers reached his ears and he shouted for the Australians to hurry. The crump of falling bombs in the distance shook the courtyard. Then the air broke over him in waves as the scream of falling bombs reverberated around the school. He dived beneath the truck. A moment later Nulsen and Halliday appeared from behind the school and began crossing the courtyard. The anti-personnel bomb which fell right in their path obliterated them. Tottle saw them disappear a split second before the shrapnel sprayed lethally along the ground, scorching into his legs and thighs. He passed out almost at once.

When he came to he began to struggle out from beneath the truck. Somehow he must climb up into the cabin. If only he could get there and get the engine started, he would drive to the Dutch military hospital. He found that he could not move his legs. He was lying in a pool of blood. He wriggled out of his shirt and tore out the sleeves, binding them tightly round his legs. He mustn't lose any more blood. Then he crawled round to the cabin and hauled his great bulk up into it. He slumped into the driving-seat and fainted.

He fainted five more times between the courtyard and the hospital. The raid was still on and the streets were almost deserted. His feet were powerless; the clutch pedal and accelerator were operated solely by his will. Once he drove the truck straight into a wall and fainted again. When he reached the hospital his eyes were half-closed and yet he steered through the gates. The hospital drive was winding and uphill. The blood had drained from his head and he saw the drive tilting upwards until he knew the engine must stall. He reached for the hand-brake as the truck began to slither backwards. His grip was firm, and then he went out cold.

When he came to he was in a hospital bed and a Dutch doctor was talking to him in English.

'You have to have an operation,' said the doctor. 'We must take the shrapnel out of your legs.'

Tottle was wheeled along to the operating theatre and put under an anaesthetic. The pieces of shrapnel were extracted from his legs, and when he recovered consciousness he found himself back in the ward. He felt weak and bemused and soon fell into a deep sleep. When he awoke it was night-time and the Dutch doctor was there again.

'How do you feel?'

'Much better, thank you.' The effects of the anaesthetic had worn off, and although his legs still felt painful his mind was clear.

'How did you get into this mess?'

'It's a long story. I stayed behind to help destroy harbour installations and stores.'

'You volunteered?'

'Yes.'

'You hoped to catch up with your friends afterwards?'

'I thought I might.'

'It is too late now.'

'I expect so.'

Tottle realised that the Dutch doctor's attitude was friendly, and he felt that all these questions must be leading somewhere. The doctor paused, and then spoke again.

'Do you still want to get out of Java?'

Tottle eyed him keenly. He might as well tell the truth.

'I realise that it doesn't seem very loyal to you people, but – yes, of course I do. Those who get away can always fight back.'

'I think I can help you. I understand there is a chance of a plane leaving early in the morning. It will be the last one. It's a Dutch plane, of course, carrying Government officials. I may be able to arrange for you to be one of the passengers.'

'That would be wonderful.'

'It is nothing.'

The doctor disappeared and Tottle was left alone for the next hour. He wanted to ask a hundred questions about the proposed flight, but he realised that he must place himself entirely in their hands. With his legs in their present state there was no longer any chance of doing much for himself.

An hour later the doctor returned.

'It is all arranged. There is a car waiting for you. Come, we must get you dressed.'

Tottle's clothing was cut to ribbons and splashed and saturated with dirt and blood. The doctor produced a varied assortment of clothes, helped Tottle into them, and then brought a pair of crutches. Tottle had never walked on crutches before. But there was no time to practise. The car was waiting.

'I don't know how to thank you, Doctor.'

'We must all do what we can. I hope you get away safely. Perhaps one day you will get back to England.'

'One day, I hope. Do you know England, then?'

'A little. I spent six months at Guy's Hospital before the war.' The doctor looked as though he was about to say something else, and then he checked himself.

'Now you must go.'

They had reached the car. Tottle, supported on one side by the doctor, turned to shake him by the hand.

'Thanks for everything. Goodbye.'

'Goodbye. Oh, one thing more. They found this in your wagon.' The doctor handed him a Mae West. 'It might come in handy.'

Tottle threw the Mae West into the back of the car and eased himself into the front seat next to the driver. He was still in much pain. At once the driver let in the clutch and the car moved off down the drive. Tottle looked at his watch. It was half-past two: twelve hours exactly since he had stopped the truck outside the Freiburg School.

They drove through the darkness for over two hours. Tottle had no idea of their direction, but imagined that they must be heading towards the west. This was confirmed when he saw the signs of first light away to his left: they had turned north a few minutes earlier. Shortly afterwards they reached the coast.

It was daylight now and Tottle watched as the driver stopped the car outside a small wooden hut overlooking a deserted cove. Lying at anchor in the cove, camouflaged by the branches of trees but just visible from the road, lay a Dutch Dornier flying-boat.

The driver of the car pointed towards the hut, and Tottle struggled out with the help of his crutches. The driver handed him his Mae West and then turned and drove off without a word.

Tottle made his way over rough ground down to the hut with difficulty. As he approached the hut he heard voices, and he walked into the hut expecting some kind of a greeting. There were eight or nine people in the hut, but no one took any notice of him. He counted three women and five men. Then he caught the eye of a tall young man with deep-set eyes standing alone. The young man came over to him.

'Are you English?'

'Yes. My name's Tottle. R.A.F.'

'My name's Mitchell. I'm a New Zealander. I had a job in a Dutch bank in Batavia. Everyone else here is Dutch. Government officials and so on. I found when I got here that I wasn't very popular. They don't seem to have exactly taken to you either, do they? They're either overloaded or they would prefer to be taking Dutchmen. Well, all I know is that we're *in* all right. The captain told me so.'

'Good show.'

'His name's Jan. He's a good type – I think he's on our side. Do you know anything about this trip?'

'Nothing.'

'I don't know much myself. I don't think anyone does. It seems to be a bit of a wild-goose chase, but it's worth a gamble to get out of Java. This flying-boat isn't really serviceable. It's been under repair. They even had to tow it to get it round here. All the others have been destroyed in air raids. No one knows if they'll ever get this one to take off, and no one seems to know where they're going to make for if they do.'

'They must have some idea, surely?'

'They say they're hoping to put down near an Allied convoy. But they don't seem to have any definite news of one. I think they're going to try and hug the Mentawei Islands at first, and only attempt the crossing of the Indian Ocean if there's no shipping about. It's a rum do, all right. Still, if it's good enough for them it's good enough for me.'

'That goes for me, too.'

After a few minutes the Dutch party began to move off down to the cove. Mitchell and Tottle followed. The bank leading down to the sea was steep and the ground rough. Tottle tried to support his weight on the crutches, but he could not get used to them and moved awkwardly. The pain in his legs intensified as he jolted from one crutch to the other. He knew that at any moment he might go crashing down the bank.

'Take it easy, old man,' said Mitchell. 'You'd better put those sticks away.' Before Tottle could protest, Mitchell had hoisted him over his shoulder and was carrying him fireman's-lift fashion down to the cove. Tottle's arms swung helplessly from side to side behind Mitchell as he clung to his crutches and the Mae West.

The flying-boat was moored alongside a narrow jetty. The Dutch pilot entered the fuselage and then signalled for the others to follow. The Dutch passengers went forward to the front cabin and Mitchell and Tottle were directed to stay in the luggage compartment, as there was no more room up front. Tottle laid his crutches down and the two men made themselves as comfortable as they could.

'We're on the short end of everything this time,' said Mitchell, 'but at least we're near the door.'

There was a stack of parachutes and harnesses in the luggage compartment and the Dutch passengers each fitted themselves before going forward. Mitchell helped Tottle into his Mae West and fastened his parachute harness. Then a motorboat appeared and towed the Dornier clear of the jetty.

'All set to go,' said Mitchell.

They listened to the whine of the starter motor as the pilot tried again and again to start the engines. There was a great deal of shouting from the front cabin and from the motorboat. At last the chatter was drowned by the roar of the engines. Then there were several abortive attempts to take off before the hull and the sea finally came unstuck and the flying-boat climbed steadily away.

Mitchell and Tottle sat crouched in the luggage compartment, waiting for disaster. But the Dornier's engines sounded strong and sure, and soon they gained confidence. Jan had said that they hoped to find plenty of small ships off Sumatra, making for Ceylon. Miraculously, they were away from the nightmare of Java, heading for freedom.

The noise of the engines and slipstream made conversation in the luggage compartment impossible, and Mitchell and Tottle dozed uncomfortably. Suddenly Tottle awoke to find that they had been airborne for an hour and a half. The endurance of a Dornier must be at least eight or ten hours. He tried to sleep again, but his legs throbbed mercilessly. Every nerve in his body seemed to be on edge. He shifted his position countless times, but found no relief.

Now his nerves were working themselves up to a terrible crescendo. When the explosion came he thought at first it was the igniting of his own nervous tension.

The flying-boat rocked and sheets of flame enveloped the cabin. Tottle saw Mitchell move quickly towards him. The New Zealander was pointing downwards, a broad grin on his face. Tottle tried to sit up, and as he did so Mitchell supported him quickly and then clipped a parachute on to his harness. Then he pulled the air bottle to inflate the Mae West. Still grinning encouragement, Mitchell half-lifted, half-dragged Tottle to the door, slid it open and pushed him out. Tottle put his hand on the ripcord handle as he went. The next thing he knew there was a fierce tug behind him and he was floating gently down. Directly above him he saw the blazing Dornier, and then another parachute opened out and he knew that Mitchell too had escaped. Then the flying-boat became an inferno as it plunged downwards to the sea.

Tottle knew no more until he too reached the sea. He released himself from his parachute and found the Mae West supported him well. He looked around for Mitchell, but there was no sign. Then he thought of the other poor devils in the crashed Dornier. Then he thought of himself.

The heat was fierce and he was intolerably thirsty. The pain in his legs was unbearable. He wondered if there were any ships near enough to have sighted the blazing wreck. That was his only chance. Then he thought of the sharks.

He had read somewhere that if you splashed the water sharks would not come near. He began to splash the water weakly. That was it. Keep on splashing. He mustn't give up. Not until they found him. Splash, splash, splash . . .

He kept saying the words to himself, repeating them over and over again for all the hours he was in the water. Splash, splash, splash.

He knew that it was many hours later when there was suddenly a closer darkness and he opened his eyes to find a native *felucca* overshadowing him. Strong hands lifted him up, and he felt himself laid gently in the bottom of the boat. As he fell back he had a brief glimpse of an inert form on the far side of the boat. It was the gallant Mitchell. Tottle saw at once that he was dead.

There was a long period of impenetrable blackness, and then he was screaming again, splash, splash, splash, and from the other side of the world a gentle English voice was saying, don't worry, you don't have to splash any more. Something welled up inside him and broke over him in a great tidal wave of emotion. Awful choking sobs convulsed him, rending his soul. He cried as only a man can cry who in a short space of time has touched the zenith and nadir of God's world.

THE GOLDFISH CLUB AND
DOWN IN THE DRINK

CHARLES A. Robertson, a designer of the equipment needed by ditching aircrew during the Second World War, was regularly brought into contact with aircrew who had come 'down in the drink'. They came into the factory to discuss their experiences with him and to assist him in his efforts to design the equipment they needed. So impressed was he by their stories of courage and endurance that he decided to establish a club to accord them the recognition that they deserved. Robertson was head of the Ministry of Aircraft Production Air Sea Rescue Equipment Drawing Office, and chief draughtsman for P. B. Cow, a company that manufactured the Mae Wests and dinghies used by the R.A.F. Thanks to the financial support of P. B. Cow, Robertson was able to found the Goldfish Club in November 1942. News of the club spread quickly, and by the end of the war, there were over 9,000 members, all issued with distinctive badges, displaying a winged goldfish above two blue waves.

Ralph Barker came to write *Down in the Drink* through a chance connection with a committee member of the Goldfish Club. While working in London at the Air Ministry in 1953, he overheard a colleague discussing the club. 'My Squadron Leader said, "I want to get away early tonight, I've got to go to a meeting of the Goldfish Club." I said, "The Goldfish Club, what's that?" He said, "You know – chaps who've come down in the drink." I said, "Has anyone ever written it up?" He said, "Lots of people were going to but nobody has." I said, "Do you think they'd mind if an outsider had a go?" He said – he was a little fellow, and he practically thumped his chest – "*I'm* on the Committee – I'll fix it!"' The committee had only just been formed, but its support was invaluable to Barker. While he was undertaking research for the book, Gerry Bowman of the *Evening News*, a London newspaper of the time, began publishing stories about members of the club; but Barker's friend on the committee requested that none of the stories selected for *Down in the Drink* be featured in the newspaper series. The *Evening News* not only refrained from covering the stories that Barker wished to include in his book, but they assisted him in securing a publisher, tipping off Ian Parsons, the managing director of Chatto and Windus, about Barker's work. If Barker owed his initial chance to be published to the loyalty and honesty of others, the success of *Down in the Drink* may be fairly ascribed to his own talents. That initial success launched a productive writing career that has spanned several decades.

Information on the present-day Goldfish Club may be obtained from www.thegoldfishclub.co.uk. All membership queries should be directed to Mr Roy Graham, 43 Churchfield, Hardon Wick, Swindon SN25 1HY.

OUT OF THE DRINK

FERRY FLIGHT

ANY hopes Bancroft and his crew may have entertained of escape were dispelled the day after their rescue, when they were taken to the Italian Naval Hospital at Messina. They spent ten days there recuperating, lazing in the hospital grounds and being well treated and well fed. They then crossed to Italy, except for Robinson, who was left behind at Messina. They had been told when they first arrived at Messina that Robinson would die, but Robinson himself evidently thought otherwise, and he recovered and was eventually repatriated at the end of the war, though some of the early surgery on his injured leg retarded rather than advanced his recovery.

The others travelled first-class to Rome on the strength of Bancroft's commission, and were then sent to a monastery north of Rome, where they were kept in solitary confinement for three weeks and interrogated daily. Their rations were one small bread roll in the morning and a plate of soup at night. Their treatment was rigorous rather than cruel. They were then sent to the notorious Campo 65 in southern Italy near Bari, where they passed the next twelve months in acute discomfort. After the invasion of Sicily in July 1943 they were moved to another camp near Genoa, and with the further advance of the Allied armies into Italy they were sent through the Brenner Pass and on to Germany.

Or, rather, some of them were. Fifty miles south of the Brenner Pass the train stopped and the prisoners were allowed out of the cattle-trucks into which they were herded for a breath of air and to stretch their legs. Bell was in a truck with several other airmen and thirty to forty South Africans. In the next truck were Irving and McNeil. When he stepped out of the cattle-truck Bell picked up an axe which was lying alongside the railway-track. An Army warrant officer stepped up at once and said, 'You've got my axe.' Taken by surprise and off his guard, Bell surrendered the axe. The Army warrant officer had worked an old trick. He had never seen the axe before either.

The axe found its way into the truck next to Bell's – the truck that held Irving and McNeil. Before they reached the Brenner Pass Irving and McNeil broke the truck open and escaped under the noses of the German guards, who were armed with tommy-guns. Fully recovered from their injuries, these two men now showed their mettle. They both succeeded in making good their escape, and both survived many months as hunted men before they reached the British lines and, finally, home. They thus joined the select band of escapers to reach England after capture by the enemy.

Bancroft finished up in Stalag Luft III, Bell in a satellite camp near by. They were released by the Americans in 1945 after surviving a forced march; and after failing to impress the Americans with the priority they felt they deserved, they made their own way back via Paris to London.

How did they come to reach the Lipari Islands on that night three years earlier?

The most likely explanation seems to be that they never saw Malta at all. The air raid that they witnessed was probably a raid on Messina by Wellingtons based at Malta. If their track took them past Malta to port, and assuming that their groundspeed was better than they computed, they might have proceeded north of Malta right up to the north-eastern tip of Sicily without seeing land. This would be quite possible on a dark night. When the flak abated and they came in over Messina, it would be quite feasible for them to mistake the narrow strip of land they crossed for Malta.

Another point in favour of this construction is that there were no Beaufighters based at Malta at this time. It would not be difficult to mistake the Junkers 88s based at Messina for Beaufighters. Again, the long duration of the flight – nine hours – suggests that the aircraft was probably a long way north of Malta.

After they were attacked, Bancroft swung the aircraft to port and ditched almost at once. The bad weather on the first day after the ditching would obscure any view they might have had of northern Sicily. They must then have been carried along by currents in a westerly direction. They thought they saw land several times after the sixth day, and they were no doubt passing south of various islands of the Lipari group.

There is one other point worth recording. The day Bell concentrated his thoughts so hard on his wife was Whit Monday, 26th May, six days after the ditching. On this day his wife, who had had an aunt staying with her for the Whitsun week-end, saw the aunt off to Birmingham by train and returned home. During the afternoon she lay down for an hour to rest. She dreamt that she saw her husband calling to her from a small round boat some distance off-shore. She awoke with a sense of impending disaster. Later that day her aunt telephoned from Birmingham to ask if she was still all right and to say that she had had a premonition that something had gone wrong since she left, something to do with water. Mrs Bell received a telegram next day to say that her husband was missing.

'CHAS'

Locke was landed at Mingaladon and taken to an R.A.F. mobile field-hospital in Rangoon. His injuries included a fractured spine, a broken right ankle, a smashed left knee, concussion, cuts, bruises, shock and exposure. He was still in hospital in Rangoon when the Japanese surrendered four weeks later.

After Locke's aircraft crashed, Pilot Officer Jimmy Laver remained on the scene for forty minutes, the limit of his aircraft's endurance. He arrived back at base an hour after the first aircraft to land. While over the wreck he saw nothing to indicate that anyone was still alive. That night, when he wrote up the operations record book, he listed Locke and Nicolson as Missing, Believed Killed in Action. 'It is feared that the squadron has lost another fine crew,' wrote Laver.

Locke was extremely fortunate that the other aircraft in the formation were able to stay with him. The positions given by Joel and Laver were plotted in the Group Operations

Room, and the air/sea rescue service was alerted. Two Spitfires were sent to locate the wreck and the dinghy, with instructions to remain on the spot until a rescue launch and the Sea Otter appeared. When they found an empty dinghy and a half-submerged wreck they returned to base and reported what they had seen. The much slower Sea Otter eventually reached the position radioed by the Spitfires, but the wreckage had drifted some miles further south in the meantime, and the Sea Otter carried out a square search without result and then returned to Rangoon, reporting that the wreckage must have sunk.

The Duty Operations Officer, however, demanded to know why the Spitfires had failed to remain on the spot for the benefit of the motor-launch and Sea Otter, and ordered them to return to the wreck immediately. His action certainly saved Locke's life.

The first motor-launch hit a submerged wreck on its way downriver, and a second launch set out. Meanwhile, a Lysander was sent to drop a dinghy near any possible survivors, and the Sea Otter took off again from Rangoon. Both the Lysander and the Sea Otter raced the second high-speed launch, which arrived when the rescue was over. Because of the presence of the Spitfires, the Sea Otter was able to fly straight to the scene of the crash this time and not waste further valuable time searching for the wreck. Such a search might have been expected to last at least twenty minutes. Locke could not possibly have held out that long. He had spent five hours forty minutes in the water, and was undoubtedly within a minute or two of drowning when he was saved. Nicolson's body was never recovered, and he was later officially posted Killed in Action.

After the war, Locke became a liaison executive in a paper-making corporation, and the Honorary Secretary of, and driving force behind, the Goldfish Club.

THE PRISONERS

Strever and Dunsmore were awarded the D.F.C. and Wilkinson and Brown the D.F.M. In their absence their kit had been divided up amongst other members of the squadron, but they got it all back except a boot-brush.

The pilot of the Baltimore which had circled the dinghy just after the ditching was a personal friend of Roy Brown's. When he got back to Malta and heard that Brown was missing he realised that it had been Strever and his crew in the dinghy and he sent a cable to Brown's next of kin. Brown got back just in time to prevent the cable leaving the island. Later, back in New Zealand, the Baltimore pilot was best man at Brown's wedding.

THE BALANCE SHEET

After completing their tour in Wellingtons, Triggs and Badham returned to Australia and converted on to Liberators at an operational training unit. They then completed another tour in the south-west Pacific, operating from Darwin, Morotai, and Cocos Island. In all they carried out 102 operational trips together, totalling 860 operational hours, and both were awarded the D.F.C. Cartwright, the wireless operator, emigrated to Australia after the war.

THE LAST DETAIL

Jordan, who lost his right eye as a result of his wounds, was awarded the Distinguished Service Order for his part in the action. He stayed on in the Service after the war, was granted a permanent commission, and became a squadron leader. Paulton and Barry, who received back-dated commissions in the R.C.A.F immediately afterwards, were awarded the D.F.C., and Vachon, Bigoray, and Grant the D.F.M. Barry became a squadron leader in the R.C.A.F. at Ottawa. The self-effacing Bigoray, who was commissioned soon afterwards, was killed on operations in 1944.

From the point of view of the Radio War the flight was completely successful, and enabled the experts to unravel the last knot in the German air defence network. To quote Churchill, 'The gap in our knowledge of the German night defences was closed.'

WINKIE AND STINKIE

Stinkie never reached his loft, and was the only casualty. Winkie, who was an unusually tough bird and had been No.1 in the National Pigeon Service 1940 breed, was given the Dickin Award (the animal V.C.). She lived another eleven and a half years, dying in August 1953. She was then stuffed, and put on view in the Dundee museum, a few miles from her old loft at Broughty Ferry. But the tale of her deed lived on, and at the annual Pigeon Show in London in November 1953 she and Cliff (by this time Wing Commander W. H. Cliff, D.S.O.) appeared together to tell the story once more in aid of charity.

Tessier and Venn also survived the war, but McDonald was killed in a Liberator on literally one of the last operations of the war, by a strange irony of fate in almost exactly the same spot as he had hit the sea with Cliff three and a half years earlier. Tessier remained in the R.A.F. after the war.

MEDITERRANEAN CRUISE

Vertican and his crew were picked up and taken back to their squadron by road next day. They found that they had drifted ashore some fifteen miles west of Homs. Vertican was honoured by the immediate award of a commission in the field and later with the Conspicuous Gallantry Medal. Tempest was awarded the D.F.C. and Curnow and Gordon the D.F.M. Taffy Smith was mentioned in despatches.

Vertican had been an aircraft apprentice at Halton – the R.A.F. school of technical training – where he began his career in 1931 and was awarded his wings as a sergeant pilot in 1938. After the war he transferred to the Aircraft Control Branch, being granted a permanent commission in 1947. He became an air traffic controller at a station in the United Kingdom. Tempest also stayed on in the R.A.F. after the war and became a squadron leader at the Air Ministry. Jock Gordon was killed on operations over Guernsey in 1944.

WHITLEYS AND HAMPDENS ON HAMM

Haffenden was later called to the group commander (Air Commodore Cunningham) and other bigwigs to tell his story, but in August 1941 came another posting, to a famous transport squadron, No. 24. He contributed to events that helped delay a Rommel breakthrough, and took part in a bid to relieve Malta, flying thirty trips to and from Gibraltar–Malta without guns or parachutes, carrying urgent freight to help boost Malta's defences.

As for his incredible survival that night in July 1941, an award was mentioned but – perhaps because of his sudden posting overseas – never came through. Haffenden himself modestly says that his reward, if any, was in his flight commander's letter, which stated: 'He showed great courage and endurance, and endeavoured to save the life of his crew.'

After the war, Haffenden worked in London, and was a director of a whisky firm.

LAST OUT OF JAVA

It seems that Tottle had been transferred from the *felucca* to a Chinese river-boat called the *Wu Sui*, which had been converted into a hospital ship. Tottle was taken in the *Wu Sui* to Bombay, and went from there to the British General Hospital at Poona. Later he was transferred to an R.A.F. hospital in the hills at Chakrata. Here he underwent treatment until December 1942, but both his legs were paralysed as a result of his wounds, and he was still unable to walk without the aid of sticks. Some idea of the terrible debilitation he had suffered may be gauged from the fact that when he first arrived at Chakrata he weighed only 6 stone 11 lb – about half his normal weight.

This was the time of the Japanese threat to India from Burma, and when volunteers were asked for from among the senior N.C.O patients in the hospital to take over routine duties at various headquarters so as to release men for the forward areas, Tottle volunteered. The prospect of being sent home to be invalided out of the Service depressed him, and he felt that his only chance of carrying on and doing his share – as if he had not done it already – lay in India, where there was a serious shortage of N.C.Os. Eventually he was posted to Lahore, amazing and to some extent disturbing the group headquarters there by arriving on sticks. But he soon broke down all the barriers that his enormous physical handicap raised, and was given a key administrative job in helping to organise and train units of the Indian Air Force. In the ensuing twenty-one months he became a familiar figure, travelling many thousands of miles in the course of his duties.

He returned to England in January 1945, and spent most of the remainder of his Service in hospital or at convalescent depots and rehabilitation units. But he never regained the use of his legs, and was obliged to use forearm crutches permanently.

After the war he held a clerical post on the Plymouth district staff of the South Western Electricity Board.

Now you can buy any of these other World War II stories from your bookshop or direct from the publisher

A Spy Has No Friends   *Ronald Seth*   £7.99
From the beginning of his mission as a secret agent, Ronald Seth was a hunted man. Shot at as he parachuted down to the Estonian coast, he suffered extremes of deprivation before being captured and sentenced to death by hanging. Seth had only one hope – could he convince his captors that he was a Nazi sympathiser and trick them into employing him as a spy? *A Spy Has No Friends* is the thrilling story of a man playing a dangerous game against a lethal opponent.

Boldness Be My Friend   *Richard Pape*   £7.99
Aggressive, impetuous and dauntless, Richard Pape was never going to sit out the war in a Nazi prison. Captured and imprisoned when his bomber crashed, his daring escape was only the beginning of a long struggle for freedom. *Boldness Be My Friend* is a gripping tale of astonishing courage.

The Honour and the Shame   *John Kenneally*   £7.99
John Kenneally won the VC in 1943 for a solo attack on a whole company of Panzer Grenadiers. Years later, he confessed that he had joined the Irish Guards under an assumed name after deserting his original regiment. *The Honour and the Shame* brings to life the adventures of a freewheeling youth and the horror and exhilaration of the battlefield.

Odette   *Jerrard Tickell*   £7.99
In the darkest days of the Second World War, a young Frenchwoman, a wife and mother, became a secret agent. Leaving England to aid the French Resistance, she was betrayed, tortured, consigned to a concentration camp and sentenced to death. Yet she kept, in the abyss, her hope. *Odette* tells the story of an ordinary woman who, when tested, displayed an extraordinary courage and compassion.

TRUE STORIES FROM WORLD WAR II
Real heroes. Real Courage.

To order, simply call **01235 400 414**
visit our website: www.madaboutbooks.com
or email orders@bookpoint.co.uk

Prices and availability are subject to change without notice.